THE BOMBERS

Other National Historical Society Publications:

THE IMAGE OF WAR: 1861-1865

TOUCHED BY FIRE: A PHOTOGRAPHIC PORTRAIT OF THE CIVIL WAR

WAR OF THE REBELLION: OFFICIAL RECORDS
  OF THE UNION AND CONFEDERATE ARMIES

OFFICIAL RECORDS OF THE UNION AND CONFEDERATE NAVIES
  IN THE WAR OF THE REBELLION

HISTORICAL TIMES ILLUSTRATED ENCYCLOPEDIA OF THE CIVIL WAR

CONFEDERATE VETERAN

THE WEST POINT MILITARY HISTORY SERIES

IMPACT: THE ARMY AIR FORCES' CONFIDENTIAL HISTORY
  OF WORLD WAR II

HISTORY OF UNITED STATES NAVAL OPERATIONS IN WORLD WAR II
  by Samuel Eliot Morison

HISTORY OF THE ARMED FORCES IN WORLD WAR II
  by Janusz Piekalkiewicz

A TRAVELLER'S GUIDE TO GREAT BRITAIN SERIES

MAKING OF BRITAIN SERIES

THE ARCHITECTURAL TREASURES OF EARLY AMERICA

For information about National Historical Society Publications, write:

The National Historical Society, 2245 Kohn Road, Box 8200,
Harrisburg, Pa 17105

THE ELITE
The World's Crack Fighting Men

THE BOMBERS

Ashley Brown, Editor
Jonathan Reed, Editor

Editorial Board

Lisa Mullins, Managing Editor, NHS edition

A Publication of
THE NATIONAL HISTORICAL SOCIETY

Published in Great Britain in 1986 by Orbis Publishing

Special contents of this edition copyright © 1989 by the
National Historical Society

Library of Congress Cataloging-in-Publication Data
The Bombers / Ashley Brown, Jonathan Reed [editors].
    p.   cm.—('The Elite : the world's crack fighting men ; v. 6)
    ISBN 0-918678-44-7
    1. Bombers.   2. Air forces.   3. Military history, Modern—20th
century.   I. Brown, Ashley.   II. Reed, Jonathan.   III. Series:
Elite (Harrisburg, Pa.) ; v. 6.
UG1242.B6B65   1988
358.4'2—dc20   89-3322
                              CIP

CONTENTS

INTRODUCTION

Destruction comes in many guises and from many directions in warfare, but surely none is more terrible or terrifying than that which rains down from the air. Shrieking dive bombers, jets rushing overhead at the speed of sound, lumbering B-17s and Henkels delivering chaos by the ton, all make and have made THE BOMBERS the messengers of devastation and, in the end, of victory and defeat. They are a special kind of ELITE, for they make of themselves and their machines living targets for the fighters and anti-aircraft batteries of the foes they seek to destroy. It takes brave men, and always has, whether in the 1940s or 1960s in Vietnam.

Fly with the Eprobungsgruppe's converted fighter-bombers, trying to knock out British radar during the Battle of Britain. Spend your own 30 seconds over Tokyo with "Jimmy" Doolittle and his intrepid B-25 Mitchell bombers, delivering the first counterblow to the Japanese mainland. Sit in the cockpit with the daring pilots of the Mosquito squadrons, or enter the skies in the formidable B-17 Flying Fortress, perhaps the finest all-around bomber ever built.

Thrill to the daring of 617 Squadron, the fabled "Dam Busters," with their bouncing bombs that knocked out a vital German power source. Or join RAAF Squadron No. 2 as the Aussies deliver stunning blows in South Vietnam. SAC B-52s carry the conflict to Hanoi in 1972, with just as much daring as the British Lancasters used to take their monster "earthquake" bombs to devastate German U-boat pens. "Pappy" Boyington's "Black Sheep" Squadron and its Corsair fighter-bombers made life hell for the Japanese in the Solomons, just as Hitler's V-1 flying bombs and Arado 234 jet bombers put terror in the skies for Britain.

From the moment that men first dropped explosives—initially little more than hand-lobbed grenades dropped out of a pilot's cockpit—the threat of death from the sky, and the danger to those who flew those missions, made the bombers a special class of men. Day after day, going into the skies to drop destruction upon an unseen enemy, whether by blockbusting huge bombs, or dropping the German glider-bombs—virtual guided missiles— the bombers have put that extra bit of risk, that special daring of life-on-the-line service, into their work. They have paid for it in their blood, for few branches of the military have suffered casualties as high as the bombers.

It has been a high price to pay, but one expected of THE ELITE.

ERPROBUNGS-GRUPPE 210

Luftwaffe Erprobungsgruppe (Experimental Group) 210, whose 'England in a bombsight' insignia is shown above, was formed in June 1940 during the latter stages of the Battle of France. The Gruppe's aircraft consisted of 24 Messerschmitt Bf 109Es and 110s, all of which had been converted to carry 500lb and 1000lb bombs. The Messerschmitts retained, however, their standard armament of cannon and machine guns, which meant that once their bomb loads had been released they could return to their fighter role and defend themselves. Between June 1940 and the autumn of 1942 the Gruppe perfected the tactics of fighter-bomber warfare. In the early days of the Battle of Britain, the Gruppe launched fairly large daylight raids against targets in Britain, but as the RAF rose to meet this challenge the Gruppe switched to hit-and-run raids, conducted by Messerschmitts flying in pairs.

In June 1941 the Gruppe was assigned to the Eastern Front, where it flew as part of Fliegerkorps II in support of Army Group Centre during Operation Barbarossa. The Gruppe flew almost non-stop, attacking Soviet airfields in the Minsk sector, and then supported the panzer divisions driving through the Pripet marshes towards Smolensk. The Gruppe's experimental status was now a thing of the past and it was redesignated Schlachtkampfgruppe (Ground Attack Group) 210. Throughout the spring and summer of 1942 its fighter-bombers supported Wehrmacht offensives. In the autumn of that year the Gruppe was finally disbanded.

In the immediate run-up to the Battle of Britain, the specially converted Messerschmitt fighters of Erprobungsgruppe 210 set out to bomb Britain's defensive radar. It was one of many fighter-bomber missions that would earn the Gruppe a place in aviation history

TARGET BRITAIN

Below: Groundcrewmen await orders to bomb up the Gruppe's aircraft while their colleagues (above) service a Bf 110 at Calais-Marck. Above right: Pilots receive a briefing before a raid. Right: A German aerial reconnaissance photo of Dover, one of the Gruppe's initial targets.

THE MORNING OF Monday, 12 August 1940, was bright and clear. The sky was a pale, translucent blue, dappled here and there with a few tufts of cirrus cloud. Over Calais-Marck airfield in northern France, an early mist had dispersed and the sun now beat down with increasing power on the lines of parked Messerschmitts. In the briefing room, the morning sun poured in through the windows and lit up the curling blue drifts of cigarette smoke.

The assembled pilots of Luftwaffe Erprobungsgruppe (Experimental Group) 210 sensed that something big was in the offing. It was nearly six weeks now since Reichsmarschall Hermann Göring had issued a General Directive calling for an all-out Luftwaffe air offensive against England: on 30 June to be precise, just one week after the close of the Battle of France. According to his directive, the main target of the Luftwaffe bombers was to be the RAF, particularly the fighter airfields and aircraft factories.

On 21 July, Göring called his air chiefs together and ordered them to work out an operational plan. There were heated arguments among the General Staff – there was no doubt that the destruction of the RAF was by far the most urgent task, but deciding the best way to go about it was a different matter.

Nevertheless, by 2 August plans for the opening move of the air offensive against England were complete. Luftflotten (Air Fleets) 2 and 3 would attack simultaneously with the objective of bringing the RAF fighters to combat, of destroying their airfields and the radar 'eyes' on the coast, and of disrupting the RAF's ground organisation in southern England. On the second day the attacks would be extended to airfields around London, and would continue at maximum effort throughout the third day. High Command hoped in this way to weaken the Royal Air Force by a few decisive blows, estab-

lishing the air superiority necessary for any further operations against Britain.

Everything was fixed except for the date. To carry out all its allotted tasks, the Luftwaffe needed at least three days of continuous good weather. The meteorologists were expecting a fine spell to continue during the first week of August, but the Luftflotten were unable to take advantage of it as they needed another week to complete their preparations for the great onslaught. Then, when the Geschwader (wings) were finally ready, the weather took a sudden turn for the worse and Adlertag (Eagle Day), which had been fixed for 10 August, had to be postponed. On 11 August the weather forecast for the next few days looked promising; the final decision

9

was made and *Adlertag* was scheduled for 13 August. H-hour was to be 0730.

Gruppe 210's baptism of fire against the British came, however, on 11 August. Following an intensive period of training in dive-bombing techniques, the pilots were ordered to attack a convoy in the Channel southeast of Harwich. The mission was a complete success. Two transports were left in flames, and the Messerschmitts suffered no damage in an ensuing skirmish with No. 74 Squadron, RAF.

On the following morning, Gruppe 210's crews were detailed to fly a vital mission as a prelude to the main attack. It was to be the culmination of their weeks of training – a mission that called for a tremendous degree of accuracy. In the briefing room at Calais-Marck, the crews listened attentively as their CO, Hauptmann Walter Rübensdorffer, and an intelligence officer outlined the plan. On the wall, three red circles stood out boldly on the map of southern England near Dover, Pevensey and Rye. At the centre of each circle was a key transmitter in the British radar network along the south coast.

Looking back in the seconds after the attack, Lutz saw a vast cloud of smoke and dust rising

The existence of Britain's radar warning system was no longer a secret; in the months before the outbreak of war the big transmitters on the coast had been photographed on many occasions by German commercial flights, and it had not taken the Germans long to divine their purpose. By the summer of 1940 General Wolfgang Martini, head of Luftwaffe Intelligence, had assembled a considerable amount of information on the British warning system, and he was also aware of its shortcomings. It worked, for example, on a wavelength of 1200 centimetres, which meant that it was virtually impossible for the British to forecast the size of an incoming enemy formation with any degree of accuracy.

It was the organisation behind the radar network that worried Martini. Inaccurate though it was, the British radar could detect the Luftwaffe's bomber formations as they assembled over France and the Low Countries, enabling RAF Fighter Command to plot their course as they headed out over the Channel and giving the Spitfire and Hurricane squadrons ample time to get airborne and intercept them en route to their targets.

The destruction of the radar transmitters on the south coast was therefore of paramount importance, and this was the task assigned to Gruppe 210 before the battle began in earnest. The plan called for an attack on the Pevensey station by No.1 Staffel, led by Oberleutnant Martin Lutz; No.2 Staffel under Oberleutnant Wilhelm Rössiger would hit the masts at Rye, leaving Oberleutnant Otto Hintze's No.3 Staffel to deal with the Dover station. As a diversion, the Dornier 17s of Kampfgeschwader 2 were to make a heavy attack on the RAF airfield at Lympne.

Twenty aircraft – eight Bf 109s and 12 Bf 110s – were detailed to carry out the mission. Rubensdörffer himself, flying another 110, was to fly along the English coast in the wake of the attack and observe results.

Take-off was at 0930. After forming up over Calais-Marck, the Messerschmitts headed out over the Channel at less than 100ft, keeping low to avoid detection by the radar. Halfway across, with the chalk cliffs of the English coastline rising out of the morning mist, the eight Bf 109s of Oberleutnant

Above: Three Messerschmitt Bf 110s, bearing the 'England in a bombsight' insignia, fly in towards their target. Far right, above: Bf 110s of Gruppe 210's 2nd Staffel (Squadron) prepare for take-off at Calais-Marck during the Battle of Britain. Far right: The underside of one of the Gruppe's Bf 110s, fitted experimentally with a 37mm cannon. Right: A Bf 110 crew prepares for take-off. Below right: The Messerschmitt Bf 110, converted for the fighter-bomber role. Bombed up, however, the Bf 109s and 110s lost many of their best flying characteristics. Their

Hintze's 3rd Staffel broke away and went into a climb, heading for Dover. The remaining aircraft turned through 50 degrees and headed southwestwards; three minutes later the formation split up, with the 1st Staffel heading for Pevensey and the 2nd for Rye. Each Bf 110 carried two 1000lb bombs, twice the load carried by the Junkers Ju 87 Stuka.

Alone now, the 3rd Staffel climbed to 9000ft and made landfall near Dover. Oberleutnant Hintze picked out the masts of the station a little further inland and gave the order to attack. With the added weight of their bombs, the Messerschmitts' acceleration in the dive was alarming. At 2000ft they released their 500lb bombs and streaked over the station at 400mph. Three bombs exploded near the masts, but when the smoke cleared the structures appeared to be still upright.

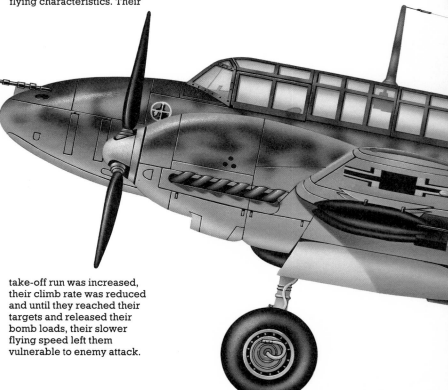

take-off run was increased, their climb rate was reduced and until they reached their targets and released their bomb loads, their slower flying speed left them vulnerable to enemy attack.

Further west, Oberleutnant Martin Lutz's 1st Staffel crossed the coast near Eastbourne and his six Bf 110s dived on their target from 10,000ft. Looking back in the seconds after the attack, Lutz saw a vast cloud of smoke and dust rising over the radar station. One of the transmitter masts appeared to be leaning at a drunken angle. A few minutes' flying time to the east, Oberleutnant Rössiger and his 2nd Staffel hurtled down on the radar station at Rye, near Hastings. Ten 1000lb and 500lb bombs exploded in the target area, destroying a number of buildings, but both the transmitter and the control room were undamaged.

Under the directions of Hauptmann Rubensdörffer, who had been circling high above the coast, the three flights dived away over the sea and headed flat-out for home. Their mission had failed; all three radar stations were fully operational again less than three hours after the attack.

As soon as the Messerschmitts arrived back at Calais-Marck they were refuelled and rearmed and their pilots were briefed for another mission. This time their target was to be Manston, a key sector station within No.11 Group RAF Fighter Command. By 1300 the aircraft were airborne once more and heading at low level towards the English coast.

The British radar stations were still suffering from the effects of the morning's attacks, and the first warning the Manston controllers received of the approaching Messerschmitts was a telephone call from a Royal Observer Corps post on the North Foreland. The pilots of No.65 Squadron raced for their aircraft, hastily strapped themselves in and started up. The leading flight of Spitfires had just opened up and begun to roll down the runway when the first Messerschmitts screamed across the airfield and unloaded their bombs.

Manston was a shambles. Twelve 1000lb high-explosive bombs and four 500lb incendiaries had scored direct hits on the hangars and other installations, and four 500-pounders had exploded among the parked fighters, destroying nine and damaging several more.

Two days later, on 14 August, Gruppe 210 struck at Manston again. On this occasion, 16 Messerschmitts dived down through the clouds on their objective; once again complete surprise was achieved and four more direct hits were registered on the airfield's installations. All the German aircraft returned safely to base.

A long burst from Crossley's guns, and a 110 burst into flames and dived into the ground

So far, Gruppe 210 had been lucky. Its surprise tactics had carried it through with minimum losses. The luck, however, was not to last. At 1835 on the 15th, 15 Bf 110s and eight Bf 109s took off from Calais-Marck and headed out over the Channel, escorted by the 109s of JG 52. The formation crossed the English coast near Dungeness; its target was the sector station of Kenley, to the south of London.

To confuse the defences, Rubensdörffer had decided to lead Gruppe 210 in a wide circle and attack Kenley from the north. He turned onto the new heading over the southern suburbs of London, and soon afterwards an airfield, which he identified as Kenley, appeared ahead. He gave the order to attack. But Rubensdörffer had made a serious mistake. His Gruppe was over Croydon, not Kenley.

A squadron of Hurricanes, No.32, led by Squadron Leader Mike Crossley, was patrolling Dover at 10,000ft when they were informed that an enemy raid was heading for Croydon. They arrived over the airfield just as Rubensdörffer's 110s were beginning their attack, and sailed in among them. A long burst from Crossley's guns, and a 110 burst into flames and dived into the ground. He immediately went after a second 110 and raked its port wing, putting the engine out of action.

Crossley's fighters had meanwhile been joined by the Hurricanes of No.111 Squadron, under Squadron Leader J.M. Thompson. Thompson caught the last 110 as it was coming out of its dive, fired, and saw chunks of metal fly off the German's starboard wing and engine. The 110 crash-landed in a field, and the pilot and observer were taken prisoner.

While the dogfight was on, the other 110s corkscrewed up in a defensive circle, waiting for an opportunity to make a break for it. Suddenly, a flight of Bf 109s dived through the fray, distracting the Hurricane pilots who thought they were the 110s' fighter escort. In fact it was Gruppe 210's 3rd Staffel, led by Oberleutnant Hintze. The 109s let go their bombs and immediately formed a defensive circle. Above them, Rubensdörffer at last saw an opening

Above: After a successful bombing mission, three Bf 110s bank steeply and head for home. Having jettisoned their bombs, both the 109s and 110s reverted to their fighter role and were able to put up a spirited defence against the attentions of the RAF. Many of the Gruppe's aircraft, however, did not escape unscathed, as can be seen in the example of flak damage, sustained by a Bf 110 on its way back to Calais-Marck (above centre). Above, far right: Flying high. A Bf 110 heads for its target.

and now broke away with the four aircraft of the Staff Flight. They were quickly lost to sight in the haze.

Their escape, however, was only a temporary respite. Just short of the coast, the Germans were sighted again and the RAF came down out of the sun. A flurry of tracer, a flicker of flame and Rubensdörffer's 110 slowly turned over onto its back. Trailing a thin stream of grey smoke, it hit the ground and disintegrated in a cloud of blazing wreckage. Neither Hauptmann Walter Rubensdörffer nor his observer had bailed out.

Back at their base, the survivors of Gruppe 210 counted the cost of the raid. Thirteen faces were missing; the crews of six Bf 110s and a 109. Overall, the Luftwaffe lost some 90 aircraft that day, which was to become known as 'Black Thursday'.

Gruppe 210 continued to operate in the fighter-bomber role during the remaining weeks of the Battle of Britain. Towards the end of September, a thick bank of cloud crept in over the British Isles and western Europe, and with the spell of bad weather came a complete revision of Luftwaffe tactics that brought the fighter-bomber idea to new prominence. On 15 September the Luftwaffe had taken a severe mauling over London, losing 56 aircraft, not counting those that limped back to their bases with

such severe battle damage that they had to be scrapped; it was clear that RAF Fighter Command was far from defeated, and was still capable of inflicting prohibitive losses.

The new Luftwaffe tactics called for penetration raids by small groups of aircraft in good weather, and interdictor missions by solitary bombers and fighter-bombers in all kinds of conditions.

The pilots pressed their bomb releases and 22 500-pounders curved down to explode in the City

The tactics were first put to the test on the morning of 20 September, when 22 Messerschmitt 109s – led by eight aircraft of Gruppe 210 – crossed the English coast at 27,000ft and went into a long, shallow dive in the direction of London. At 13,000ft the pilots pressed their bomb releases and 22 500-pounders curved down to explode in the City.

Small hit-and-run missions formed the main part of Gruppe 210's task during the winter months of 1940-

41, although a good deal of experimental work was also carried out with various bomb-load combinations dropped from high, medium and low level. By the early spring of 1941 Gruppe 210 had developed fighter-bomber tactics into a fine art. With the advent of better weather the pilots were anticipating a renewed offensive against British targets when, early in May, the whole of Luftflotte 2 received orders to move east, to Poland.

Fighting in the vanguard of the Luftwaffe's tactical experiments, in both the Battle of Britain and later on the Eastern Front, Gruppe 210's place in aviation history was assured. The fighter-bomber tactics it had pioneered were to become classic.

THE AUTHOR Robert Jackson is a freelance aviation writer who has contributed a number of articles to military publications. He has written a great many books including *The Royal Air Force in Action*.

Main picture: Four Bf 109s, flying low to evade British radar interception, head for action along the south coast, near St Margaret's Bay, during the Battle of Britain.

MOSQUITO SQUADRONS OF NO. 140 WING

Of the three squadrons that made up No. 140 Wing, only No. 21 Squadron was a Royal Air Force unit. Re-formed as a bomber unit in December 1935, the squadron was equipped with Bristol Blenheim bombers and carried out reconnaissance missions and shipping searches during the early months of World War II. After the German offensive in the Low Countries, it became involved in attacks against enemy columns. In October 1940 the squadron moved base from Lossiemouth, Morayshire, to Norfolk, tasked with attacking enemy coastal targets. In December 1941, No. 21 Squadron was deployed to Luqa airfield in Malta, attacking Mediterranean shipping and land targets in North Africa.

After being disbanded in March 1942, the squadron was re-formed on the same day at Bodney, in Norfolk. It converted to Lockheed Venturas in May 1942, and carried out numerous daylight bombing missions before being incorporated into the Second Tactical Air Force (2 TAF) and converting to Mosquitos in September 1943.

No. 464 Squadron, Royal Australian Air Force, was formed as a Ventura unit at Feltwell, Norfolk, on 1 September 1942. It operated as part of No. 2 Group. In July 1943, the group was transferred from Bomber Command to 2 TAF, and the squadron began conversion onto Mosquitoes the following month. It operated these aircraft for the remainder of the war, and was eventually disbanded on 25 September 1945.

No. 487 Squadron, Royal New Zealand Air Force, was formed at Feltwell two weeks after No. 464, and carried out daylight operations with Venturas until late June 1943. The unit converted onto Mosquitoes in August 1943, and continued bombing missions for the remainder of the war. It was disbanded in September 1945.

JAIL

Experts in the art of low-level, precision bombing, the pilots of the Mosquito squadrons flew some of the most daring missions in the history of aerial warfare

BUSTERS

Right: The team from No. 105 Squadron that spearheaded the RAF's first daylight attack on Berlin. On the right is the newly promoted Wing Commander Bob Reynolds, shown here with his navigator, Pilot Officer E.B. Sismore. Below left: Pilots and navigators from the squadron run over pre-flight details. By the summer of 1943, No. 105 Squadron's Mosquitoes had been equipped with the 'Oboe' navigation aid, enabling the unit to perform a Pathfinder role. Far left: The insignia of No. 21 Squadron. Armed with a pair of 500lb bombs (below right), a flight of Mosquitoes sets out for France (bottom right).

30 JANUARY 1943 was a very special day for Adolf Hitler. Exactly 10 years earlier, he had brought the Nazi Party to power in Germany – and embarked on a path that was to lead his country into the holocaust of World War II. The Nazis had planned huge celebrations to mark their tenth anniversary. There was to be a massive military parade in Berlin, and Hitler himself would make a radio broadcast at 1100 hours. His propaganda minister, Joseph Goebbels, would make another speech five hours later. The Germans had made no secret of their anniversary celebrations. Although Berlin had been raided many times at night, they believed that the Royal Air Force (RAF) had no aircraft capable of striking at the capital in daylight and surviving. At 0830 hours, with the military parade already starting to assemble in Berlin, Hitler sat at breakfast and waded through the mound of telegrams and presents that had come flooding in from party members all over Germany. Unknown to the Führer, however, one present had yet to arrive. It would be delivered in exactly two and a half hours time – by the RAF.

If attacked, and forced to take evasive action, the chances of making it back to base were small

Five hundred miles from Berlin, three sleek aircraft were running up their engines on the RAF airfield of Marham, in Norfolk. They were twin-engined de Havilland Mosquitoes, the RAF's newest and fastest bombers. The Mosquitoes had entered service with No. 105 Squadron less than a year earlier, and had already carried out several daring low-level attacks on enemy targets. Now, on this clear January morning, No. 105 was about to take the war right into the heart of the Third Reich.

As the three Mosquitoes thundered away from Marham and set course for Germany, Squadron Leader Bob Reynolds – the man selected to lead the attack – knew that the success of the mission depended on split-second timing. The plan was to bomb the Berlin radio station, just off the Wilhelmstrasse, at exactly 1100, coinciding with the start of Hitler's speech. Reynolds' navigator, Pilot Officer E.B. Sismore, was one of the best in his field, and needed to be. In addition to the crucial aspect of timing, the five-hour round trip would leave only a small margin of fuel. There was thus no room for error. If attacked, and forced to take evasive action, the chances of making it back to base were small. The Mosquito bombers carried no defensive armament; they had to rely on speed alone to evade enemy fighters. The aircraft raced across the North Sea at low level, climbing slightly as they crossed the German coast. The morning was brilliantly clear, and Sismore had no difficulty in picking out landmarks as the bombers sped towards their target. Reynolds climbed hard, taking the three aircraft up to 20,000ft for their final approach. The lakes around Berlin came up under the nose, glistening like metal in the sunshine.

In Britain, linguists monitoring the German radio shortly before 1100 heard an announcer tell the audience to stand by for an important speech. Disappointment followed – the speech was to be made not by Hitler, but by Hermann Göring, chief of the German Luftwaffe. Hitler had developed a sore throat at the last minute, and Göring was standing in for him. The only consolation was that Göring was ranked second in the Third Reich hierarchy behind the Führer.

MOSQUITO SQUADRONS: WORLD WAR II

Split-second timing and deadly precision were crucial to the success of the Amiens raid. Four sections of three Mosquitoes swept in at 'deck' level, the first two tasked with breaching the perimeter walls. Following this, six aircraft from No. 464 Squadron, Royal Australian Air Force (badge shown right), attacked designated objectives in the southeast and northeast of the prison complex. Below right: An illustration of the level of accuracy achieved by the Mosquito aircrews. The southern wall has been breached with minimal damage to the prison cells.

The Mosquitoes were now over Berlin. With 30 seconds to go, Sismore centred the broad ribbon of the Wilhelmstrasse in his bomb-sight. A few tufts of scattered flak burst around the speeding aircraft, but there was no sign of any enemy fighters.

All over Germany, millions of people listened to their radios as a fanfare of trumpets died away and the announcer began to introduce Göring's speech. Suddenly, his words were cut short. Clearly audible over the radio was the crump of exploding bombs as the 500-pounders dropped by the three Mosquitoes whistled down to erupt around the broadcasting station. There was a long pause, punctuated by sounds of confused shouting in the background. Then, breathlessly, the announcer informed listeners that there would be some delay. His voice faded out and was replaced by martial music. It was nearly an hour before Göring finally came on the air. He was clearly harassed and angry. Only a couple of years earlier, he had announced confidently that no enemy aircraft would ever fly over the Third Reich. Yet, today, the RAF had visited the Reich's capital in broad daylight.

All three Mosquitoes returned safely to base – but, for the RAF, the day's work was not over yet. Goebbels was due to speak at 1600 hours, and a hot reception had been planned for him too. At 1235 three more Mosquitoes, this time drawn from No. 139 Squadron and led by Squadron Leader D.F.W. Darling, took off from Marham. They flew at wave-top level to a point north of Heligoland, then turned in towards Lübeck. By this time, the weather had deteriorated, and the aircraft ran through squalls along the whole of their route. As the Mosquitoes climbed to 20,000ft, Sergeant R.C. Fletcher, the navigator in the number two aircraft, shouted a warning that Messerschmitt 109s were attacking from astern. Fletcher's pilot, Sergeant J. Massey, and Flight Sergeant P.J. McGeehan, who was flying the third aircraft, both took violent evasive action and managed to shake off the fighters. Squadron Leader Darling was not so fortunate. He was last seen diving down into cloud, apparently out of control, and failed to return from the mission.

The two remaining Mosquitoes flew on above a dense cloud layer. At 1555 they arrived over Berlin and Sergeant Massey dropped his bombs through a gap in the clouds. The flak was now intense, and it was another eight minutes before Flight Sergeant McGeehan could get into position to make a successful bombing run. His bombs burst half a mile south of the city centre. As the Mosquitoes turned for home

Below: 'Master bomber'. Group Captain Percy Pickard, shown here shortly before taking off on the Amiens mission. The raid was Pickard's last as commander of No. 140 Wing. His Mosquito was ambushed by a pair of enemy fighters on the way home – he never made it back to base. Insets (clockwise from top left): Several weeks after the raid, aerial reconnaissance reveals the full extent of the precision bombing. A Mosquito banks over the Amiens road after delivering its payload on the southeast sector of the prison. As the bombs hit their mark on the northeast wing, falling debris sends a cloud of dust into the air.

Mosquito Raids
Northwest Europe, 1943-45

NORWAY **DEC 1944**
Oslo
SWEDEN

Lossiemouth

SCOTLAND

Glasgow
Edinburgh

NORTH SEA

DENMARK
OCT 1944 Copenhagen
Aarhus

NORTHERN IRELAND

MARCH 1945

Heligoland Lübeck

ENGLAND

Hamburg

NETHERLANDS
Marham
Bodney Feltwell Amsterdam
Berlin
Hunsdon
APRIL 1944 The Hague
JAN 1943

London
WALES Dover Calais GERMANY
Lasham Brussels
Southampton Cologne
Littlehampton BELGIUM
Albert LUX
ENGLISH CHANNEL Amiens
Le Havre **FEB 1944**

FRANCE Paris

Key
+ Mosquito bases
* Mosquito raids
→ Route to Amiens

Goebbels' speech went out as planned – from the safety of an underground bunker. Their noses down to gain speed, the two bombers raced for the coast, evading the worst of the flak, as well as a swarm of Focke-Wulf 190s. The Mosquitoes landed safely at Marham shortly after 1830.

Just over one year later, on 18 February 1944, the Mosquitoes carried out what has since become one of the most famous low-level daylight attacks of all time. Aircraft of No. 140 Wing, part of the recently formed Second Tactical Air Force, bombed and destroyed the walls of Amiens Prison, allowing over 200 French Resistance fighters to escape.

The attack was to go ahead, as many of the French prisoners were in danger of imminent execution

Commanded by Group Captain Percy Pickard, No. 140 Wing was essentially a Commonwealth outfit, made up of No. 21 Squadron RAF, No. 487 Squadron Royal New Zealand Air Force (RNZAF), and No. 464 Squadron Royal Australian Air Force (RAAF). Six crews were selected from each squadron to make the attack, codenamed Operation Renovate. The day fixed for the attack dawned overcast and grey, with storms of sleet sweeping across the Mosquitoes' base at Hunsdon, Hertfordshire. The forecast indicated that the route to the target would also be covered by heavy, low cloud. Nevertheless, it was decided that the attack was to go ahead, as many of the French prisoners were in danger of imminent execution. The raid was to be led by No. 487 Squadron. At noon precisely, three Mosquitoes were to blast a hole in the eastern wall of the prison, and, three minutes later, three more aircraft would bomb the northern wall. The Australians of No. 464 Squadron would then go in; one section of three aircraft bombing the southeast corner of the prison while the other section attacked the northeast wing. The third squadron, No. 21, was to remain in reserve in case any of the other attacks failed. The RAF pilots were not happy about their watch-and-wait role, but all three squadrons had clamoured for first place in the raid and Pickard had settled on the easiest way to decide the order of attack – by the flip of a coin.

The three squadrons took off at 1100 hours on 18 February, flying straight into the teeth of a blinding snowstorm. Each aircraft carried a pair of 500lb bombs with 11-second delayed-action fuzes. The Mosquitoes made rendezvous with their fighter escort over Littlehampton, and together with the three squadrons of Typhoons they headed out over the Channel at low level. Despite the poor visibility, Amiens proved easy to locate and the Mosquitoes skirted the town to the north and thundered towards their target along the straight, poplar-lined Albert-Amiens road. The New Zealand squadron attacked bang on schedule, bombing from as low as 50ft. The bombs of the leading aircraft slammed into the eastern wall about five feet off the ground. Meanwhile, the second section of three aircraft swept round to strike from the north. Wing Commander R.W. Iredale, leading the first section of No. 464 Squadron, later described the attack:

'From about four miles away I saw the prison and the first three aircraft nipping over the top. I knew then it was OK for me to go in. My squadron was to divide into two sections, one to open each end of the prison, and it was now that one half broke off and swept in to attack the far end from the right. The rest of us carried on in tight formation. Four

hundred yards before we got there, delayed-action bombs went off and I saw they had breached the wall. Clouds of smoke and dust came up, but over the top I could still see the triangular gable of the prison – my aiming point for the end we were to open.

'I released my bombs from 10ft and pulled up slap through the smoke over the prison roof. I looked round to the right and felt slightly relieved to see the other boys still 200yds short of the target and coming in dead on line. They bombed and we all got away OK, re-formed as a section, and made straight for base.'

Meanwhile, Pickard, who had gone in with the Australians, now broke off to act as master bomber. He flew low over the prison, examining the damage, and only when he was satisfied that all the objectives had been attained did he order the Mosquitoes of No. 21 Squadron to set course for home, their bombs still on board. As the Mosquitoes roared away, prisoners – many of whom had escaped from their death cells with the help of explosives smuggled in by the Resistance – streamed through the breaches in the walls, and raced across the snow-covered ground to the shelter of the woods beyond. A massive German search operation later rounded up some of the fugitives, but many got clean away.

As the Mosquitoes sped away from their target,

Above: Wing Commander R.W. Iredale, who led the first section of No. 264 Squadron during the daring low-level raid on Amiens Prison. Precision bombing became a hallmark of No. 140 Wing and, nine months later, the three squadrons involved in the attack repeated their success during a mission to destroy the Gestapo Headquarters in Aarhus, Denmark. Top left: As the Mosquitoes set course for home, the Gestapo building lies devastated in their wake. Once again, the men of No. 140 Wing had hit the target dead centre, resulting in minimal civilian casualties.

one of them – a No. 464 Squadron aircraft flown by Squadron Leader I.E. McRitchie – was hit by light flak and went down out of control. Pickard immediately turned back to fly over the wreck, presumably to see what had happened to the crew. His Mosquito was caught by a pair of Focke-Wulf 190s and shot down. He and his navigator, Flight Lieutenant Alan Broadley, were killed instantly. All the other Mosquitoes returned safely to base.

Two months later, in what an Air Ministry bulletin described as 'probably the most brilliant feat of low-level precision bombing of the war', the Mosquitoes struck again. This time, their attack was directed against the Gestapo headquarters at The Hague, the nerve-centre of German operations against the Resistance in the Low Countries. The Gestapo HQ was a 90ft-high, five-storey building tightly wedged among the other houses in the Schevengsche Weg. It was strongly defended by light anti-aircraft weapons, a factor that would make the Mosquitoes' mission even more hazardous.

The task of destroying the building was given to No. 613 Squadron, commanded by Wing Commander Bob Bateson. It would be the most difficult job a

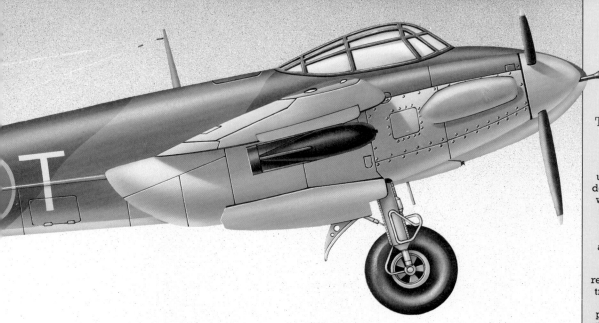

THE DE HAVILLAND MOSQUITO

Conceived in 1938 as an unarmed day bomber, the de Havilland Mosquito (left) went on to perform a wide variety of roles: high and low-level day and night bomber, long-range day and night-fighter, fighter-bomber, minelayer, pathfinder, photo-reconnaissance, trainer and transport aircraft. A grand total of 43 marks were produced and, apart from the Ju 88, no other military aircraft has been built in so many versions.

The prototype, W4050, flew in November 1940, and reached a speed 20 miles per hour in excess of the fastest British fighter of the time. The first deliveries of B. Mk IV bombers went to No. 105 Squadron in January 1942.

Numerically the most important variant of the Mosquito was the FB. Mk VI, which entered service with the tactical squadrons of the RAF's No. 2 Group in 1943. Equipped with eight 60lb rocket projectiles, the FB. Mk VI also served with several strike squadrons of RAF Coastal Command. From 1943 to 1945 the Mk VI was employed by 44 RAF squadrons.

Powered by two Rolls-Royce Merlin 21 inline piston engines, the Mk VI had a maximum speed of 380 miles per hour at 17,000ft, and a service ceiling of 31,000ft. Armament comprised four 20mm cannon and four 0.303in machine guns, in addition to two 500lb bombs and eight rocket projectiles. The Mosquito was also built in Canada and Australia, and 40 of the Canadian reconnaissance variants were supplied to the USAAF and used under the designation F-8. The final total of Mosquito production reached 7781, of which 6710 were built during the war. As the NF.30 and NF.36 night-fighter, the PR.34 reconnaissance and B.35 light bomber variants, the ubiquitous Mosquito remained in front-line service until the 1950s.

bomber squadron ever had to face, and planning for the raid had to be meticulous. A scale model of the Gestapo HQ was built, perfect in every detail, right down to the thickness and composition of the walls. Alongside the planners, scientists worked hard in order to develop a new bomb – a mixture of incendiary and high explosive – that would have a maximum destructive effect on the mass of Gestapo files and records. Bateson picked his crews carefully, and put them to the test during several weeks of intensive training. At last, everything was ready. In the early hours of 11 April 1944, Bateson led six Mosquitoes away from their base at Lasham in Hampshire, and set course over the Channel.

As they approached The Hague, the Mosquitoes split up into pairs and swept across the rooftops, the narrow streets shuddering to the din of their engines. As Bateson's Mosquito streaked towards the target, bomb-doors open, its port wing-tip missed the spire on top of the Peace Palace by inches. Flight Lieutenant Peter Cobley, following in line astern behind Bateson, saw the leader's pair of bombs drop away. He had a hazy impression of a German sentry throwing away his rifle and running for his life, and

Right: The badge of No. 487 Squadron, Royal New Zealand Air Force. The insignia is based on Maori legend. Tribal meeting houses usually had a similar figure above each entrance – brandishing a weapon as a challenge to the enemy. Left: 'Wooden Wonders'. Mosquitoes from No. 487 Squadron set out for France.

then he saw Bateson's bombs literally skip through the front door of the HQ. Cobley dropped his own bombs in turn, pulling up sharply over the roof of the building. Two minutes later, with dense clouds of smoke already pouring from the shattered building, the second pair of Mosquitoes made their attack. After a further interval, the third pair finished the job. The raid was a complete success. The Gestapo building had been utterly destroyed, and the buildings that surrounded it had suffered only slight damage. All six Mosquitoes got back safely, without a single shot being fired at them.

On 31 October 1944, another Gestapo Headquarters – this time at Aarhus, in Denmark – was attacked by 25 Mosquitoes of No. 140 Wing. The squadrons involved were Nos. 21, 464 and 487, the same units that had carried out the Amiens Prison raid. Led by the newly promoted Wing Commander Bob Reynolds, they took off from Thorney Island and set out over the North Sea, escorted by eight Mustang fighters. The Mosquitoes carried a total of 35 500lb bombs, again fitted with 11-second delayed-action fuzes.

The Gestapo HQ was located in two adjoining buildings that had previously formed part of the University of Aarhus. Once again, the squadrons were confronted with the problem of making an effective attack while causing minimum damage to civilian property. The target area was reached without incident, the Mustang fighter escort 'beating up' trains and other targets of opportunity as they raced across Denmark at low level. The Mosquitoes swept across the Gestapo HQ like a whirlwind and unloaded their bombs into the centre of it, leaving the building shattered and ablaze. One Mosquito actually hit the roof of the building, losing its tail-wheel and half its port tailplane. It nevertheless managed to reach England safely, as did the other aircraft. More than 200 Gestapo officials were killed in the attack, and all the files on the Dutch Resistance

Of all the Mosquito operations, one of the most spectacular was that flown on 11 April 1944 by six aircraft of No. 613 (City of Manchester) Squadron. Led by Wing Commander Bob Bateson (below), the Mosquitoes completely destroyed the German Gestapo archives housed in the Kleizcamp Art Galleries in The Hague. Skimming the rooftops as they streaked towards their target, the aircrews unleashed a hail of bombs that found the target with uncanny accuracy. Main picture: Huge palls of smoke shroud the Schevengsche Weg as the bombs, a mixture of incendiary and explosive, devastate the Gestapo HQ.

movement were destroyed in the subsequent fire.

On 31 December 1944, Mosquitoes of No. 627 Squadron carried out an equally successful attack on the Gestapo Headquarters in Oslo, Norway, and on 21 March 1945 it was once again the turn of the three squadrons of No. 140 Wing, when Bob Bateson led them in a daring low-level attack on the main building of the Gestapo HQ in Copenhagen, Denmark. Although the target was completely destroyed, the success of the mission was tragically marred when one of the Mosquitoes, striking an obstacle with its wingtip, crashed on a convent school and killed 87 children.

The Danes, however, were forgiving. Such tragedies, they said, were inevitable during times of war. When Bob Bateson visited Denmark after the war, he was treated like a hero. During his visit, he met several men who had been undergoing torture in the Copenhagen HQ when the Mosquitoes arrived overhead. They owed their lives to him. But that was all in the past; of far greater significance to Wing Commander Bateson was the day when he led his Mosquitoes over Copenhagen for the last time, taking part in a flypast to raise money for Danish orphan children, the victims of the tyranny he and his men had done so much to help stamp out.

THE AUTHOR Robert Jackson is a professional aviation historian and the author of over 50 books, including *The Royal Air Force in Action*.

NETTLETON'S LANCS

The Augsburg raid of 1942 was one of the most daring and heroic missions ever undertaken by RAF Bomber Command

ON 17 APRIL 1942, an audacious daylight bombing mission was flown by RAF Bomber Command against the MAN diesel engine factory at Augsburg, in Bavaria, which was responsible for the production of roughly half of Germany's output of U-boat engines. The raid was notable for two main reasons: it was the longest low-level penetration ever made

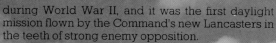

during World War II, and it was the first daylight mission flown by the Command's new Lancasters in the teeth of strong enemy opposition.

Because of the havoc wrought by Hitler's U-boats, the MAN factories at Augsburg had long been high on the list of priority targets, but there was a problem. Getting there and back involved a round trip of 1250 miles over enemy territory, and the MAN factories

occupied a relatively small area. With the navigation and bombing aids then available, the chances of a night attack pinpointing and destroying such an objective were very remote, and a daylight precision attack, going on past experience, would be prohibitively costly.

Then, in early 1942 the Lancaster arrived. With its relatively high speed and strong defensive armament, it was possible that a force of Lancasters could reach Augsburg if they went in at low level, underneath the German early-warning radar. Also, Lan-

Below: Three Avro Lancaster bombers of No.44 (Rhodesia) Squadron in flight. Inset: The man who led the daring daylight raid against the diesel-engine factories at Augsburg, Squadron Leader John Nettleton. Nettleton won the Victoria Cross for his part in the mission.

NO.44 (RHODESIA) SQUADRON

No.44 Squadron, RFC, was formed on 27 July 1917 and made a name for itself during the remainder of World War I, pioneering the use of the Sopwith Camel for night operations. One of its early commanding officers was Major A.T. Harris, who rose to fame during World War II as Sir Arthur 'Bomber' Harris. The squadron was disbanded in 1919 but reformed in 1937 as a bomber squadron. At the outbreak of war No.44 was equipped with Handley Page Hampdens. Early operations consisted mainly of North Sea sweeps, security patrols and minelaying. In May 1940 the squadron switched to attacks on enemy lines of communication, followed by raids on the invasion barges assembled by the Germans in the Channel ports for Operation Sealion. Soon after the Augsburg raid, in which the squadron flew its newly acquired Lancasters, No.44 Squadron had the unique distinction of numbering two VC holders among its personnel: John Nettleton and the then commanding officer, Wing Commander R.A.B. Learoyd. No.44 Squadron saw unbroken service with RAF Bomber Command throughout the war, flying 4362 Lancaster sorties on 272 bombing and 27 minelaying operations. In 1947 No.44 re-equipped with Lincolns, and in 1951 moved onto Washingtons. Two years later it was re-equipped yet again, this time with Canberras. In 1956, as part of the Suez campaign, the squadron took part in the bombing of Egypt. In July 1957 the squadron was disbanded but reformed again in 1960 as part of V-Force, flying Vulcan B.Mk Is. No. 44 Squadron was finally disbanded at Waddington on 21 December 1982.

casters flying 'on the deck' could not be subjected to attacks from below on their vulnerable underbellies. With the new aircraft, the idea of a deep-penetration, precision attack in daylight was resurrected.

The operation was to be carried out by six crews from No. 44 Squadron, based at Waddington, and six from No. 97, stationed at Woodhall Spa in Lincolnshire – the two most experienced Lancaster units. A seventh crew from each squadron would train with the others, to be held in reserve in case anything went wrong at the last moment.

Training for the mission began on 14 April 1942, and for three days the two squadrons practised formation flying at low level, making 1000-mile flights around Britain and carrying out simulated attacks on targets in northern Scotland. Speculation ran high over the nature of the target. To most of the experienced crews, a low-level mission signified an attack on enemy warships, a long, straight run into a nightmare of flak. When they eventually filed into their briefing rooms early on 17 April, and saw the long red ribbon marking their attack route on the map stretching to Augsburg, a stunned silence descended on them. Even an attack on a major battleship would have been preferable to this.

Flying south to their departure point on the coast, the Lancasters were to cross the English Channel at low level and make landfall at Dives-sur-Mer, on the French coast. Shortly before this, bombers of No. 2 Group, covered by a massive fighter 'umbrella', were to make a series of diversionary attacks on Luftwaffe airfields in the Pas de Calais, Rouen, and Cherbourg areas. The Lancasters' flight track would take them across enemy territory via Ludwigshafen, where they would cross the Rhine, to the northern tip of the Ammersee, a large lake to the west of Munich and about 20 miles south of Augsburg..

If all went well the first Lancasters would reach the target at 2015, just before dusk

As they approached the target, the bombers were to spread out and create a three-mile gap between each section. Sections would then bomb from low level, in formation, each Lancaster dropping a salvo of four 1000lb bombs. The ordnance would be fitted with 11-second delayed-action fuzes, which would give the bombers time to get clear, and would explode well before the next section arrived over the target. Take-off was to be at 1500 hours. This meant that, if all went well, the first Lancasters would reach the target at 2015, just before dusk. They would thus have the shelter of darkness by the time they reached the danger areas along the Channel coast on the homeward flight.

The Lancasters of No. 44 Squadron were to form the two leading sections. This unit was known as the 'Rhodesia' Squadron, and with good reason – about a quarter of its personnel came from that country. No. 44 also contained a number of South Africans, and one of them was chosen to lead the mission. He was Squadron Leader John Dering Nettleton, a tall, dark-haired 25-year-old, who had already shown himself to be a highly competent commander, rock-steady in an emergency.

There was a fleeting glimpse of the 109's pale grey, oil-streaked belly as it flashed overhead

At three o'clock in the afternoon of 17 April, the quiet Lincolnshire village of Waddington was rudely shaken by the roar of 24 Rolls Royce Merlins as No. 44 Squadron's six Lancasters took off and headed south for Selsey Bill, the promontory of land jutting out into the Channel between Portsmouth and Bognor Regis. Ten miles due east, at Woodhall Spa, the six bombers of No. 97 Squadron, led by Squadron Leader Sherwood, were also taking off.

Each section left Selsey Bill bang on schedule, the sea a blurr below the Lancasters as they sped on. The bombers to left and right of Nettleton were piloted by Flying Officer John Garwell and Warrant Officer Rhodes; the Lancasters in the following section were flown by Flight Lieutenant Sandford, Warrant Officer Crum, and Warrant Officer Beckett. The sky was clear and the hot afternoon sun beat down through the perspex of cockpits and gun turrets. Before they reached the French coast, most of the crews were flying in shirt sleeves.

The bombers were flying over wooded, hilly country near Breteuil when the flak hit them. Lines of tracer from concealed gun positions met the speeding Lancasters, and the ugly black stains of shell-bursts dotted the sky around them. Shrapnel ripped into two of the aircraft, but they held their course. The most serious damage was to Warrant Officer Beckett's machine, which had its rear gun turret put out of action.

Then, near Evreux, the Lancaster formation was spotted by enemy fighters. A Messerschmitt Bf 109 came streaking in, singling out Warrant Officer Crum's Lancaster (in 44's second section) for his first firing pass. Bullets tore through the cockpit canopy, showering Crum and his navigator, Rhodesian Alan Dedman, with razor-sharp slivers of perspex. Dedman looked across at the pilot and saw blood streaming down his face, but when he went to help, Crum just grinned and waved him away. The Lancaster's own guns hammered, there was a fleeting glimpse of the 109's pale grey, oil-streaked belly as it flashed overhead, and then it was gone.

The Lancasters closed up into even tighter forma-

Below: A Lancaster of No.44 Squadron warms up on the airfield before taxiing into take-off position. Above: A No. 44 Squadron flight commander and his crew pose for the camera before setting out on a bombing mission in 1942.
Above right: A last-minute check on the course to be flown is made before boarding the Lancaster. Right: En route. A Lancaster navigator at work as the aircraft heads out over the English Channel towards an appointment with a German industrial target.

AVRO LANCASTER B.MK I

In 1936, in response to an Air Ministry specification for a new tactical bomber, work began on the twin-engine Avro Manchester. However, it soon became obvious that the Manchester suffered from directional instability and a lack of power. In an attempt to solve these problems, the designers, led by Roy Chadwick, converted the Manchester airframe with enlarged outer panels, a tail with taller fins and rudders, and four 1145hp Rolls-Royce Merlin engines.

The first prototype Lancaster, BT308, flew on 9 January 1941 and was a resounding success, being pronounced 'eminently suitable for operational service.'

The first production Lancaster, L7527, was flown on 31 October 1941. Over 300 Manchesters were quickly converted into Lancasters, and full-scale production was under way by early 1942. The earliest production models retained the Manchester's two-gun ventral turret, but this was rarely used and soon discarded. Total production during World War II was 7377, of which 3425 were B.Mk 1s. Powered by four Rolls-Royce Merlin XX (1280hp), 22 (1460hp) or 24 (1640hp) engines, the seven-seat Lancaster B.Mk 1 had a maximum speed of 275mph and a range of 2530 miles. Armament comprised nine 0.303in Browning machine guns (one in a Frazer-Nash FN.60 ventral turret, two each in FN.5 nose and FN.50 dorsal, and four in FN.20 tails turrets), in addition to 22,000lb of bombs.

During the course of 156,000 sorties, the Lancaster flew with at least 59 Bomber Command squadrons – making it the most important British heavy bomber of World War II.

tion as 30 more Messerschmitts pounced on them like sharks. It was the first time that Luftwaffe fighters had encountered Lancasters, and to begin with the enemy pilots showed a certain amount of caution until they got the measure of the new bomber's defences. As soon as they realised that its defensive armament consisted of .303in machine guns, however, they began to press home their attacks skilfully, coming in from the port quarter and opening fire with their cannon at about 700yds. At 400yds, the limit of the .303's effective range, they broke away sharply and climbed to repeat the process.

The mid-upper and rear gunners were wounded, and then the port wing fuel tank burst into flames

Warrant Officer Beckett was the first to go. A great ball of orange flame ballooned from a wing of his aircraft as cannon shells hit a fuel tank. Seconds later, the bomber was a mass of fire. Slowly, the nose went down. Spewing burning fragments, the shattered Lancaster hit a clump of trees and disintegrated.

Warrant Officer Crum's Lancaster, its wings and fuselage ripped and torn, came under attack by three enemy fighters. Both the mid-upper and rear gunners were wounded, and then the port wing fuel tank burst into flames. The bomber wallowed on, almost out of control. Crum, half-blinded by the blood streaming from his face wounds, fought to hold the wings level and ordered Alan Dedman to jettison the bombs, which had not yet been armed. The 1000-pounders dropped away, and a few moments later Crum managed to put the crippled aircraft down on her belly. The Lancaster tore across a wheatfield and slewed to a stop on the far side. The crew, badly shaken and bruised but otherwise unhurt, broke all records in getting out of the wreck, convinced that it was going to explode in flames. But the fire in the wing went out, so Crum used an axe from the bomber's escape kit to make holes in the fuel tanks and threw a match into the resulting pool of petrol. Within a couple of minutes the aircraft was burning nicely, and there would only be a very charred carcase left for the Luftwaffe experts to examine.

Crum and his crew split up into pairs and set out on the long walk through Occupied France to Bordeaux, where they knew they could make contact with members of the French Resistance. All of them,

however, were rounded up by the Germans and spent the rest of the war in POW camps.

With Beckett and Crum gone, only Flight Lieutenant Sandford was left of the three Lancasters in the second section. Sandford, a quiet lover of music who amused his colleagues because he always wore pyjamas under his flying suit for luck, was one of the most popular officers on No. 44 Squadron. Now his luck had run out, and he was fighting for his life. In a desperate bid to escape from a swarm of Messerschmitts, he eased his great bomber down underneath some high-tension cables. But the Lancaster dug a wingtip into the ground, cartwheeled and exploded, killing all on board.

The enemy fighters now latched onto Warrant Officer Rhodes, flying to the right and some distance behind John Nettleton. Soon, the Lancaster was streaming fire from all four engines. Rhodes must have opened his throttles wide in a last-ditch attempt to draw clear, because his aircraft suddenly shot ahead of Nettleton's. Then it went into a steep climb and seemed to hang on its churning propellers for a long moment before flicking sharply over and diving into the ground. There was no chance of survival for any of his crew.

There were now only two Lancasters remaining in the 44 Squadron formation – those flown by Nettleton and his number two, John Garwell. Both aircraft were badly shot up and their fuel tanks were holed, but the self-sealing 'skins' seemed to be preventing leakage on a serious scale. Nevertheless, the fighters were still coming at them like angry hornets, and the life expectancy of both crews was now measured in minutes.

The gunners reported seeing fountains of smoke and debris bursting into the evening sky

Then, a miracle happened. Singly, or in pairs, the enemy fighters suddenly broke off their attacks and turned away. They were probably running out of fuel or ammunition, or both. Whatever the reason, their abrupt disappearance meant that Nettleton and Garwell were spared, at least for the time being. But they still had more than 500 miles to go before they reached the target. Behind them, and a little way to the south, Squadron Leader Sherwood's 97 Squadron formation had been luckier; they saw no German fighters, and flew on unmolested.

The Augsburg Raid 17 April 1942

Key
→ The flight to Augsburg

Flying almost wingtip to wingtip, Nettleton and Garwell swept on in their battle-scarred aircraft. There was no further enemy opposition, and the two pilots were free to concentrate on handling their bombers. This task grew considerably more difficult when, two hours later, they penetrated the mountainous country of southern Germany and the Lancasters had to fly through turbulent air currents boiling up from the slopes.

They finally reached the Ammersee and turned north, rising a few hundred feet to clear some hills and then dropping down again into the valley on the other side. And there, dead ahead of them under a thin veil of haze, was Augsburg.

As they reached the outskirts of the town, a curtain of flak burst across the sky in their path. Shrapnel pummelled their wings and fuselages but the pilots held their course, following the line of the river to find their target. The models, photographs and drawings

Top: The cockpit layout of an Avro Lancaster. Right: Ordnance personnel bomb up a Lancaster. The early versions of the aircraft carried their bomb loads in flush-fitting bomb bays, but as bombs increased in size the bomb bays had to be made deeper so that they protruded below the line of the fuselage. The largest bomb carried was the 22,000lb 'Grand Slam', or 'earthquake' bomb. Below: A side-view of the Avro Lancaster, the finest British heavy bomber of World War II.

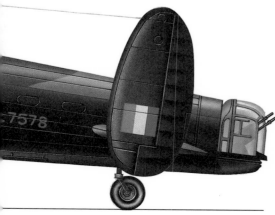

WING COMMANDER J.D. NETTLETON, VC

John Dering Nettleton came from a naval background – his grandfather had been an admiral in the Royal Navy – and after leaving school in Natal he spent two years in the Merchant Navy.

After this period at sea, Nettleton trained as a civil engineer. While pursuing this profession he decided to take a holiday in England, but three days before he was due to return to South Africa he made an impulsive decision to join the Royal Air Force.

Nettleton turned out to be an above average pilot, which had its own penalty; like many others, he was 'creamed off' to be an instructor. Finally, however, he got an operational posting to No.44 (Rhodesia) Squadron and rose to the rank of flight lieutenant while flying Handley Page Hampden bombers on operations over Germany. When the squadron re-equipped with Lancasters, Nettleton became flight commander and was promoted to the rank of squadron leader. On the Augsburg raid of April 1942, for which Nettleton was awarded the Victoria Cross, he was still on his first operational tour.

Later, Nettleton was promoted to wing commander and was given command of No.44 Squadron. On the night of 12/13 July 1943, while returning from a raid on Turin, his Lancaster was shot down over the English Channel by a German nightfighter. Nettleton and his crew perished.

Above: A flight of Lancasters unleashes its bombs over Germany. Right: An aerial photograph showing the target of No.44 Squadron's raid of April 1942 – the MAN diesel-engine works at Augsburg. The sketch of the area (bottom) was part of the briefing material shown to the crews before they embarked on the mission. When Nettleton and Sherwood's aircraft arrived over the works, they found their specific targets with ease, due to the high quality of their pre-flight briefing. Unfortunately, many of their bombs did not explode and the factory suffered little damage. They did, however, succeed in punching a huge hole in the roof of the diesel-engine assembly shop (marked Ⓐ on sketch) and demolished a crank-grinding shop (marked Ⓑ).

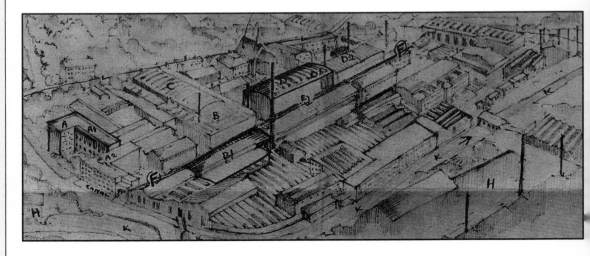

they had studied at the briefing had been astonishingly accurate and they had no difficulty in locating their primary objective, a T-shaped shed where the U-boat engines were manufactured.

With bomb-doors open, and light flak continually hitting the Lancasters, they thundered over the last few hundred yards. Then the bombers jumped as the eight 1000lb bombs fell from their bellies. Nettleton and Garwell were already over the northern suburbs of Augsburg when the bombs exploded, and the gunners reported seeing fountains of smoke and debris bursting high into the evening sky above the target.

The Lancaster pilots had battled their way through against appalling odds and had successfully accomplished their mission, but the flak was still bursting around them and now John Garwell found himself in trouble. A flak shell turned the interior of the fuselage into a roaring inferno and Garwell realised that this, together with the severe damage the bomber had already sustained, might lead to her breaking up at any moment. There was no time to gain height so that the crew could bale out; he had to put her down as quickly as possible. Blinded by the smoke pouring into the cockpit, Garwell eased the Lancaster gently down towards what he hoped was open ground. All he could do was to try and hold the bomber steady as she sank.

A long, agonising minute later the Lancaster hit the ground, sending earth flying in all directions as she skidded across a field. She slid to a stop, and Garwell, with three other members of his crew, scrambled thankfully out of the raging heat and choking, fuel-fed smoke into the fresh air. Two other crew members were trapped in the burning fuselage and a third, Flight Sergeant R.J. Flux, had been thrown out on impact. He had wrenched open the escape hatch just before the bomber touched down; his action had given the others a few extra seconds in which to get clear, but it had cost Flux his life.

By the time he reached his target the Lancaster was little more than a plunging sheet of flame

As Nettleton turned for home, alone now, the leading section of No. 97 bore in across the hills towards Augsburg. All three Lancasters released their loads on the target and thundered on towards safety, their gunners spraying any anti-aircraft position they could see. The bombers were flying so low that, on occasion, they dropped below the level of the roof tops, finding some shelter from the murderous flak.

They almost made it, all three of them. But then Sherwood's aircraft, probably hit by a large-calibre shell, began to stream white vapour from a fuel tank. A few moments later flames erupted from it and the bomber went down out of control, a mass of fire, to explode just outside the town. Sherwood alone was thrown clear and survived. The other two pilots of the section, Flying Officers Rodley and Hallows, returned safely to base.

The second section consisted of Flight Lieutenant Penman, Flying Officer Deverill and Warrant Officer Mycock. All three pilots saw Sherwood go down as they roared over Augsburg in the gathering dusk. The sky above the town was a mass of vivid light as the enemy gunners hurled every imaginable kind of flak shell into the Lancasters' path. Mycock's aircraft was hit and caught fire, but the pilot held doggedly to his course. By the time he reached his target the Lancaster was little more than a plunging sheet of

flame, but Mycock held on long enough to release his bombs. Then the Lancaster exploded, its burning wreckage cascading into the streets below.

Deverill's aircraft was also badly hit and its starboard inner engine set on fire, but the crew managed to extinguish it after bombing the target and flew back to base on three engines, accompanied by Penman's Lancaster. Both crews expected to be attacked by night fighters on the home run, but the flight was completely uneventful. It was just as well, for every gun turret on both Lancasters was jammed.

For his part in leading the Augsburg raid, John Nettleton was awarded the Victoria Cross. He was promoted to Wing Commander, and the following year he was flying his second tour of operations. But sadly, death and John Nettleton were destined to keep a long-delayed rendezvous. On the night of 12/13 July 1943, he was shot down and killed while returning from a raid on Turin.

Tragically, the sacrifice of seven Lancasters and 49 young men on the Augsburg raid had been in vain. Many of the delayed-action bombs failed to explode, and the effect on production at the MAN factory was negligible. Never again would the RAF send out its four-engined bombers on a daylight 'extreme danger' mission of this kind.

Fate sometimes plays strange tricks. Some 40 years later, a Vulcan jet bomber carried out the longest-range bombing mission in the history of air warfare, against Stanley airfield in the Falklands. That Vulcan, and its crew, belonged to No. 44 Squadron.

THE AUTHOR Robert Jackson is a professional aviation historian and the author of over 50 books, including *The Royal Air Force in Action*.

Above: Four of the surviving members of the No.97 Squadron element of the raid on Augsburg. From left to right they are: Flying Officer B.R.W. Hallows, Flying Officer E.E. Rodley, Flight Lieutenant D.J. Penman and Flying Officer E.A. Deverill.

Above: The latter-day wings of No.44 Squadron, the Vulcan bomber, which saw service recently in the Falklands campaign of 1982.

379TH BOMBARDMENT GROUP

Nicknamed 'Triangle K', the 379th (Heavy) Bombardment Group, consisting of four bomber squadrons, the 524th 525th, 526th and 527th, was formed in November 1942 at Gowen Field, Idaho. A few weeks later it was stationed at Wendover Field in Utah, some experienced fliers from existing formations were drafted in and a commanding officer, Colonel Maurice 'Mo' Preston, was appointed. Despite many early teething problems, progress in building up the 379th was rapid and, with a further move to Sioux City Air Base, the group was pronounced ready for overseas duty in mid-April 1943.

Over the next few weeks the group travelled to Britain – aircrews collecting their new B-17s and flying across the Atlantic.

Once in Britain, the group came under the command of the US Eighth Army Air Force and was immediately sent on a familiarisation course at Bovington. In mid-May the unit moved on to Kimbolton and a few days later, on the 29th, took part in its first mission. Losses in this and later raids were extremely high and Preston was forced to introduce a series of measures to improve the group's performance in every department.

Preston's re-training programme achieved good results and the group went on to earn a first-rate bombing record. By the close of the war, it had flown 10,492 sorties, dropped over 26,000 tons of bombs and had won two Distinguished Unit Citations. Over 140 B-17s had been lost to enemy fire.

As a group the 379th did not survive after the war – it was formally de-activated at Casablanca on 25 July 1945. Its distinctive tail insignia is shown above.

FLYING FORTRESS

Below: The B-17 Flying Fortress was the mainstay of the USAAF's daylight offensive against Hitler's Europe. Here, a B-17 of the 379th 'Triangle K' Group heads for the Channel.

The Flying Fortresses of the USAAF's 379th (Heavy) Bombardment Group fought their way through the hostile skies over Nazi Germany to strike deep into the industrial heartland of the Third Reich

UNDER FULL POWER, with its speed gauge indicating 120mph, the B-17 Flying Fortress thundered off the end of the runway and then climbed away over the little Huntingdonshire town of Kimbolton. At 30-second intervals, another 23 B-17s followed, straining under heavy loads of fuel and bombs to gain take-off speed. Each carried 2800 US gallons in its tanks, two 2000lb demolition bombs in the bay and a crew of 10

young men whose feelings switched between excitement and apprehension. They knew that take-off in a bomber loaded to capacity was not without risk. If an engine faltered at the moment of lift-off a crash was almost inevitable – a crash that would most probably result in explosion, fire and their premature deaths. But on this day, 29 May 1943, their apprehension and excitement were all the greater because they, the men of the 379th (Heavy) Bombardment Group of the United States Eighth Army Air Force (USAAF), were going to war for the first time.

In the leading Fortress Colonel Maurice 'Mo' Preston, the group commander, called up his rear gunner, Lieutenant Francis, on the intercom and received confirmation that all 24 B-17s were airborne, gaining altitude and beginning to move to their pre-arranged places in the formation. Usually, Francis was the bomber's co-pilot, but on this flight he had been displaced by the 379th's 'boss' and was monitoring the movements of the following B-17s. For nearly an hour the bombers circled, establishing the close, staggered formation known as a 'box', which was designed to give the B-17s' guns unobstructed fields of fire and bring the maximum number of weapons to bear on attacking fighters. Observed either from the ground or the air, these bomber boxes did not appear to conform to any planned pattern. In fact, they were carefully arranged and built from three-plane 'vees' echeloned back and to left and right. Once satisfied that all his group's aircraft were in position, Preston headed northwest over Molesworth. The plan was to swing in behind another, more experienced group which had already left that airfield and form a larger formation known as a combat wing. Continuing northwest after this manoeuvre, the bombers reached

Left: A record-breaking team posing for the camera. The crew of 'Ol' Gappy' completed over 150 missions before the end of the war. Below: Six Fortresses, flying in a box formation, circle Kimbolton.

the prominent landmark of Eye Brook reservoir, near Corby, for a rendezvous with other USAAF formations.

The 379th was part of a force of 169 B-17s bound for the German U-boat base at St. Nazaire on the west coast of France – a target with one of the heaviest anti-aircraft defences in Western Europe. The US Eighth Air Force's campaign against the U-boat bases on the Atlantic coast had been so costly that Fortress crews were calling St. Nazaire 'Flak City'. The novice 379th Group had been thrown in at the deep end; St. Nazaire was no kindergarten target.

As the bombers soared above 10,000 feet, the crews put on their face masks and began to breathe oxygen. Everything seemed to be going according to plan but, as the B-17s flew over the Thames, one of the engines on Lieutenant Zucker's Fortress began

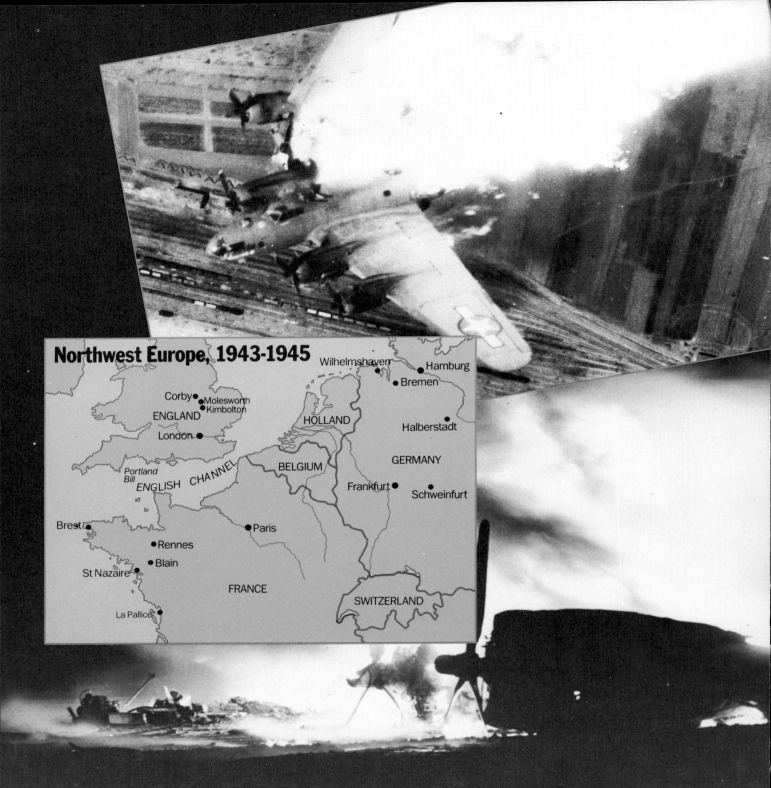

Northwest Europe, 1943-1945

Wilhelmshaven
Hamburg
Bremen
Corby • Molesworth
Kimbolton
ENGLAND
HOLLAND
London
Halberstadt
BELGIUM
GERMANY
Portland
Bill
ENGLISH CHANNEL
Frankfurt
Schweinfurt
Brest
Paris
Rennes
Blain
St Nazaire
FRANCE
SWITZERLAND
La Pallice

to lose power: a turbo-supercharger, an essential piece of equipment when operating at high altitudes, had failed. Zucker had no alternative but to abort – to abandon the mission. Waggling his wings to signal his departure, as radio silence had to be observed, Zucker edged out of the formation and returned to Kimbolton. Another Fortress drew up to take his place. A little later, the prominent landmark of Portland Bill appeared through the haze below, and the formation made a slight change of course.

The Eighth Air Force's plan for the attack involved two forces of Fortresses and a small formation of B-24 Liberators. Some 70 B-17s were to strike at a naval depot near Rennes and divert enemy fighters away from the St. Nazaire force and, 40 minutes after the

diversionary raid, the B-24s would hit the U-boat pens at La Pallice. Timing was crucial if losses were to be kept to a minimum.

At 20,000 feet over the Channel, vapour trails began to stream back from the B-17s' engines as hot gases mingled with the thin, sub-zero air. As the aircraft headed towards the Brest peninsula, the untried crews of the 379th saw their first flak: red flashes, leaving ugly black smudges of smoke. The formation was off course and attracting the fire of German flak batteries on Guernsey. Fortunately, the flak was light and too inaccurate to harm the aircraft. At this point, however, another B-17 suffered mechanical failure and had to turn back. The remaining crews donned steel helmets and body armour as the

Enemy ground fire was the scourge of the 379th during the Allied bomber offensive against occupied Europe. Above left: Hit by flak over Nis, Yugoslavia, on 15 April 1945, a B-17 bursts into flames and disintegrates. The tail section has already broken off. Right: US groundcrew inspecting the damaged tailplane of a B-17 hit by debris from another bomber. Main picture: After a crash landing, fiery wreckage litters Kimbolton airfield.

Brest peninsula appeared. Tense gunners scanned the sky with their 0.5in machine guns at the ready, expecting an immediate assault by German fighters, but none appeared. Even when the Allied fighter escort, flying high above, was forced to turn back through lack of fuel, there was still no sign of the Luftwaffe. The bombers droned on until the bombardier in the lead aircraft picked out Blain, the French town that was to act as the 'Initial Point': the place where the B-17s would turn towards their objectives, open their bomb-bay doors and prepare for the final approach to the targets, with each formation getting in trail. Preston could see the barrage of flak exploding around the leading formations; the intensity of the reception at St. Nazaire had not been exaggerated. Individual aircraft began weaving to confuse the flak batteries but there was no escaping the murderous salvoes.

At precisely 1711 hours, however, the 379th's lead bombardier released his aircraft's lethal load and, following his example, every other bombardier in the group did the same. By this time, two of the 379th's B-17s had been hit by enemy flak. That flown by Captain John Hall, the commanding officer of the group's 526th Squadron, was on fire and falling out of formation. Five men were seen to parachute clear of the flaming aircraft. Another B-17 from the same squadron also went down.

Flying on out over the sea, the 379th escaped the flak and then turned right to re-establish battle formation with the Molesworth group before re-crossing the Brest peninsula. Suddenly, intercoms crackled with shouts of 'Bandits'. A pack of Fw 190s swept through the leading squadron, and the Fortresses shook from the recoil of their defensive guns. The air battle was brief and confused: Lieutenant Hale's aircraft dived under attack, while Lieutenant Francis, in the tail turret of Preston's B-17, fired several rounds into an Fw 190 and claimed its destruction. The French coast was reached and crossed, and the Channel Islands avoided – at last the crews felt relieved of their ordeal. Not so Lieutenant Earl Carlson and his men. Their B-17 had been having mechanical problems and these, plus flak fragments, caused two engines to be shut down by the time Portland Bill came into view again. Carlson thought he could regain home base, but, with only a few miles to go, a third engine failed under the strain and he was forced to make a crash-landing in a field near Little Staughton. The crew emerged uninjured.

FLYING FORTRESS

In May 1934 the US Army issued its requirements for an advanced, multi-engined bomber. Of the many designs submitted, the Boeing Company's proposal was accepted and in August 1935 the prototype Model 299 completed its first endurance flight: over 2100 miles at an average speed of 252mph. Its prominent positions for five machine guns earned the new bomber the nickname 'Flying Fortress'.
The United States Army Air Corps, the forerunner of the US Army Air Force (USAAF), placed its first orders with Boeing and 12 B-17s were delivered between January and August 1937.
Over the following years,

the B-17 was built in a number of models, but it was the 'E' and 'F' variants that first saw service with the Eighth Army Air Force. Experience showed that the Fortress was particularly vulnerable to head-on attacks from enemy fighters. To off-set these weaknesses, a new model, the B-17G, was brought into service. Unlike its predecessors this aircraft had a 'chin' turret mounting two 0.5in machine guns beneath the fuselage nose. In all it carried a total of 13 machine guns. Four turbocharged radial piston engines provided a speed of 287mph at 25,000 feet, and the aircraft had a range of 2000 miles with a 6000lb bombload.
Its main failing was that it could easily catch fire if hit by flak.
Despite this problem, 12,731 aircraft were produced, and the Fortress remained the USAAF's standard heavy bomber throughout World War II.

It was a sober crowd of men who gathered for interrogation at Kimbolton airfield that evening. Bombing had been inaccurate, three of the group's bombers had succumbed to mechanical failure, another had been written off in a crash and three others shot down. The 379th alone had suffered half the losses of the St. Nazaire force. It was a rude introduction to the daylight precision-bombing campaign conducted by the US Eighth Army Air Force.

With a total complement of 36 crews and B-17s in the group, it did not take much arithmetic for the aircrews to work out that at this rate of loss their chances of survival were slim. A tour of combat was 25 missions; from mission number 10 they would be living on borrowed time. But Preston, a big, genial Californian who had nursed the 379th from its earliest days, knew there was much that could be done to improve their performance and reduce losses. His men were novices and he was intent on turning them into bombing experts. On that May evening the 379th Bomber Group was a sore and shaken outfit, and not even their ambitious commanding officer could have foreseen the future accomplishments which were to

make it the most efficient bomber group of the USAAF.

Following the unit's painful combat initiation over St. Nazaire, inclement weather postponed further operations, as clear skies were essential for accurate bombing from high altitudes. During this lull, the 379th licked its wounds, trained and prepared for its next mission. Two weeks were to elapse before this event. The target on 11 June was the U-boat yards at Wilhelmshaven and the 379th again bore the brunt of the US losses. Frontal attacks by German fighters on the inexperienced group downed six of its 29 B-17s, three-quarters of the total Eighth Air Force's losses on that day. In addition, 13 men in the returning bombers were wounded and one other killed. Losses might have been higher but for the efforts of the top-turret gunner in Lieutenant Bill Jones' B-17, nicknamed 'Dangerous Dan'. When fighters attacked, the bomber received many hits. Jones had a bullet pass through his mouth and out of his right shoulder, while his co-pilot was knocked unconscious by the explosion of a 20mm cannon shell. However, the gunner, Cliff Erikson, with only a little experience of flying, took over the controls and brought the aircraft back to base. Although Erikson had never landed a B-17 before, the wounded pilot was able to give instructions and the aircraft was brought down safely.

Understandably, such punishing losses had a further dramatic effect on the group's morale. Two days later a raid on Bremen was undertaken with a great deal of apprehension, but to everyone's relief all the bombers returned safely. Although all the bombers made it back to Kimbolton, many had been hit by flak during the raid. Lieutenant Hale remembered the horror of flak striking home:

'I guess the nearest I came to not coming back from a mission was when a flak fragment went into No. 1 engine. By the time I saw something was wrong most of the oil had gone and there was no response to attempts to feather. Very soon the prop on No. 1 had run away and set up heavy vibration. The knowledge that at any moment the 500lb prop could twist itself off its hub and come slashing across towards the cockpit didn't make for a happy situation.

'When it did finally separate, it took off down without damaging No. 2 engine. By that time we were out of formation and alone, and lucky to make it back without being picked off by a fighter.'

The group's fourth raid brought a single loss, but in a failed attack near Hamburg on 25 June the 379th again ran into the Luftwaffe and six of its B-17s failed to return. In just under a month nearly half its initial complement had been lost or destroyed. People were beginning to say that the 379th had a jinx.

Preston, however, was not going to let his men become preoccupied with thoughts of their own survival; he could see that the losses were not just due to bad luck. Formations had to be tighter, gunners more capable, navigation more precise and bombing more accurate. Preston wanted to know why his group was performing so badly and set his staff to find out. They analysed the first 20 missions and found that poor bombing was due to the bombardiers being unable to locate targets in time to set up their intricate Norden sights. Bombardiers were given intensive instruction and practice in 'pin-point' pilotage – relating observed landmarks to map details. Further, bombardiers were found to be relying too heavily on navigators to find their targets, so Preston sent his lead crews on training flights without navigators so that their bombardiers were forced to identify targets themselves. On combat missions, bombardiers were required to pin-point

Above left: Palls of black smoke shroud the bearings factory at Schweinfurt in Germany during a raid by the Eighth Air Force. On 13 April 1944, a large formation of B-17s returned to hit the few buildings left standing after a previous raid in February. Heavy concentrations of bombs also hit machine shops and warehouses as well as the city's main railway lines and marshalling yards. **Above:** The weapons that did the job: groundcrew loading a pair of bombs into the bay of a B-17 at Kimbolton. Each Fortress could carry up to 6000lb of bombs, but a normal load was nearer 4000lb. **Left:** A Fortress cockpit. **Above left:** 'Ol' Gappy', a B-17G.

from take-off to landing and were also forbidden to put down their maps to shoot at enemy fighters.

Other evidence showed that the bomb run from the Initial Point had often been little more than a haphazard search for the target which disrupted the formation and ruined its bombing pattern. A new procedure was introduced whereby target runs were on pre-determined headings; usually in a straight line with the pilot in control until the aiming point was in view. He would then hand over to the bombardier who would make the necessary flight adjustments through his bombsight controls. Preston found that straight runs might increase losses to flak, but, in practice, losses on bomb runs remained the same but bombing accuracy improved. Preston's persistence began to pay off: in August 1943 the 379th suddenly came from the back to lead all the Eighth Army Air Force groups in the percentage of bombs dropped within 100 feet of the mean point of impact on targets attacked during the month.

A similar campaign of intensive study and hard training was used to develop navigational skills. It was found that when formations strayed from the briefed route or did not make check-points on time, their fighter escorts were often thrown off balance and the loss of B-17s to enemy fighters increased. A formation had to be at the right place at the right time.

Gunnery also came under the spotlight. Despite the high claims of enemy fighters shot down, it was evident that the average gunner scored hits more by chance than by expertise. Ingenious gunnery rigs were constructed to aid gunners in mastering deflection shooting (firing in anticipation of a moving target). One of these devices consisted of a gun turret mounted on a truck which sped round the airfield perimeter while the gunner sighted on aircraft flying overhead. Improvement in combat performance resulted in one tail gunner, Sergeant Michael Arooth, running up a score of nine credited 'kills'.

There was also the problem of aborts – turnbacks due to mechanical, equipment or human failure. Often, 15 per cent of all the bombers taking part in a mission returned to base without having reached the target. This was wasted effort and, with the aid of his engineering officer, Captain Conrad Hunt, Preston set out to obtain better servicing and maintenance of the group's bombers. Aborts were analysed and measures taken to prevent persistent types of failure. Under Preston's reforms, there was a gradual improvement, with a notable decline in bombers despatched on a mission returning early.

Improving the group's expertise, however, was not easy while its bombers continued to mount regular operations. Men who had been groomed for leadership were lost, and heavy battle damage grounded bombers. Indeed, it was not until their 87th mission in March 1944 that the 379th's B-17s first returned without any flak damage.

However, the Fortress was renowned for its ruggedness and ability to absorb battle damage, and most were soon back in service. Lieutenant Hale was later to praise these characteristics:

'On the reckoning of one of the members of my crew we took 16 hits to our aircraft in 31 missions. Eight of the hits were 20mm cannon shells which knocked large pieces out of the tailplane and stopped an engine but luckily didn't hit a gas tank. A rocket hit took out a number of control cables which would have been fatal on a less stable ship.

'It was because the '17 handled so well that you could compensate for such damage. I did know of a pilot who made our field with only one prop

turning, but that is not a situation I would like to have experienced. Photographs showing "Forts" that came home with complete tail stabilisers missing and other severe damage prove what a tough old lady she was, worth all the praise she collected.'

During the difficult winter of 1943/44, progress towards Preston's goal of seeing the 379th become the most efficient bomber group in the Eighth Air Force was often marred by reverses. Weather thwarted accurate bombing, and the group often came under massive assault by the Luftwaffe. On its second mission to the Schweinfurt bearing factories, six B-17s failed to return and during the raid on an aircraft plant at Halberstadt on 22 February, five went down. Mo Preston led his men on this last raid and received a foot wound. Although senior officers tried to relieve him of his command, he refused, and for a while continued his administration, hobbling around Kimbolton on crutches. He had imbued others with his enthusiasm and members of his staff including Bob Kittel, Louis Rohr, Lloyd Mason and Jim DuBose offered ideas and support.

Preston's attempts to make technical changes in the conduct of bombing missions were an irritation to his immediate superiors in the Eighth Air Force, who were not always receptive to change. Nevertheless, the 379th became the greatest single influence in the Eighth Air Force, fostering practices designed to increase the probability of hitting targets. The group evolved a larger squadron formation to achieve better bomb patterns and this was eventually adopted by all other groups.

By April 1944, the 379th had the lowest number of aborted sorties in the Eighth Air Force

By April 1944 there was no denying the ascendancy of the 379th. It had achieved an operational 'grand slam' by leading all the Eighth Air Force groups in every phase of offensive warfare. It despatched the most aircraft, dropped the greatest weight of bombs, had the highest bombing accuracy and the lowest number of aborted sorties and losses. It was a position that the 379th was to maintain for most operational months until the end of hostilities.

Strangely, despite its transformation from the most ill-fortuned to the best group in the Eighth Air Force, little acknowledgement was accorded the 379th. It remained very much an unknown unit while publicity was lavished on Fortress groups which had suffered particularly cruel losses in the great air battles over Europe. Most of these units had popular names – 'The Ragged Irregulars', 'The Bloody Hundredth', 'Hell's Angels', 'Can Do' and so on. The 379th gained no such sobriquet and was generally known among US personnel in Britain as the 'Triangle K' group, the identification marking carried on the fins of its B-17s. However, the 379th, proud of its achievement, incorporated in its group insignia a motto meaning 'Power and Precision'. There was only one black mark against its good record, one which, much to the annoyance of Mo Preston and his staff, they never could erase; the highest VD rate in the Eighth

Above right: Despite severe flak damage, the crew of this B-17F, 'Nine Yanks and a Jerk', nursed their aircraft back to base and made a safe landing. Far right: A rear gunner, with two 'kills' to his credit, sighting his twin 0.5in machine guns. Right: A waist gunner checking his machine gun prior to a raid.

BEATING THE BANDITS

Although enemy flak accounted for a fair proportion of USAAF losses during the daylight bombing campaign against occupied Europe, the greatest threat to the B-17s came from German fighters. The USAAF evolved a system of formation flying to minimise its casualties.

Fortresses usually formed up into 'combat wings' prior to the beginning of the approach to their target. Each wing consisted of three group 'boxes' of 18 to 21 aircraft, flying one above the other.

The theory was that, in this formation, the bombers could bring the maximum firepower to bear against attacking enemy fighters. Generally, the larger and more compact the bomber force, the greater its defensive capabilities, but, unfortunately, very close flying produced accidents and spoiled bombing accuracy.

Experience soon taught crews to be more flexible in their flying. Boxes were often sloped upwards and backwards but this system also had its drawbacks – enemy fighters nearly always went for the vulnerable lower group. Better protection was afforded by formations leading with the middle group, placed above and ahead of the lower group. Despite these precautions, the lower groups continued to suffer heavy losses and crews dubbed the position 'Purple Heart Corner'. There was little enthusiasm for flying this post and a system of rotation was introduced. When under attack gunners used a technique of aiming called 'the zone system' which, despite its scientific sounding name, involved little more than pointing the machine gun in the general direction of the enemy and blazing away. Most gunners admitted that a 'kill' was more a case of luck than judgement.

In spite of their defensive armament, the B-17s relied on long-range fighter escorts for their security.

Air Force. Evidently, the men were as careless at home as they were careful at war.

In October 1944 Colonel Preston was given command of the 41st Combat Wing that controlled the 379th and two other groups. He had been in command of one group longer than any other officer in the Eighth Air Force and had personally flown on more than 40 raids. Despite his promotion, he continued to fly the occasional mission with his old group. His replacement, as head of the 379th Bombardment Group, was Lieutenant-Colonel Lewis 'Lew' Lyle. Lyle was one of the real veterans of the B-17's war, having flown his first sortie back in November 1942 and who by October 1944 had nearly 60 to his credit. Lyle was imbued with the same spirit as Preston, and possessed extraordinary energy. Under his leadership the group continued to prosper.

The high standard of engineering continued to help reduce losses and many Fortresses survived to complete record numbers of missions. In the autumn of 1944 one, nicknamed 'Swamp Fire', became the

Below left: Colonel 'Lew' Lyle, the 379th's second commanding officer, sharing a joke with Majors 'Ed' Millison (centre) and Jim Edwards (left). Lyle flew 69 missions between late 1942 and April 1945, a record surpassed by only one other pilot of the Eighth Air Force. Below right: Major Lloyd Mason, the group's mission leader, meeting British royalty, with the commander of the Eighth Air Force, Lieutenant-General Jimmy Doolittle, looking on. Main picture: A close formation of B-17s heading for Germany. The vapour trails indicate that they are flying above 20,000 feet.

first in the Eighth Air Force to complete 100 missions without a turnback for mechanical reasons. There were many other veteran B-17s in the 379th, and by early 1945 one, 'Birmingham Jewel', led all other Fortresses in the number of missions completed. Sadly, this bomber was shot down over Berlin on its 128th raid. However, when the 379th completed its 330th and final operation on 25 April 1945, one of its veteran B-17Gs, nicknamed 'Ol' Gappy', had 157 raids to its credit, far more than any other Fortress in the Eighth Air Force.

At the end of hostilities, the 379th Bombardment Group stood supreme in operational efficiency. It had flown more credited sorties, had dropped a higher tonnage of bombs with greater overall accuracy and with a lower drop-out rate than any of the other 41 bombardment groups in the Eighth Air Force. The 379th also had the lowest total of aircraft lost of any B-17 group over the whole of the campaign in Western Europe. During his retirement, Preston recalled his days at Kimbolton as the most significant of his career. When asked to identify the reasons for the 379th Bombardment Group's outstanding record, he quoted the group's motto: 'Power and Precision', adding 'and a lot of guts'.

THE AUTHOR Simon Clay is a leading authority on the history of the US Air Force in World War II and has written numerous books on the subject.

Continually in the vanguard of the American bomber offensive, the aircrews of the 91st Bombardment Group led the way to Allied victory

RAGGED IRREGULARS

91ST BOMBARDMENT GROUP

The 91st Bombardment Group was activated on 15 April 1942, at Harding Field, Louisiana, one of the initial batch of heavy bomber groups scheduled for service in Europe. Its four combat component squadrons were also activated on the same date. These were the 322nd, 323rd, 324th and 401st Bombardment Squadrons, although for the first few days of its existence the 401st was designated the 11th Reconnaissance Squadron. Expansion began with the first phase of training at McDill Field, Florida, and the major part of flying training was carried out at Walla Walla in Washington State during the summer of 1942. The air echelon brought their new B-17Fs to Britain via the North Atlantic air route in late September, while the ground complement sailed on the *Queen Mary* to the Clyde.

During the course of its 340 combat bombing missions the 91st Bomb Group flew 9591 individual aircraft sorties, dropping a total of 22,142 tons of bombs on enemy targets. The group returned to the USA in the summer of 1945, where it was run down and inactivated in November. Reactivated as part of Strategic Air Command in 1947 to perform a strategic reconnaissance role, flying RB-17 and RB-29 aircraft, it later converted to the new RB-45 and RB-47 jets. In the mid-1960s it was based on Guam with B-52 bombers, and combat missions were flown during the Vietnam War. Today, its successor unit, the 91st Strategic Missile Wing, is equipped with Minuteman intercontinental ballistic missiles (ICBMs) and is based in central USA.

WHILE OVER 100 United States Army Air Force (USAAF) bombardment groups saw combat during World War II, one more than any other has come to epitomise their effort. The men and machines of the 91st Bombardment Group, 'The Ragged Irregulars', were fortunate in attracting a great deal of press coverage, but their subsequent acclaim was well earned. Within the USAAF's premier formation, the Eighth Army Air Force, the group was the most distinguished unit of the 1st Bombardment Wing, itself an outstanding wing of the 1st Bombardment Division.

In November 1942 the Allies invaded North Africa and the supporting American air units were drawn largely from those that had operational experience flying from England. As a result, the Eighth Air Force was left with a few untried heavy bomber units recently arrived from the United States. Of these, only four B-17 groups were large enough to pursue the American plan for daylight bombing over Hitler's 'Fortress Europe'. Among the four was the 91st Bomb

Group, and in the course of the next six months the groups pioneered the special techniques of high-altitude precision attack which they were later to use in the vanguard of the mightiest bomber armada ever committed to battle.

The 91st had arrived in England from its Washington State training base in September 1942, and it was initially deployed on Kimbolton airfield in Huntingdonshire. This, like the airfields occupied by the three other freshman Flying Fortress groups, was a wartime base with sparse accommodation for personnel, mostly Nissen hut barracks. Kimbolton's runways quickly showed signs of wear under the heavy Fortresses, however, and a move became necessary while repairs were carried out. It was at this point that the group had an unexpected stroke of luck.

When the commanding officer of the 91st, Colonel Stanley Wray, heard that an airfield at Bassingbourn was being considered for them, he drove south to inspect it. Finding a fully-fledged RAF base with centrally-heated accommodation, he immediately ordered the group to move house. By the time headquarters discovered what was happening, it was too late – the 91st was in possession.

The group's first mission was flown on 7 November 1942, when 14 B-17s left Bassingbourn to attack U-boat facilities at Brest in Brittany. The strike was not very successful as only eight aircraft bombed, while the rest of the force abandoned the raid after encountering bad weather. Missions which followed in the first month often met similar frustrations.

It was during a trip to St Nazaire, on the Bay of Biscay, that the 91st had its first serious encounter with the Luftwaffe. Part of the formation had become separated in heavy cloud and had turned back, while the remaining five Fortresses flew on. This small force was subjected to head-on attacks by Fw 190s near the target. In the course of the battle two bombers flown by squadron commanders were shot down, and another was so badly damaged that it crash-landed near Watford on return. The German interceptors were led by Oberstleutnant (Lieutenant-Colonel) Egon Mayer, commanding the Third Gruppe of Jagdgeschwader 2 (III/JG 2), who was trying out new tactics against the B-17s. Thereafter, the 91st frequently tangled with the Luftwaffe, their fierce fights resulting in both losses and victories. Before the end of the year another 91st squadron commander was killed, and by the early spring of 1943 the loss rate was such that on average only one

Page 37, background and inset left: Gunners of the 91st Bombardment Group, manning 0.5in Brownings, claimed the highest total of enemy aircraft destroyed of any group in the Eighth Army Air Force. Inset right: B-17 'Nine-0-Nine', which completed 140 missions without a single mechanical breakdown. Top left: Men of the 91st's 322nd Bomb Squadron examine their objective before take-off. Far left: Major Charlie Hudson, one of the group's most highly skilled bombardiers, and the bombsight he used to devastating effect over Germany. Bottom left: Boeing B-17F-10 B0 of the 322nd Bomb Squadron was lost during a raid on Stuttgart on 6 September 1943. Above left: Colonel Stanley Wray, the 91st's original and charismatic commander. Left: Lieutenant-Colonel 'Russ' Milton is decorated for his courageous leadership during bombing operations.

in three of the group's airmen had a chance of completing the 25 combat missions required to complete a tour of duty.

Nevertheless, morale was high under the leadership of Stan Wray, a tough, resourceful leader with a great sense of humour. It was during this period that the 91st picked up the nickname 'Wray's Ragged Irregulars', a self-mocking quip at the group's performance during these early days. The courage and fighting spirit of its aircrews was exemplified by their operation of 4 March 1943. On this date the Eighth Air Force's four B-17 groups were despatched to attack rail targets at Hamm. Previous attempts to strike the German industrial heartland in the Ruhr had been frustrated by bad weather, and thick cloud had made accurate high-altitude bombing impossible. On this occasion it again appeared that the bombers would have to be recalled, as cloud was forming in their path. The recall signal was finally sent, but by this time the leading 91st unit was well into Germany and did not receive the message. The air commander, Major Paul Fishbourne, soon became aware that his formation was alone but decided to forge ahead. The sky cleared, enabling the 91st to make the first American bombing attack on the Ruhr. This bold step was not made without cost, however, as the Fortresses had a running fight with the Luftwaffe both to and from the target. Three B-17s were shot down and another had to ditch in the North Sea. The 91st later became the recipient of the coveted Distinguished Unit Citation, and this was the earliest action by an Eighth Air Force unit for which the award was made.

The 91st came under ferocious attack, losing 10 of its B-17s but claiming 13 enemy fighters

By the summer of 1943, the Triangle A was the proud emblem of the most blooded of the Eighth Air Force's growing number of Fortress-equipped groups. The 91st's gunners had become the first to be credited with more than 100 enemy aircraft destroyed in air fights. Moreover, the group always seemed to be in the van of the great air battles. On the first strike against the Schweinfurt ball-bearing factories (17 August 1943), major source of that vital component of the German fighting machine, the 91st led the Eighth Air Force and came under ferocious attack, losing 10 of its B-17s but claiming 13 enemy fighters. On this occasion General Robert Williams, the commander of the 1st Division, who had lost an eye in the London Blitz, flew in the lead bomber and survived the ordeal. On the second disastrous Schweinfurt mission, flown on 14 October 1943, the 91st was again the lead group, although this time by default since the planned leaders did not assemble and place their formations on time.

The 91st was also the leading group on 11 January 1944, when a mission to attack aircraft production facilities at Oschersleben went badly wrong in deteriorating weather and the Ragged Irregulars came under vicious fighter attack. When the Eighth Air Force launched its first major mission against Berlin on 6 March the same year, the 91st headed the bomber stream. That day saw the heaviest losses ever of American heavy bombers – 69 aircraft – but such strain was imposed on the resources of the Luftwaffe fighter organisation that it never fully recovered.

The Berlin, Oschersleben and Schweinfurt missions were led by Lieutenant-Colonel Theo-

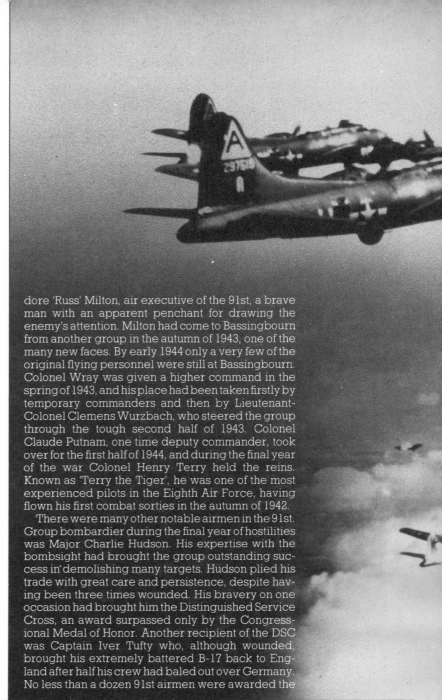

dore 'Russ' Milton, air executive of the 91st, a brave man with an apparent penchant for drawing the enemy's attention. Milton had come to Bassingbourn from another group in the autumn of 1943, one of the many new faces. By early 1944 only a very few of the original flying personnel were still at Bassingbourn. Colonel Wray was given a higher command in the spring of 1943, and his place had been taken firstly by temporary commanders and then by Lieutenant-Colonel Clemens Wurzbach, who steered the group through the tough second half of 1943. Colonel Claude Putnam, one time deputy commander, took over for the first half of 1944, and during the final year of the war Colonel Henry Terry held the reins. Known as 'Terry the Tiger', he was one of the most experienced pilots in the Eighth Air Force, having flown his first combat sorties in the autumn of 1942.

There were many other notable airmen in the 91st. Group bombardier during the final year of hostilities was Major Charlie Hudson. His expertise with the bombsight had brought the group outstanding success in demolishing many targets. Hudson plied his trade with great care and persistence, despite having been three times wounded. His bravery on one occasion had brought him the Distinguished Service Cross, an award surpassed only by the Congressional Medal of Honor. Another recipient of the DSC was Captain Iver Tufty who, although wounded, brought his extremely battered B-17 back to England after half his crew had baled out over Germany. No less than a dozen 91st airmen were awarded the

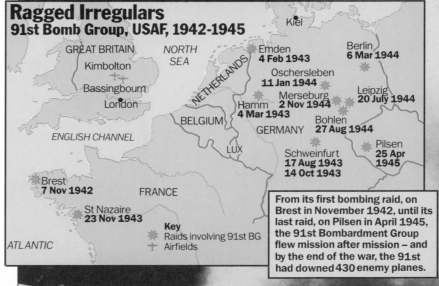

Ragged Irregulars
91st Bomb Group, USAF, 1942-1945

Kiel
GREAT BRITAIN NORTH SEA Emden 4 Feb 1943 Berlin 6 Mar 1944
Kimbolton NETHERLANDS Oschersleben 11 Jan 1944
Bassingbourn Merseburg 2 Nov 1944 Leipzig 20 July 1944
London Hamm 4 Mar 1943
BELGIUM Bohlen 27 Aug 1944
ENGLISH CHANNEL GERMANY
LUX Pilsen 25 Apr 1945
Schweinfurt 17 Aug 1943 14 Oct 1943
Brest 7 Nov 1942 FRANCE
St Nazaire 23 Nov 1943
Key
Raids involving 91st BG
Airfields
ATLANTIC

From its first bombing raid, on Brest in November 1942, until its last raid, on Pilsen in April 1945, the 91st Bombardment Group flew mission after mission – and by the end of the war, the 91st had downed 430 enemy planes.

Above: Three scenes from the USAAF documentary film *The Memphis Belle*, one of the best records of American bomber operations to survive the war. The crew of this aircraft was the first to be returned to the United States after completing their 25-mission tour of duty. The aircraft was taken on a 'bond tour' of the USA.
Background: B-17s of the 91st flying a mission in the summer of 1944.

A STARRING ROLE

In early 1943 the United States Army Air Force (USAAF) determined to make a film documentary publicising the role of the Eighth Army Air Force bombers in the European Theatre of Operations (ETO). General Arnold, head of the USAAF, handed the task to Major William Wyler, formerly the Hollywood producer of such films as the acclaimed *Mrs Miniver*. Wyler's brief was to show the American public the scope of B-17 operations, at the same time providing evidence to counter some of the US Navy's criticisms of the strategic bombing campaign.

Since its move to the pleasant accommodation of the former RAF base at Bassingbourn, nicknamed 'the Country Club of the ETO', the 91st Bomb Group had, not unnaturally, become a favourite call for newsmen from nearby London. As a consequence, its career was receiving the best coverage of an American formation in the war. Wyler selected the 91st for the film, and his first weeks were spent in obtaining action footage of combat with German fighters. The plot of the documentary then came to centre on the crew of the aircraft most likely to be the group's first to complete 25 missions. Titled after the B-17's nickname, 'The Memphis Belle', Wyler's film is now regarded as a classic documentary of the air war. The 91st Bomb Group was to receive further acknowledgement in postwar films. Its aircraft identity symbol, the letter A in a triangle, appeared in several films, including the excellent *Twelve O'Clock High*.

Above right: Clark Gable after a publicity flight in a B-17 of the 91st Bomb Group.

DSC by the end of the war, a greater number than in any other bomber group.

While the chances of an individual completing a tour of operations had improved to a healthy 78 per cent by the second half of 1944, the sky over Germany was still a very dangerous place. The flak emplacements defending the installations most vital to Hitler's war effort contained as many as 400 guns, and they sent up the most formidable barrages. The Luftwaffe, although it had lost air supremacy to the Allied fighters, was still able to give a good account of itself on occasion. On 20 July the 91st suffered the fury of the Luftwaffe during a raid on Leipzig, when it came under fire from a mass formation of Fw 190s that brought down eight Fortresses. On 2 November, while heading for the Merseburg oil plants, the group went off course above a 'solid' undercast and met a similar force which inflicted the group's highest loss on a single mission – 13 bombers. Flak, however, was to be the principal danger in the last months of the war, and it brought down several of the Ragged Irregulars. The final exchange with an enemy fighter took place in April 1945, at which time the 91st gunners had been credited with 420 enemy fighters destroyed since November 1942, a total greater than that of any other bomber group in Eighth Air Force. On the other hand, the 91st had sustained the highest aircraft losses of any bomber group, 197 planes missing in action and some 30 wrecked in accidents. While the gunners' claims were probably exaggerated through the confused nature of air fighting, considered in conjunction with the loss figure, they emphasise the 91st's ceaseless involvement in air fighting.

The group was credited with having flown 340 bombing missions, although it had been alerted, and often briefed and airborne, for another 160. Sometimes adverse weather would develop on route and

the operation would be abandoned. With the increasing supply of radar devices during 1944, 'blind' bombing could be successfully undertaken, although this was no substitute for the accuracy of visual attack. Those recalled or abandoned missions were always frustrating, and sometimes harrowing, experiences for the crews. Such an occasion was recorded in the diary of Lieutenant Paul Chryst, a bombardier in the 401st Squadron:

'The entire 36-ship formation was all over the sky, going 36 different ways at 36 different altitudes'

'My 10th mission; Sunday 27 August 1944. We were awakened about 5.30. Briefing at 6.30. The big wall map showing the route of the day's mission was covered by a screen when we entered the room but you could get an idea of the duration of the mission by the position of the pulley that held the map. Today it was way up the wall, showing we were in for a long, dangerous mission somewhere. S-2 Intelligence removed the screen at the commencement of briefing and we saw the route went way out to 13 degrees east, to Bohlen, Germany. We started engines at 8.20, taxied at nine o'clock, left the base and assembled at 5000ft before heading for the North Sea. We were carrying a maximum load of 10 500lb General Purpose bombs and about 2680 gallons of gasoline per aircraft. At 12.30 we started to climb into an approaching weather front and visibility suddenly went to zero. The entire 36-ship formation, the whole 91st Bomb Group, was scrambled all over the sky, going 36 different ways at 36 different altitudes. You just prayed no other ship was trying to fill your space. The VHF was crowded with ships calling for instructions and directions. We flew blind up to about 15,000ft and hit a heavy snow concentration which collected on the wings. As we could not find the formation we lowered altitude until we broke out somewhere near Kiel. Immediately, flak started to burst around us so we turned and headed for home. We then saw some B-24 Liberators going west and desperately tried to catch this formation so we could obtain defensive protection.

'Part of my function as a bombardier was to monitor two of the radio channels, so that if the pilot was busy on the interphone or other channels I

could forward messages to him. I listened to our pilot, Harry Garner, using the radio code signal for the day, calling several times to the B-24 formation ahead for permission to tack on to the tail end of this group, but the message never got through. I heard the B-24 tail gunner that I was staring at telling his leader that there was a strange-looking B-17 trying to follow them. They were not receiving our transmissions but we were receiving theirs. The last warning that came from the B-24 formation was to the effect, "Keep that B-17 in your sights and if he gets too close shoot him out of the sky." Fortunately the B-24s have a 15mph edge over us in top speed and we had never been able to close up. Nearer England we saw a B-17 group and tacked on to them. I hope we get credit for this mission, it was a harrowing experience.'

The Ragged Irregulars flew their last operation on 25 April 1945 to attack targets at Pilsen. It brought them two champions. One of them, a B-17G nicknamed 'Nine-O-Nine', completed 140 combat operations without ever having to turn back through mechanical failure. One or two other B-17s had flown more missions, but these aircraft had at some time or other suffered mechanical lapses, forcing abandonment of their missions. 'Nine-O-Nine' had an unblemished mechanical record, unequalled by any other Fortress in the Eighth Air Force.

The other champion was Lieutenant-Colonel Immanuel Klette, a command pilot. Klette had flown a tour of operations with another B-17 group in the spring and summer of 1943, before having to crash-land a B-17 he was piloting in a wood during darkness. Although badly crushed, he survived and, overcoming his injuries, he persuaded Henry Terry to let him take over the vacant command of the group's 324th Squadron. Klette, whose parents had been forced to leave Germany under the threat of racial persecution, had a relentless hatred for the Nazis and flew every mission he could, particularly those that looked difficult. It was soon noted at Bassingbourn that losses were few or nil when 'Manny' Klette flew, an achievement which

Below: Celebrating their completion of 25 missions, the crew of a B-17 take their aircraft low to 'buzz' the control-tower of the 91st Bomb Group's base at Bassingbourn airfield. **Bottom:** Returning from a mission to Kassel in Germany, the hydraulics of this B-17 failed as it attempted to land. Without brakes, it overshot the Bassingbourn runway and ended up severely damaged in a cornfield.

could be attributed to his intensive study of all intelligence information on enemy defences and his skilful leadership. Although every pilot would happily follow whenever Klette led the mission, higher authority decided that he was ignoring the law of averages and had seen enough action. But orders to reduce the number of missions he undertook were circumnavigated and Klette kept on flying. On 25 April 1945 he completed his 91st sortie, a total higher than that of any other US heavy-bomber pilot in Europe. He had also undertaken seven other missions that had been recalled.

The 91st Bombardment Group is proud of its reputation, evidenced by the strong veterans association that has continued down the years. Most certainly the organisation stands as one of the most famous of the United States air force units of World War II, and as one with an incomparable record of combat between bomber and fighter.

THE AUTHOR Simon Clay is a leading authority on the history of the US Air Force in World War II and has written books on its aircraft and personnel.

NO.609 (WEST RIDING) SQUADRON

No.609 Squadron was originally formed as a bomber unit at Yeadon on 10 February 1936, but at the outbreak of World War II, it was equipped with Spitfire Mk.1s.

During the early months of the war the squadron was engaged in flying convoy patrols. However, after Dunkirk in May 1940, it was moved to provide air defence for the area around Southampton.

The unit was heavily involved in the Battle of Britain and claimed to have destroyed 100 enemy aircraft by 20 October. In early 1941 the squadron was moved to Biggin Hill and took part in fighter sweeps and bomber escort duties over northern France until the following November when it moved north, to Digby, for flying training. In March 1942, 609 returned to active duty at Duxford and a month later began to convert on to Typhoons. Its first action with the new aircraft came on 30 June. Combats, however were few, and it was not until the unit moved to Manston in November that its pilots got a real taste of battle. After a period of engine modification in July 1943, the squadron went onto the offensive against enemy targets in northern France.

In February 1944 the squadron undertook further training at Armament Practice Camp and then, after joining the 2nd Tactical Air Force, converted to rocket projectile missions. After the Allied invasion of Europe in June 1944, the squadron transferred to France and launched attacks against enemy ground targets. It remained in action until the end of the war, when it was withdrawn from front-line service. No.609 Squadron's insignia is shown above.

TALLY HO!

With their devastating armament of rockets and cannon, the Typhoons of No. 609 Squadron, RAF, took a deadly toll of the German armoured forces in Normandy

A FEW weeks after the Allied landings in Normandy on 6 June 1944, Group Captain Desmond Scott, the commander of No. 123 Wing was flying with the ground-attack aircraft of No. 609 (West Riding) Squadron. Somewhere below lay the target: a German convoy of tanks, soft-skinned vehicles and troops. Suddenly, movement in the distance attracted Scott's eye – it was the convoy. The Group Captain signalled his fellow pilots, and they headed towards the sighting. Scott remembered the attack:

'Swirling clouds of yellow dust hung over the busy roads beneath us, and further to the southeast the battered city of Caen flickered and smouldered under a huge mushroom of pink and black smoke. In the more open country the fields were strewn with the bloated carcasses of hundreds of tan and white cattle. Shell craters, bomb holes and burnt-out tanks littered the tortured countryside.

'To the south of Potigny we began climbing but streams of light flak came racing up towards us. So, I hastily sank down again to the comparative safety of the taller trees and hedgerows. I caught sight of the object of our early-morning mission.

'The road was crammed with enemy vehicles – tanks, trucks, even horse-drawn wagons and ambulances, nose to tail, all pressing forward in a frantic bid to reach cover before the skies once more became alive with the winged death of the 2nd Tactical Air Force. As I sped to the head of the mile-long column, hundreds of German troops began spilling out into the road, to sprint for the open fields and hedgerows.

'The convoy's lead vehicle was a large half-track. In my haste to cripple it and seal the road, I let fly with all eight rockets in a single salvo; I missed, but hit the truck that was following. It was thrown into the air along with several bodies, and fell back on its side. Two other trucks in close attendance piled into it.

'Within seconds the whole stretch of road was bursting and blazing under streams of rocket and cannon fire. Ammunition wagons exploded like multi-coloured volcanoes. Several teams of

operations. With their eight rockets and four 20mm Hispano cannons, they would make sure that the lumbering metal giants of Hitler's prized panzer divisions were no longer the undisputed victors of the Blitzkrieg days.'

The squadron had to practise to perfect their art. In late February 1944 they had joined the 2nd Tactical Air Force (TAF) and, together with No. 198 Squadron, they had come under the command of Scott's No. 123 Wing. A few months before the invasion, its pilots had spent three weeks' detachment at Llanbedr in Wales, where the squadron trained in the use of rocket projectiles.

No. 609 Squadron resumed operations in May, attacking a road bridge on the Cherbourg peninsula on the 2nd, and railway sheds at Amiens on the following day. Apart from transportation targets, several radar sites were attacked and, on the eve of D-day, the squadron severely damaged a chateau housing Rommel's headquarters, although the field marshal himself was not there at the time. Flak was the Typhoon's greatest enemy and it accounted for five of the squadron's pilots in May. 'It seems like the war has started,' Flight Lieutenant Eric Roberts, newly appointed to command A Flight, confided to his diary.

On 6 June the squadron had supported the Allied forces invading northwest Europe with another attack on a radar site, followed by two strikes against German military convoys moving up to the beach-heads. A couple of enemy tanks and various other vehicles were knocked out. One of the successful pilots was Roberts, who missed a PzKpfw IV with his rockets but then opened fire on it with his 20mm cannon. 'It just belched flame and black smoke – completely burned out,' the surprised pilot reported. However, Warrant Officer George Martin – 'tough, strong and troublesome' – was hit by flak and took to his parachute. After a series of narrow escapes, he finally evaded capture and was liberated by advancing troops.

During most of the remainder of June the squadron's efforts were concentrated on attacking enemy troop trains and road convoys, although bad weather often hampered these operations. Three pilots were

Below left: In late May 1944 the Allies were poised to launch their invasion of Northwest Europe. In the build-up to the landings, ground-attack Typhoons of No.609 Squadron were used to blast enemy radar stations along the Normandy coast. The Typhoon packed a fearful punch: eight rockets and four 20mm cannon. Both weapons were capable of smashing tanks and concrete emplacements. Here, two of the squadron's groundcrew look aloft as a fully-armed Typhoon streaks towards the enemy-held territory. The squadron had several mascots; 'Sarah – a duck for luck' (above) and 'Group Captain Goat' (right).

horses stampeded and careered wildly across the fields, dragging their broken wagons behind them. Others fell in tangled, kicking heaps, or were caught up in the fences and hedges. It was an awesome sight: flames, smoke, bursting rockets and showers of coloured tracer – an army in retreat, trapped and without air protection.'

By the summer of 1944, No. 609 Squadron was fast developing into one of the finest ground-attack units in the 2nd Tactical Air Force. Its pilots were flying the deadly Hawker Typhoons, aircraft Scott believed, were:

'To change the whole concept of close-support

THE HAWKER TYPHOON

Despite its later fame, the Typhoon's operational debut as an interceptor, in the middle of 1941, was a failure. Its Napier Sabre 1 engine was not fully developed; the aircraft performed poorly at high altitudes and had a slow rate of climb. With an improved version of the Sabre engine and a switch to low-level operations, however, the aircraft came into its own. The original versions of the Typhoon were armed with 12 .303in machine guns, but later 'tank-busting' aircraft, fitted with four 20mm Hispano cannons, carried either a variety of bomb-loads or eight rocket projectiles with 60lb warheads.

The RAF took delivery of its first production aircraft in July 1941 and No.609 Squadron was one of the first units to fly the Typhoon. The aircraft's change of role to ground-attack missions in 1942 was a great success and Typhoons were claiming to have destroyed up to 150 trains a month by the middle of 1943.

Their speed, 412mph at 12,000ft, enabled them to hit the targets with impunity and escape before the enemy could respond. Typhoons were also used to attack pin-point targets; on 24 October 1944 they were able to kill two German generals in their headquarters at Dordrecht and wound Rommel during an attack on his staff car on 17 July 1944. Such accuracy was a testament to the Typhoon's quality as a strike aircraft and the pilots' skill.

lost to flak during the month, and on 23 June Luftwaffe fighters put in one of their comparatively rare appearances. Six Messerschmitt Bf 109s attempted to 'bounce' a formation of eight Typhoons, but they were spotted by Flight Officer 'Spud' Holmes who alerted the squadron. In the dogfight that followed, Roberts shot down one of the Bf 109s. Other pilots claimed a 'probable' and four enemy aircraft were damaged. Next day, Squadron Leader Wells, who had led the unit since February, handed over command to Squadron Leader L.E.J.M.'Manu' Geerts, the first Belgian to command 609 Squadron. Geerts, in his late 30s, was rather old by the standards of fighter pilots. Indeed, he had taught his eventual successor, Raymond Lallemant, to fly. Nonetheless, he was described as 'a brilliant pilot, perhaps the most experienced of the former Belgian Air Force.'

On 27 June Geerts was leading the squadron north of Le Mans when they again clashed with enemy fighters. On this occasion their opponents were FW

Right: Squadron Leader Roland Beamont led 609 Squadron between October 1942 and May 1943. At 22, he was the unit's youngest ever commander and did much to convince the RAF of the Typhoon's value as a ground-attack aircraft. His own Typhoon is shown above.

190s. Roberts was one of the pilots present:

'Two of them got on my tail and a third was in front. I had to break again and, after dicing like this for what seemed ages, thought discretion was the better part of valour and beat it down to the deck, there to proceed flat out for about 10 miles.'

Since 14 June, 609 Squadron had made use of an airstrip within the Normandy beach-head as an advanced landing ground, but, at the beginning of July, it moved across the Channel permanently to B-10 airstrip near Plumetot, only four miles north of enemy-occupied Caen. Scott remembered the dangers of fighting in the front line:

'B-10, like some of the other hurriedly-constructed airfields, was still repeatedly shelled and this dusty airstrip was a most uncomfortable place to live.'

On 9 July the squadron moved to B-5 at Camilly and, 10 days later, to B-7 at Martragny. Nonetheless, life on the bridgehead continued to be characterised by 'dust, dry rations, drama and dysentry,' thought Scott. However, one member of the squadron who seemed unaffected by the harsh conditions was the goat mascot Billy, who remained with the unit until the end

of the war. Scott was struck by his unusual diet:

'He would eat almost anything, being particularly partial to cigarettes and starter cartridges, spitting the brass caps out of the side of his mouth like corks from a pop gun.'

Attacks on transportation targets and armed reconnaissances over enemy-held territory continued in July, but the squadron was increasingly called on for close-support missions to assist the Allied advance. Typical targets were gun positions, strongpoints, armour and troop concentrations, often located only a few hundred yards from friendly forces. Close-support missions were precisely controlled, using the Visual Control Point (VCP) technique developed in Italy. An RAF officer would accompany the forward troops and direct air attacks by means of a VHF radio link. Sometimes the Typhoons would be airborne on a 'Cab Rank' patrol awaiting a call from the controller. However, so close were the Normandy beach-head airstrips to the fighting front, that the aircraft were usually kept on ground alert, ready to take-off, with their pilots strapped into the cockpits.

The Wing's aircraft strength was doubled in late July, when No. 164 and 183 Squadrons joined No. 198

Above: A Typhoon pilot, framed by the menacing barrels of two 20mm Hispano cannon, climbs into his cockpit. Left: Scenes of destruction in Normandy. Two German tanks, a Panther and PzKpfw IV, after a Typhoon attack. Right: 609 Squadron prepares to take off.

and 609 Squadrons. At the same time, a new Wing Leader, Wing Commander Walter 'Farmer' Dring, replaced Wing Commander R.E.P. Brooker, although Scott continued in overall command of the Wing. On 7 August Dring led 32 of the Wing's aircraft against a German armoured counter-attack in the Mortain area and such was the rocket-firing Typhoons' success that the attack was defeated.

Within a week of this action, the Germans had conceded defeat in the battle for Normandy and began to retreat northwards across the Seine. Geerts was leading eight of his squadron's Typhoons on an armed reconnaissance in the Falaise-Vimoutiers-Argentan area on the morning of 13 August and, finding a gap in thick cloud cover, he brought his aircraft down to attack German road columns. Four tanks were immediately knocked out by rocket fire and a blazing fuel dump crowned the success of the squadron's mission with a 4000ft-high column of dense, black smoke.

It was a fitting end to Geerts' period of command. The following day he was relieved by his former pupil, Squadron Leader Raymond Lallemant. The ever-smiling Lallemant, nicknamed 'Cheval', was no stranger to the squadron, as he had first joined the unit as a sergeant pilot back in the summer of 1941. He had taken part in the early air battles of the Normandy campaign as a flight commander of 609 Squadron's sister unit, No. 198 Squadron, and had taken command of the West Riding Squadron in time to participate in the campaign's climax – the Falaise Gap action.

By the third week in August a pocket of enemy-held territory had formed around Falaise, flanked by British and Canadian forces to the north and by the Americans to the south. Within this area, the remnants of 16 German divisions were almost completely encircled, with only a 25-mile-wide gap open for their escape. The Typhoons of 2nd TAF, 18 squadrons strong, took full advantage of this situation and, flying an average of 1200 sorties per day, turned the German defeat into an utter rout.

Lallemant had good reason to remember his last sortie of 18 August, a day of especially heavy fighting

during which the 2nd TAF mounted 1471 sorties, and later claimed 90 tanks and 1100 vehicles destroyed:

'Finding some tanks, I was glad to get rid of my burdensome rockets; but one or two others, who made the mistake of letting theirs off prematurely at lorries, now found themselves restricted to peppering the Tigers with their 20mm cannon.

'On my first swoop I was surprised by the number of tanks that still seemed to be around, but then noticed that many of them had already been put out of action. Another swoop was greeted by a burst of 88mm [flak] from a battery hidden in the Gouffern forest, which I promptly signalled my colleagues to avoid. Then I spotted a troop of soldiers brandishing a white flag, marching in fours towards Vimoutiers. They appeared to have had enough, but with the flak still firing at me, I decided to quench their thirst for war for good with a few bursts of cannon fire, and they went somersaulting into the ditches.

'Next, my attention was attracted by a tank screened by a hedge lining the road. Two pairs of rockets, and it went up in flames...'

The gap was closed on 19 August, but on the following day German armoured forces counter-attacked in an attempt to re-open the escape route. Dring led his squadrons into an attack on these forces and careful briefing, good control, excellent leadership and accurate flying combined to make the operation a brilliant victory. Dring was awarded a well-deserved DSO. Cheval Lallemant, at the head of No. 609 Squadron, remembered that 'the road from Trun to Vimoutiers was on fire. At "de-briefing" it was established that 13 tanks had been destroyed and seven damaged. 609 had destroyed 10.' The scene from ground level amply justified the claims of the 2nd TAF pilots. Scott recalled that 'the roads were choked with wreckage and the swollen bodies of men and horses.'

The enormous destruction wrought on the German armour by 609 Squadron on 19 August was widely recognised as a great feat of arms. A few weeks later, the US military magazine 'Stars and Stripes' asked 2nd TAF headquarters to nominate the finest Typhoon squadron. Air Marshal Leigh-Mallory demanded that his staff nominate the best Group. No. 84 Group was put forward and its commander was asked to decide his best wing. The honour went to No. 123 Wing under Scott, who immediately declared that No. 609 Squadron was his best unit – a fitting tribute to the pilots' skill.

THE AUTHOR Anthony Robinson was formerly on the staff of the RAF Museum, Hendon and is now a freelance military aviation writer.

Three scenes from Normandy. Left: A Typhoon, its wings painted with black and white invasion stripes, takes off in a thick cloud of dust. Main picture: Rockets are launched against a vital railway bridge. The interdiction of enemy transport was vital to the Allied build-up. Above: Loading rockets onto underwing racks. Below: Squadron Leader Raymond Lallemant.

TYPHOON TACTICS

Raymond Lallement, the Belgian pilot who flew with, and later commanded, No. 609 Squadron, became acutely aware of the problems associated with ground-attack missions:

'Rocket firing did require great experience and skill; do not forget that we had no elaborate gunsight. The best we had was a squadron-level modification of the standard sight made by Roland Beamont [one of the unit's early commanders].

'Most of the rockets did end up short of the target due to pilot inexperience, and because of the flak. We had to be very low to escape that accurate German flak. That led to fear of collision with obstacles on the ground. Don't think the German tanks were silly enough to park in the middle of a field. They knew about camouflage.

'However, the real point was to trace the tanks and kill them before they could run for shelter. When they were in the open a vertical dive was best.

'When a tank was hiding the only way was to go down almost straight and level, holding the aircraft very steady, particularly during the firing of the rockets until they had cleared the long launching rails.'

TARGET FOR TONIGHT

Among the aircrews of No.9 Squadron, RAF, *Spirit of Russia* built up an impressive, albeit eccentric, operational record

'SPIRIT OF RUSSIA' was the name given to Lancaster EE136 'R-Robert' by Flight Sergeant James 'Tiger' Lyon and his crew from No.9 Squadron, Royal Air Force (RAF). This remarkable bomber began operations with a night raid on Düsseldorf on 11/12 June 1943, and, over the next 16 months, amassed an impressive combat record and a reputation as a 'charmed' aircraft. For Lyon and his crew, the most important operation was that against the Peenemünde V-2 testing station on the shores of the Baltic, on the night of 17/18 August 1943.

One month earlier, on 25 July, Hitler had expressed his determination to 'break terror by terror.' It was clear that he was referring to the use of saturation V-2 bombing to decimate London and bring Britain to its knees. Allied air reconnaissance showed that research at Peenemünde had reached an advanced stage, and Bomber Command decided to bring forward its projected assault on the establishment when further intelligence revealed signs of light anti-aircraft defences being constructed.

Ten crews from No.9 'Bat' Squadron were designated to join the 597-strong bomber force. Practice for the mission was undertaken at Wainfleet bombing range, with the Lancasters of No.9 achieving pinpoint accuracy on their time-and-distance runs. For security reasons, the aircrews involved in Operation Hydra were not told the exact nature of their targets.

At 2120 hours, *Spirit of Russia* rumbled down the runway of RAF Bardney, Lincolnshire, and took to the air with Lyon in the pilot's seat. The force attacked in three waves, with the Lancasters of No.9 hitting 'aiming point E' – the experimental station. At 0044, Lyon's bomb-aimer acquired the target from 5000ft and sent *Spirit of Russia's* ordnance tumbling out of the bomb-bay. One 4000lb 'cookie', and two 1000lb and 500lb bombs started their irreversible descent towards the German V-2 base. The mission was carried out with magnificent dash and was an unqualified success, with minimal interference from enemy nightfighters. The Mosquitoes of No.8 Group had dropped incendiary flares on Berlin and deceived the Luftwaffe into thinking that the capital city was the main target. Although this ruse was eventually discovered, most of the bombers had released their bombs and turned for base by the time enemy fighters arrived over Peenemünde. Out of 597 aircraft, Bomber Command lost 40, with no loss to No.9 Squadron. Sergeant R.W. Corkhill, the navigator aboard *Spirit of Russia*, later recalled a particularly hazardous incident during the operation:

'Jeffrey the bomb-aimer had just dropped the bombs in the centre of a group of Pathfinder Force green target indicators when Jimmy Lyon called out "hold tight" and side-slipped the Lancaster. Luckily, he had been looking up and saw another Lanc above us opening its bomb doors – no doubt

Attacked by wave after wave of Lancaster bombers (left), the experimental V-2 station at Peenemünde suffered extensive damage (bottom left). Below right: The 'Battle Honours Board' of No.9 Squadron. Below: With Flight Sergeant James Lyon in the cockpit, members of the squadron pose for a group photograph around *Spirit of Russia*. Below left 'Tiger' Lyon.

NO.9 SQUADRON

No.9 Squadron, Royal Flying Corps, was formed at St Omer, France, on 8 December 1914. After being disbanded in early 1915, it was re-formed in April under the command of Major Hugh Dowding. The squadron crossed to France in December 1915, and was equipped with B.E.2cs for operations with Allied artillery units. The unit stayed on the Western Front until the Armistice, having been involved in night raids, offensive patrolling and tactical bombing. It was disbanded on 19 December 1919.

The squadron re-formed as a bomber unit on 1 April 1924, flying the Vickers Vimy and later the Handley Page Heyford. Towards the end of 1939, No.9 Squadron converted to the Vickers Wellington and took part in the first raid against Germany – attacking Brunsbüttel on 4 September. In May 1941, No.9 Squadron turned its attention to industrial targets in the Ruhr. In August 1942 the squadron re-equipped with Avro Lancasters and was transferred to No.5 Group. At the end of World War II, the squadron moved to Binbrook, Lincolnshire, and in 1952 became the first unit to convert to Canberra jet bombers. After overseas trips to Sweden, North Africa, Malaya and the Philippines, the squadron was eventually disbanded on 13 July 1962.

The unit was re-formed in March 1962 as part of Britain's nuclear deterrent – the V-Force. Flying the Vulcan B.Mk 2, the squadron was stationed in Cyprus as part of the Near East Bomber Wing until 1975. In 1982, No.9 Squadron became the first operational squadron to be equipped with the Tornado GR.Mk 1. Above: The badge of No.9 Squadron, RAF.

thinking it safer to fly a bit higher than instructed!' Lyon and his crew flew in *Spirit of Russia* on a further two occasions before completing their tour of operations with a night raid on Kassel on 22 October 1943. This tour had seen Lyon's crew awarded an 'aiming point' certificate for a high-level mission over Cologne on the night of 3/4 July 1943.

When not operated by Flight Sergeant Lyon and his crew, *Spirit of Russia* was flown by several other pilots from No.9 Squadron. On the night of 5/6 September 1943, Pilot Officer Jimmy McCubbin and his crew flew EE136 to Mannheim during a night bombing mission. Aboard the aircraft during this eventful 'op' were Sergeants Norman Owen (flight engineer), Bart Sherry (navigator), Joe Dagnell (bomb aimer), Andy Smith (wireless operator), Charlie Houbert (mid-upper gunner) and George Elliot (rear gunner). *Spirit of Russia* set off from Bardney as part of a 605-aircraft formation from Bomber Command. The weather conditions were clear, however, providing the Luftwaffe's nightfighters with a perfect hunting ground.

The target was bombed from 19,000ft at 2330 hours, but *Spirit of Russia* was attacked by enemy

No.9 Squadron, RAF Western Europe, 1939-45

fighters as she set course for base. Sergeant Smith recalls the occasion in his diary:

'A nasty day of heavy rain, clearing in the evening. We're on ops again tonight, in Jimmy Lyon's kite – "R-Robert, *Spirit of Russia*". Tonight's target is Mannheim, 550 aircraft on. Another nasty night, when we were again shot up...We had just bombed and had turned onto the short leg southwards from Mannheim when the rear gunner, Geordie Elliot, reported an unidentified aircraft coming up astern. A second or two later, the rattle of his guns came over the intercom and Jimmy put "R" into a corkscrew. The engagement lasted only four minutes but it seemed a long time. The Jerry was a single-engined job and made five attacks, while Jimmy kept twisting and weaving. We were hit twice by cannon shells – on both occasions there was a tremendous bang from down the rear of the fuselage where the shells hit. Charlie in the mid-turret was wounded at the beginning and almost blinded by blood from a gashed forehead.

'Geordie's voice would come over the intercom: "He's comin' in again skipper," and the guns would rattle as Geordie opened up, leaving us to wonder when another smack was coming. But after the fifth attack, with Geordie blazing away, the fighter didn't come out of his dive...Joe and Norman saw him go down below us with flames streaming from him. So it ended. Just in time...a hole about three foot across was blasted in the port fin and one of the internal rudder controls was half shorn through. Jimmy was called upon to do some delicate flying...

'I got the first-aid kit out and did what I could for Charlie. He had three bullet wounds high in the right chest, just under the collar bone, and bad gashes on the forehead. I gave him a shot of morphine...

'Bart proceeded to do some fine navigation, picking up the threads of our course bit by bit. We'd strayed somewhat off track and had to alter course to avoid Paris...One of life's tenser moments came when the indicator light flicked on the "Boozer" instrument, warning that an enemy fighter was behind and within range. Jimmy immediately swooped, climbed and twisted until Geordie was satisfied that there was nothing there.'

Making it safely back to base, McCubbin's crew were told that, at 28 ops, they could consider their tour of duty completed. After inspecting the damage to *Spirit of Russia* and marvelling at their lucky

In May 1942, determined to demonstrate the effectiveness of strategic bombing, the Air Officer Commanding in Chief Bomber Command, Air Marshal Arthur Harris, chose Cologne as the target for a massive saturation raid. Wellington and Stirling bombers, equipped with the 'Gee' navigation aid, were in the vanguard of the main force, closely followed by Lancasters and Halifaxes. More than 900 bombers, including a large contingent from No.9 Squadron, arrived over the target on the night of 30 May. Photographic reconnaissance (far left) later revealed the devastating effect of strategic bombing given sufficient aircraft, bombs and navigational aids. Far left, below: Silhouetted against the night sky by flares and anti-aircraft fire, a Lancaster flies over Hamburg during a Bomber Command operation in July 1943. Below left, centre: With typical good humour and high spirits, Flight Lieutenant J.A. Wakeford steps into Lancaster ED689 prior to his 50th operation with No.9 Squadron. Bottom left: The aircrews of No.9 Squadron are briefed at RAF Bardney before a night raid on the German radio factory at Friedrichsagen. Wakeford and his crew are seen here on the extreme right of the picture. Below: Once the briefing has been completed, Lancaster 'M' for Mother is one of the first aircraft to take off for the target.

escape, Sergeant Smith commented: 'All in all, quite a finish to the tour.'

For the next year, until she was transferred to No.189 Squadron in October 1944, *Spirit of Russia* built up a colourful and unique reputation among the aircrews of No.9 Squadron that flew in her. The most consistent crews were those of Pilot Officers W.E. Ling, W.E. Siddle, R.C. Lake, and Flying Officer R.W. Mathers.

The aircraft had already amassed an impressive operational record of 22 missions – eight of which had been flown by 'Tiger' Lyon and his crew – but had been badly shot up on a number of occasions. This inevitably gave rise to certain misgivings among the aircrews when they were allotted *Spirit of Russia* prior to an op. Pilot Officer Siddle's rear gunner, Sergeant Clayton Moore, later recalled his first introduction to the aircraft:

'Shortly after joining the "Bat Squadron", we were allocated Lancaster ED975 as our personal property. But we treated this aircraft to a gross injustice on the night of 5/6 September 1943, and (it is rumoured) we were duly punished for having done so when we were presented with *Spirit of Russia*.

'We took it up on the morning of 3 November for an air test, and found to our considerable consternation that the thing would not fly straight!...For some days, the impression had been filtering through to us that the aircraft was not particularly popular with the other crews. We held a conference and decided we would "show" them by accepting *Spirit of Russia* without further procrastination. Whether the other crews' dislike of the aircraft was attributable to its in-built instability or its strong Communist connections – both of which could be described as strong leanings towards the left – was not clear to us.'

'We decided to go around again, by which time the hapless train would have reached the station'

Despite this initial scepticism, Moore soon began to appreciate the merits of this remarkable aircraft. It may have flown well over its quota of operational sorties, but there was still plenty of life in the old bird. On the night of 10/11 November, the chocks were removed from under the wheels of *Spirit of Russia* and, with Siddle at the controls, she took off from Bardney for a raid on Modane, 100 miles southeast of Lyons. For the crew, it was to be a memorable operation, ending with the award of an aiming point certificate by the Air Officer Commanding of No.5

Group, Air Vice Marshal R.A. Cochrane. Sergeant Moore takes up the story:

'Modane was an important rail junction on the French-Italian border. It is in a valley with the Alps towering above it on either side; at the far end of the valley is a tunnel into which the line runs. We were just making our bombing run when I noticed a steam train approaching Modane about a mile astern of us. I interrupted Flight Sergeant Norman Machin's "left...left...steady" to inform the crew of this new development. We decided to go around again, by which time the hapless train would have reached the station. This we did, and bombed the train as it was drawing into the station. Our bombing photographs indicated a direct hit...the train (believed to be carrying troops) had been bombed throughout its length, and our last bomb had succeeded in blocking off the end of the tunnel.'

On their return to Bardney, the crew embarked on an intensive training programme with Spirit of Russia, enabling Siddle to familiarise himself with the somewhat wayward tendencies of the aircraft. It did not take long for the men to reassess their new charge in a much more favourable light – after all, she had furnished them with an aiming point certificate, a much-coveted award in the RAF.

Following their successful raid on the Modane railway junction, the bomber crews of No.9 Squadron participated in the 'Battle for Berlin' during the long winter nights between 18 November 1943 and 31 March 1944. Sixteen raids were undertaken, involving a total of 215 sorties. Spirit of Russia took to the air on the first night of operations, flown by Pilot Officer Blair. Blair and his crew completed a further 11 sorties against Berlin, leading to the award of the Distinguished Flying Cross to Blair himself, and the Distinguished Flying Medal to Sergeant R. Smith and Flight Sergeant W. Miller. The onslaught on Berlin reached a peak on the night of 15 February 1944 when 21 Lancaster crews from No.9 Squadron set out for the German capital. On this occasion, Spirit of Russia was flown by Flying Officer W. Mathers, who dropped his bombs from 20,000ft. Pilot Officer Ling and his crew took part in 10 of the raids, two of which were flown in Spirit of Russia.

From April to June 1944, nearly 90 per cent of Bomber Command's efforts were redirected in support of the forthcoming 'second front'. The operational records of No.9 Squadron reflected this. The raids into France were of short duration and encountered only marginal enemy resistance. As a result, each operation was only counted as a 'half', thereby doubling the number of ops required to complete a tour. These 'half operations' were flown largely against the French rail centres of Tours and Lachapelle-aux-Pots.

The German-occupied areas of northern France received the full weight of Bomber Command's attention during the run-up to D-day. On 6 June, 20 crews from No.9 Squadron bombed Argentan, with Pilot Officer Roy 'Puddle' Lake at the controls of Spirit of Russia. During the next few weeks, the squadron's aircrews flew their Lancasters during raids on Rennes, Portieux, Chatellerault and the centres of the German oil industry.

On 24 June 1944, No.9 Squadron raided Prouville and encountered heavy resistance from enemy nightfighters. Three crews failed to return from the mission. But once again, Spirit of Russia was in the thick of the fighting. With one swastika already painted on their aircraft's fuselage, the crew of R-Robert were eager to add another. Pilot Officer Lake later recounted the action:

'On paper, this particular raid was a piece of cake – just across the Channel to the Pas de Calais area, in order to bomb V-1 rocket sites. Unfortunately, we

On 12 November 1944, a detachment of Lancasters from No.9 Squadron teamed up with the legendary No.617 Squadron for an attack on the German battleship, Tirpitz. Using 12,000lb 'Tallboy' bombs (below right), the Lancasters roared into Tromsø fjord, Norway, and delivered their explosives with pinpoint accuracy. Tirpitz keeled over, digging her superstructure into the mud at the bottom of the fjord (below). Inset, below left: The aiming point certificate awarded to Flight Sergeant Lyon and his crew for their raid on Milan on 7/8 August 1943. Inset, bottom left: Aircrews gather their kit together prior to an operation. Bottom right: Still going strong! Groundcrew pose next to the Lancaster bomber named Johnny Walker.

were covered by about 50 searchlights and then attacked by three Ju 88s. Things got a little hectic for a while and some of the acrobatics became rather violent as we fought for our lives. The old *Spirit of Russia* creaked and groaned and eventually we found ourselves upside down. All the gyro instruments toppled. More by good luck than good airmanship, we found ourselves going the right way and managed to lose the searchlights. Of course, all guns were blazing continuously and it was subsequently confirmed that one of the Ju 88s had been shot down in flames. No-one in my crew had been injured and as far as I knew we had suffered no damage... it subsequently transpired that we had 72 holes all over the fuselage and

wings. Of course, the groundcrew were a little upset that I had damaged their baby, but, when I told them that they could paint another swastika on her side, I guess they forgave me.'

On 4 July, bombing operations commenced against the V-1 sites at Creil, north of Paris, and *Spirit of Russia* was one of the first aircraft from the squadron to enter the fray – flown by Pilot Officer G.A. Langford. From 30 July, the squadron undertook operations on seven consecutive nights against both French and German targets. *Spirit of Russia* flew on all seven of these missions, bringing her total number of ops to 76. On the night of 13 August, it was the turn of Brest harbour to feel the full force of No.9 Squadron's precision bombing. The objective was to sink an oil tanker that the Germans had intended to use to block the harbour entrance. Coaxing *Spirit of*

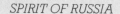
Lancaster EE136 was issued to No.9 Squadron on 31 May 1943 as a replacement for ED838. The latter had been downed by enemy anti-aircraft fire during a night raid on Essen one month earlier. The operational career of *Spirit of Russia* was to span 109 missions, during which she was flown by pilots of the British, Australian, New Zealand and Canadian air forces. A total of 36 pilots took over the controls of *Spirit of Russia* while she was in service with No.9 Squadron. The Lancaster was sent for repairs on four separate occasions, but maintenance was generally within the capabilities of the local service unit.

On 24 October 1944, when No.9 Squadron re-equipped with new Lancasters, the old airframes were given to the re-formed No.189 Squadron, also based at RAF Bardney. Now designated CA-R, *Spirit of Russia* carried out her 93rd operation on 1 November 1944 with a raid on Hamburg. She completed a further 16 operations before touching down at RAF Bardney for the last time on 3 February 1945, following a raid on Karlsruhe. The Lancaster was then transferred to No.20 Maintenance Unit, until a damage report of Category E/FB effectively took her out of service. As a result of extensive repairs, however, *Spirit of Russia* was later deemed fit for use as an instructional airframe. Thus, on 2 May 1946, she was allotted to No.1 Radio School with the instructional airframe identity of 5918M. At some point during the 1950s, *Spirit of Russia* was consigned, along with several other wartime aircraft, to the RAF Fire Training School at Sutton-on-Hill, Yorkshire.

Russia up to 15,000ft, Pilot Officer Lake held her on course until the shout 'bombs away' was heard from the nose of the Lancaster.

Operations continued throughout the months of August and September, with *Spirit of Russia* flying a further eight sorties against targets in Germany and France. October was equally hectic for the bomber crews of No.9 Squadron, but *Spirit of Russia*'s long association with the unit was drawing to a close. Her last operation with the squadron was flown on the night of 15/16 October when, along with 17 other Lancasters, she carried out an attack on the Sorpe Dam, in western Germany. Each aircraft carried a 'Tallboy' bomb, and the formation was escorted to its target by a squadron of Mustangs. *Spirit of Russia* was piloted by Flying Officer A.L. Keeley and, while the dam was not breached, the assault force did score several direct hits and forced the Germans to lower the water level.

After being transferred to No.189 Squadron on 24 October 1944, *Spirit of Russia* completed a further 17 operations before her final mission-tasking on the night of 2/3 February 1945. Flown by Flight Lieutenant F.J. Abbott, she took part in a successful raid against Karlsruhe in southwest Germany.

During an operational career that spanned 109 sorties, *Spirit of Russia* had taken part in all of the major battles of Bomber Command. From the Battle of the Ruhr during March-July 1943, to the precision bombing attacks on enemy targets prior to D-day, the aircraft amassed a 16-month combat record with No.9 Squadron. This represented a remarkable achievement at a time when the average life of a Lancaster was only three weeks. The regular crews of *Spirit of Russia* seemed to possess similar good fortune – some completed over 10 operations on this aircraft alone, even though the average life of an aircrew was calculated to be five flight ops. In the

Above: Following a raid on Stettin in April 1943, the crew of *Johnny Walker* enjoy a post-operational smoke while they wait for the transport that will take them to the debriefing. Below: 1954, and a poignant end for one of the most remarkable bombers of World War II. Having flown into the face of enemy fire on over 100 occasions, but now ravaged by the elements, *Spirit of Russia* plays host to a group of servicemen who, perhaps, are remembering the daring exploits of their predecessors.

course of 109 missions, 92 of which were with No.9 Squadron, *Spirit of Russia* had without doubt lived up the unit's motto: 'Throughout the night we fly'.

THE AUTHOR Bruce Blanche has contributed a number of articles to military publications, specialising in the history of the RAF during World War II.

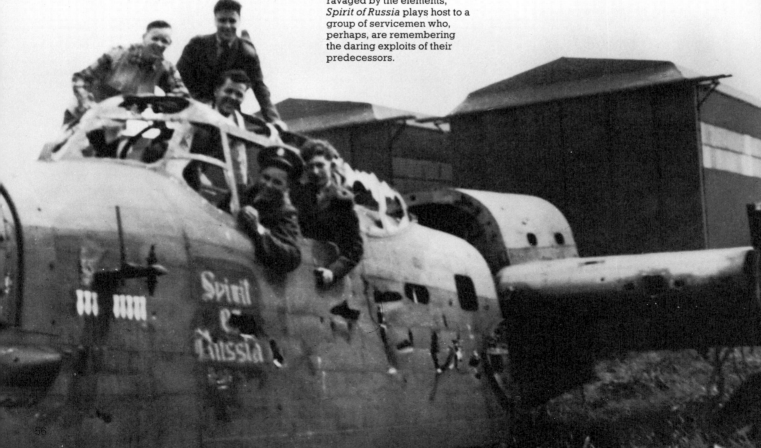

PRECISION AND POWER

After the Dams raid, the men of 617 Squadron developed new techniques to make their bombing the most accurate in the world

ONCE PUBLICITY about its spectacular attack on the German dams in May 1943 had subsided, 617 Squadron faced an uncertain future. Both flight commanders were among the eight crews shot down on Operation Chastise and Wing Commander Guy Gibson, VC, had since been taken off operations. Yet C-in-C Bomber Command, Sir Arthur Harris, was determined to use the squadron 'for the performance of similar (specialist) tasks'.

So replacement crews were brought in and Squadron Leader George Holden, DSO, DFC – slight, fair-haired and abrasive – assumed command. Not until mid-July, though, did the reshaped squadron fly operationally. Then, six Lancasters bombed power-stations in northern Italy, flying on to North Africa where they acquired a huge supply of oranges, figs and dates for the return flight. Back at

Above: The Avro Lancaster, undoubtedly Britain's finest four-engined heavy bomber in World War II. Invariably the main bomber aircraft flown by 617 Squadron, the Lancaster proved itself capable of carrying much greater bombloads than those originally envisaged by the manufacturer – 13,000lb over a range of 650 miles or 5500lb up to 2350 miles – and its deep, wide bomb-bay was readily adapted to carry the specialised weapons devised by Barnes Wallis.

Scampton, repetitive training was broken by a leaflet excursion to Milan, which prompted Flight Lieutenant Joe McCarthy (the American who had attacked the Sorpe dam) to complain bitterly of 'selling goddam newspapers'.

A fortnight after moving to their new base at Coningsby, on 14 September eight Lancasters from 617 Squadron, each carrying a 12,000lb, thin-cased, blast bomb, set out to break the banks of the Dortmund-Ems canal from a height of 150ft. Due to poor weather, they were recalled over the North Sea. But, in turning back, Squadron Leader David Maltby (who had breached the Moehne dam) hit the sea causing 'a terrific explosion'.

Returning from leave the next morning, Flight Lieutenant Micky Martin heard that the operation would be remounted that night and insisted on taking Maltby's place. His rear gunner thought him a 'bloody fool' in volunteering for something so obviously dangerous, and his fears were soon justified. On the way to the target, Holden, who was to co-ordinate the attack by radio telephony (R/T), ran into flak over Noorhorn and crashed in an enormous

NIGHT BOMBING

In 1941 the Butt Report evaluated the effectiveness of RAF Bomber Command's night blind-bombing missions. Its conclusions, based on analysis of 600 aerial photographs, were devastating. On average only one-third of the crews claiming to have reached their targets came within five miles, and for the Ruhr the figure was one in 10. Clearly the most serious problem was navigation. Britain's first navigation aid, named Gee, involved three radio stations on the ground transmitting pulse signals so that the bomber's navigator could accurately fix his position. But the system could easily be jammed. Radar then provided more reliable aids. 'Oboe', whereby two ground stations in England tracked an aircraft over the target, lacked range. But in 1943 H_2S was introduced, a plane-mounted radar system that scanned the surface directly below the bomber to produce images that could be 'read' by the navigator in conjunction with maps.

The task of pinpointing the target for the approaching bombers became the responsibility of the Pathfinder Force. The Pathfinder navigators identified the target and incendiary marker bombs were dropped on the site. The red flares burned for eight minutes and during the course of the bombing were reinforced by additional marker runs. The stream of bombers, broken into a series of waves, then homed in on the flares blazing below.

The Pathfinder Force achieved many outstanding operational successes, but it was not until 617 Squadron showed how the problem of poor marking could be eliminated that high-level night bombing reached its full potential in World War II.

Top: The badge worn by all navigators in the RAF.

ball of fire. His men included four of Gibson's crew at the dams. Yet more misfortune lay ahead. At the canal, dense fog obscured the target. Four Lancasters were lost there and another jettisoned its bomb after failing to find the canal. That left Martin and Flight Lieutenant David Shannon, another dams veteran, who managed to drop one bomb in the canal and one on the tow-path. Close, but not close enough.

The day after the Dortmund-Ems disaster, Martin was temporarily put in command. That same night, he led six 617 Lancasters to the undefended Antheor viaduct in southern France, which carried the main railway line into Italy, and attacked with 1000lb bombs from 350ft. Once more bombing accuracy was insufficient, and this reinforced the doubts of Air Vice-Marshal R. A. Cochrane, Air Officer Commanding No.5 Group to which 617 Squadron belonged, about the worth of low-level attacks by heavy bombers. He therefore ordered 617 to practise with the new Stabilising Automatic Bomb Sight (SABS) to achieve a maximum 100yds error from 20,000ft.

Using this tactic, Martin took the squadron to Antheor again three weeks later. Encouraging results in training led Cochrane to expect errors of 50yds or less from 10,000ft. But of the 10 Lancasters that bombed on 11 October 1943, six dropped their 12,000lb loads on the wrong target and the other four did not fulfil Cochrane's hopes.

Thus neither from high level nor low level could 617 Squadron destroy precision targets at the time when Wing Commander Leonard Cheshire, DSO & Bar, DFC, took over from Martin. A tall, thin Oxford graduate of 25 with two bomber tours behind him, Cheshire was a mixture of quietness, boisterous humour and ruthless efficiency. Soon after his arrival the Air Ministry ordered an all-out assault on 60 special targets in northern France. On 16 December 1943, therefore, Cheshire led nine Lancasters armed with 12,000lb bombs to a V1 launching site (approximately 300 by 250yds in area) near Abbeville. Preceded by marking aircraft of the Pathfinder Force, 617 achieved an average error of 94yds, but the markers were some way from the target and it survived intact. Further attacks on this and similar sites during the next month underlined the problem of accurately marking a small target from high level.

During their training in January 1944, therefore, Cheshire and Martin worked on a system of low-level marking. They used it unofficially in action, after flares had been dropped to illuminate the target, by diving their Lancasters to an unprecedented 400ft to mark another 'special target'. Although this technique produced better bombing results, the markers skidded on impact. When 617 moved to Woodhall Spa, Cheshire and Martin concentrated on eliminating this fault, and towards the end of the month they were ready to try again. This time Flight Lieutenant Les Munro dropped flares then Cheshire and Martin released their spot markers just before pulling out of the dive. The markers did not skid.

Cheshire now approached Cochrane, explaining that he had developed in practice a method of low-level marking by diving at an angle of 30 degrees once the target had been identified and illuminated. It promised a high degree of accuracy. Cochrane suspected that the 'practice' had been under operational conditions, he gave no hint agreeing to an experiment against the 'distinctive target' of the Gnome-Rhône works near Limoges. However, he cautioned that 300 French girls would be working on the night shift and civilian homes were nearby. Neither must be harmed.

So Cheshire led 12 Lancasters to Limoges on 8/9 February 1944, carrying in his own aircraft an RAF film crew. As the Lancasters approached, troublesome cloud dispersed and, 'we could see the moon behind the cathedral on the banks of the river.' The target was undefended, except for a few machine guns, and Cheshire made three low runs over it, being rewarded by a stream of figures rushing away from the buildings. On the fourth run, he marked the aiming point with incendiaries from 200ft, then Martin dived with red spot markers and the remaining 10 617 Squadron Lancasters dropped back-up markers for the main force from 10,000ft with the SABS. Reconnaissance photographs were striking: only seven of the 48 bays in the factory escaped severe damage; the residential areas were untouched. Sir Charles Portal, Chief of the Air Staff, signalled: 'Warmest congratulations to this squadron on the extreme accuracy of their bombing.'

With his flight engineer wounded and bomb-aimer dead, he nursed a crippled Lancaster to Sardinia

The Antheor viaduct, now surrounded by searchlights and installations of heavy and light flak, would provide a sterner test, however. Four nights after the Limoges operation, 617 made another attempt to destroy this valuable Axis communication link, knowing that their 12,000lb bombs must land within 10yds of the arches. Repeated attempts by Cheshire and Martin to mark the target by flying in from the sea failed, and eventually Martin approached overland at low level, while Cheshire drew enemy fire in the bay. But Martin's courageous effort also failed. With two engines damaged, his flight engineer wounded and bomb-aimer dead, he was left to nurse a crippled Lancaster to Sardinia, where he landed with no brakes on a small runway.

In the meantime, at Antheor Cheshire tried unsuccessfully five more times to mark at low level, eventually dropping his spots from 5,000ft. They missed by 100yds. He warned the nine orbiting Lancasters to compensate for this error and, press-

Left: Increasingly heavily defended by flak installations, the Antheor viaduct near Cannes carried the important coastal rail link between France and Italy. Its destruction depended on extremely accurate marking as a bomb had to fall within 10yds of the structure. 617 Squadron attacked the viaduct three times, but all three of their raids took place before the development of Cheshire's technique of marking from low level in a Mosquito. The viaduct was finally destroyed by American bombers. Below right: Cheshire made the first official trial of his new low-level marking technique over the lightly defended target of the Gnome-Rhône aero-engine factory at Limoges. The sequence of photographs shows his incendiary markers lighting up the factory workshops. Below: A plume of smoke streams from the plant in a daylight reconnaissance photograph. The factory was utterly destroyed and the civilian work force suffered no casualties.

ing home their attack, they dropped eight bombs within 20yds of the viaduct – just 10yds from success. Cochrane now grounded Martin after an arduous tour, and Cheshire divided the squadron into three flights under the remaining dams veterans Munro, McCarthy and Shannon.

During the spring of 1944, 617 successfully attacked factory targets in France with remarkable accuracy, sustaining few casualties or aircraft losses. Bad visibility foiled an operation against La Ricamerie near St Etienne, causing Cheshire acidly to report by wireless telegraphy (W/T): 'Attack unsuccessful. Refer to your weather forecast' (which had predicted clear skies). At Clermont-Ferrand,

WING COMMANDER LEONARD CHESHIRE, VC.

Leonard Cheshire learned to fly in the biplanes of the Oxford University Air Squadron in 1937. He applied for a commission in the RAF and when war came he was posted to the Whitley bombers of No. 102 Squadron. Cheshire strove for a full understanding of his aircraft, the beginning of a practice that was to save many crewmen's lives. On a raid on Cologne a shell burst in his plane yet he flew on to release his bombs, and for this he won the DSO. Transferred to the Halifaxes of No. 35 Squadron, he completed 50 raids in a long tour of duty and was awarded the DFC. He immediately volunteered for another tour.

In August 1942 he became commander of No. 76 Squadron and led raids over Italy and Germany, winning a bar to his DSO.

On 1 April 1943 he was posted to Marston Moor by Air Vice-Marshal Carr to supervise the conversion of aircrews from medium to heavy bombers.

He then relinquished his

new rank of Group Captain to become commander of 617 Squadron in October 1943.

While awaiting the completion of the Tallboy bomb Cheshire developed his radical low-level marking technique, carrying out the task in Lancasters, then Mosquitoes, and finally in a US P-51 Mustang. Cheshire flew on 40 raids with 617 Squadron, destroying key German targets.

Having flown 100 missions with four squadrons Cheshire was awarded a third DSO and the VC. He left 617 Squadron in July 1944.

Precision bombing
617 Squadron RAF
July 1943 - June 1944

RAF Scampton
RAF Woodhall Spa
RAF Coningsby
GREAT BRITAIN
HOLLAND
RAF High Wycombe
Noorhorn
London
RAF Manston
14 Sept 1943
Berlin
Calais
Dortmund
Brussels
BELGIUM
Abbeville
16 Dec 1943
GERMANY
Paris
Karlsruhe
24 April 1944
Mailly-le-Camp
3 May 1944
Munich
24 April 1944
FRANCE
SWITZERLAND
8/9 Feb 1944
Limoges
16 Mar 1944
Clermont-Ferrand
Milan
15/16 July 1943
Bergerac
18 March 1944
St Etienne
4 March 1944
Turin
Toulouse
5 April 1944
16/17 Sept 1943
11 Oct 1943
12/13 Feb 1944
Antheor viaduct
ITALY

Key
■ RAF stations
● 617 Squadron targets
— Boundaries, 1943 – 1944

however, he could signal after a mere seven minutes: 'Michelin's complexion seems a trifle red,' following low-level marking by himself, Munro, Shannon and McCarthy. Nevertheless, Cochrane insisted on marking from 5000ft at Bergerac, where Cheshire radioed that 'the powder works would seem to have outlived their usefulness'. Officially, 617 achieved 'outstanding operational success and big strides forward in the development of precision bombing' in March, but Cheshire was convinced that low-level marking employed all the time would bring consistently better results.

He persuaded Cochrane to let him try a further refinement of this method. On 5 April 1944 Cheshire set out in a Mosquito, whose speed and manoeuvrability made it superior to the Lancaster for this task, in what has been described as 'the most important stage in the development of night precision bomb-

Above: The Mosquito F.B.VI bearing the marking NS993 that was flown by Wing Commander Leonard Cheshire in the raid on Munich of 24 April 1944. It was one of the first raids on the city.

ng'. He marked an aircraft repair factory at Toulouse from low level, enabling 140 Lancasters of 5 Group to bomb 'with tremendous effect'. So stunning was his achievement that Bomber Command decided to give 5 Group an 'independent role in attacking precision targets by night,' moving 627 Mosquito Squadron from the Pathfinders so that, spearheaded by 627 and 617 Squadrons, 5 Group could do its own marking. Soon afterwards, four more Mosquitoes arrived at Woodhall Spa for McCarthy, Shannon, and Flight Lieutenants R.S.D. Kearns and G.E. Fawke.

From mid-April until the end of May the average bombing error for 617-led attacks was 380yds, as compared with 680yds for high-level attacks on similar targets. Not all operations went smoothly, however. At the large military depot at Mailly-Le-Camp on 3 May, night fighters savaged main-force Lancasters, claiming 42 out of 338, for which Cheshire blamed 'inflexibility' on the part of the controller over the target, whose delay in sending in second-wave bombers had been strictly in accordance with the prepared plan. In contrast, 'flexibility of tactics' had much to do with 617's success.

The value of Cheshire's technique was underlined on 24 April 1944 at Munich, the historic centre of

Above: A 'Wooden Wonder' warms up for a night flight. Introduced into service in early 1943, the Mosquito F.B.VI was an ideal craft for low-level marking, being fast (it was capable of 278mph at sea level, 329mph at 20,700ft) and manoeuvrable. Designed to carry up to 1000lb of bombs, it was armed with four 20mm cannon and four .303in Browning guns. **Below right:** Leonard Cheshire's flight log-book. Among the routine local sorties are two operations in which he carried out low-level marking. He was awarded the VC after the 24 April raid on Munich. In the raid of 3 May, he and Squadron Leader Shannon made successful dive drops on the large military depot of Mailly-le-Camp prior to D-day.

Nazism and an important railway junction. As 250 Lancasters approached from the unusual direction of southeast France, six 617 Lancasters would drop diversionary flares and markers on Milan. 627 Squadron Mosquitoes would scatter 'Window' (metallic foil strips that created false images of planes on German radar) over Munich and another bomber force attack Karlsruhe. Four 617 Squadron Mosquitoes, operating at extreme range and piloted by Cheshire, Kearns, Shannon and Fawke, were to mark the target from low level. Cheshire's navigator, Flying Officer Pat Kelly, on learning that extra tanks could not be secured, decided that they must refuel at RAF Manston in Kent. Even then he cheerfully predicted: 'We might get back, but probably won't.' As the four crews walked out to their waiting aircraft at Manston, Cheshire remarked on the 'glorious sunset'. Shannon spoke for the others when he retorted: 'Damn the sunset. I'm only interested in the sunrise.'

In the early stages of the flight, over the North Sea and European mainland, the Mosquitoes encountered poor weather. When Cheshire called up Shannon to discuss the visibility, he was astonished to

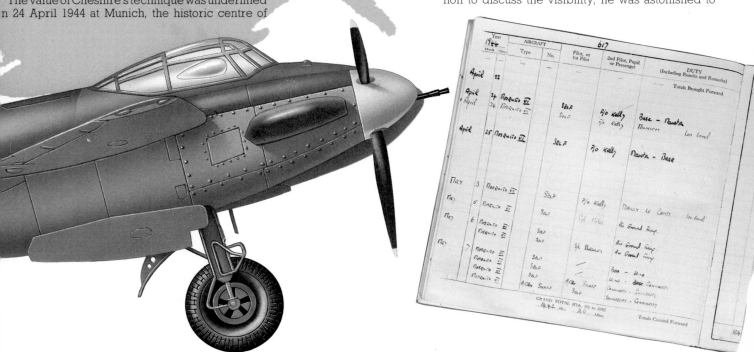

GERMAN NIGHT FIGHTERS

As World War II progressed, German radar-equipped night-fighter squadrons became increasingly adept at intercepting Britain's bomber formations. In early 1944 German night fighters were fitted with a new radar system, the Lichtenstein SN-2. Unlike its predecessor, the Lichtenstein C-1, it was not disrupted by Window and was capable of picking up a bomber at four miles' range. Once a bomber was located, it was tracked from the stern until the night-fighter pilot made visual contact with his quarry. The orthodox night-fighter attack was known as 'von unten hinten' (from under and behind). The fighter approached from as low as possible to avoid the bomber's rear-turret armament and fired its forward-firing guns from a nose-up position into the bomber's fuselage.

The discovery that Lancaster and Halifax crews could not see directly beneath their planes led to an entirely new nightfighter weapon code-named 'Schräge Musik' (slanting, or jazz, music). It consisted of a pair of 20mm cannon mounted in the fighter's canopy to fire almost vertically upwards. This enabled the pilot to fly in just beneath the bomber, unseen by its crew, and cripple it from close range.

hear a different familiar voice reply. Martin was engaged in intruder raids against enemy airfields to distract night fighters for them. After a short exchange, Martin wished Cheshire the 'best of luck', and the Mosquitoes flew on through thinning cloud and increasingly heavy flak. Soon they could see searchlights ahead and angry flashes pierced the darkness. They had reached Munich, and Cheshire began his dive through flak, flares and balloon cables from 5000 to 700ft to mark the aiming point. Resisting the urge to drop and pull out early in the cauldron of exploding metal and glaring beams, he placed his red spots accurately. Almost blacking out with the force of gravity, Cheshire skimmed the roof-tops before climbing to circle back. The other three Mosquitoes then backed up his markers and 617 Squadron Lancasters reinforced the original spot fires as the main force bombed.

Despite shortage of petrol, Cheshire continued to orbit the target below the discharging bombers at a height of 1000ft for 12 minutes after dropping his markers, his plane illuminated by fires below and flares above, ready to correct any gross inaccuracy in the main-force bombing. He reasoned that the chances of his being hit by a falling bomb were 'very, very slight', but his Mosquito sustained heavy damage from flak and once, coned by searchlights, he all but lost control. At length, satisfied that he had done

everything possible, Cheshire turned for home. Leaving the target area, as usual and contrary to regulations, he and Kelly lit cigarettes to relax. Suddenly, the Mosquito was flooded with light and buffeted by flak as it ran into a defensive belt. For 40 miles Cheshire sweated, twisted and cursed until they were through.

Now Kelly was able to devote his whole attention to conserving their dwindling fuel supply, eventually guiding them to Manston with 10 minutes of petrol remaining. However, their ordeal was not yet over. Approaching the runway, Kelly remarked on 'funny lights' below. Swiftly Cheshire realised that these were from the guns of a German fighter that was attacking Fawke who, with flaps down and committed to landing, was presenting an easy target. Fortunately the German's aim was off-centre. Cheshire snapped urgently for Kelly to 'turn the bloody navigation lights off,' and in panic Kelly switched off everything he could lay his hands on. As the runway lights had also been hastily extinguished, and being unable to risk staying in the air longer for lack of fuel, Cheshire made an intuitive landing in utter darkness. None of the Mosquitoes returned with more than 15 minutes of petrol on their gauges.

Next day reconnaissance aircraft confirmed both the accuracy and effectiveness of the operation. Cheshire had proved that a well-defended target in Germany could be visually marked without using a bomb-sight by diving to a low level. The method developed against precision targets in France had been conclusively proved for main-force operations against the enemy heartland.

617 Squadron's contribution to the D-day landings

Left: Two Messerschmitt Bf 110s equipped with the Lichtenstein C-1 radar installation. Though designed as a long-range escort fighter, the Bf 110 proved too unwieldy and sluggish in acceleration to match Britain's nimble single-seat fighter planes, and later models were built specifically for the night-fighter role. Background: A drop of Window, metallic foil strips which successfully jammed German radar until the introduction of Lichtenstein SN-2 radar equipment.

Flying officer, 617 Squadron 1944-45

A member of the Royal Australian Air Force serving in 617 Squadron, this Lancaster crewman wears standard Air Force battledress, over which is an inflatable life vest. His nationality badge is worn on the upper left arm and rank is indicated on the shoulder strap. Large numbers of Commonwealth servicemen served with the RAF during World War II, and they made a valiant contribution to Britain's strategic offensive against Germany.

was considerably less dramatic. Operation Taxable entailed a spoof raid to convince the enemy that a convoy was approaching the French coast in the region of Calais, instead of Normandy.

Several weeks of intricate and tiresome training in keeping formation according to a stop-watch preceded the take-off by eight Lancasters at 2300 hours on 5 June: each carried 12 men, including an extra pilot and navigator.

Eight Lancasters took over in a precise manoeuvre to ensure absolute continuity in the course of the ghost convoy

Starting from a predetermined point over the Channel, the aircraft took up a set formation to drop Window at four-second intervals for 35 seconds, then turn back for 32 seconds before repeating the process for another 35 seconds, simulating a convoy proceeding at 7mph for the benefit of enemy radar. After four hours a second group of eight Lancasters took over in a precise and delicate manoeuvre to ensure absolute continuity and no interruption of the course of the ghost convoy. This second group broke off at dawn within sight of the French coast. The operation went perfectly and the Germans were fooled. But Cheshire still regarded it as a 'stooge job', and Shannon wrote in his log book: 'Successful, but bloody browned off.'

Operation Taxable was the logical successor to earlier precision work in France. 617 Squadron had by now established its reputation as a specialist marking and bombing unit, quite apart from the Dams Raid. It had also acquired a second VC – awarded to Cheshire after Munich. He insisted, however, that the decoration was 'for all of 617 Squadron' and paid special tribute to Shannon and Martin, who had 'paced' him by their achievements.

617 Squadron could no longer be classed as a 'single operation squadron' or, for that matter, a 'suicide' one. Moreover, after an interval of 13 months, it was about to resume close association with Barnes Wallis, who would soon have two more of his special bombs for them: Tallboy and Grand Slam.

THE AUTHOR John Sweetman is currently Head of the Department of Political and Social Studies at the Royal Military Academy, Sandhurst and has written *Operation Chastise, The Dams Raid: Epic or Myth*.

'We arrived over the target at about 4000/5000ft some five minutes before 'H' hour, when the first parachute flares were due to be dropped. There was no moon but it was beautifully clear and we could see the built-up area below us, but no easily identifiable detail. I confirmed with 'Flare Leader' that the Illuminators were on time and running in to drop the dual line of flares.

'The defences were responding in strength. Searchlights were probing the sky, and considerable heavy and light anti-aircraft fire was being directed at the incoming Lancasters. The flares came down perfectly and on time – two lines of powerful lights on parachutes at

BOMBER RAID

One of the Mosquitoes that marked with Leonard Cheshire on the Munich raid of 24 April 1944 was piloted by Flight Lieutenant Terry Kearns, DSO, DFC, DFM. A New Zealander, he is seen above (third from left) with crew members of the Lancaster that he also flew on operations with 617 Squadron.

3000ft and some 200/300yds apart. The aiming-point – a large square in the centre of the city – was clearly visible within the two lines of light. My attack entailed a steep dive through the burning parachute flares, releasing the marker bombs at about 1500ft, then a sharp pull out from the dive and a steep climb away, avoiding the burning flares and other obstacles. On the climbing turn we looked back and saw that the markers had landed and were burning in front of what looked like a town hall. The marker force had enjoyed scant attention prior to this, but now searchlights and light 'Ack Ack' fire made marking runs more difficult. When we had broken clear of the defences, I circled to observe the accuracy of the bombing and the continuity of the aiming-point markers; these were satisfactory so we set course for home.'
Flight Lieutenant Terry Kearns, DSO, DFC, DFM.

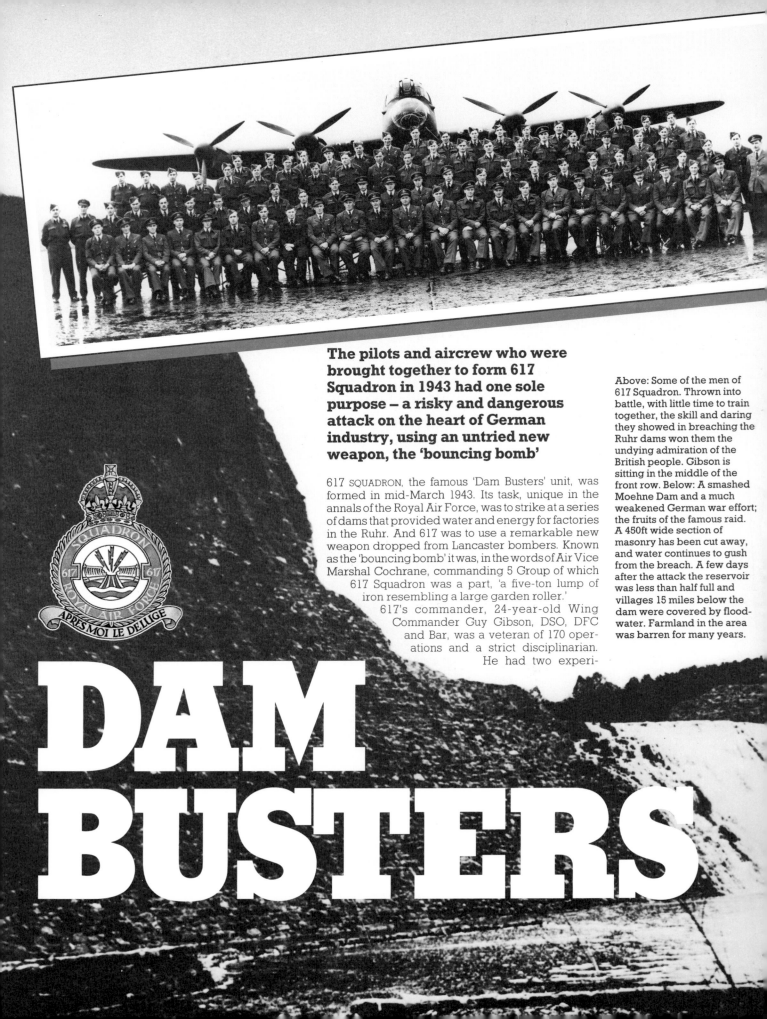

The pilots and aircrew who were brought together to form 617 Squadron in 1943 had one sole purpose – a risky and dangerous attack on the heart of German industry, using an untried new weapon, the 'bouncing bomb'

617 SQUADRON, the famous 'Dam Busters' unit, was formed in mid-March 1943. Its task, unique in the annals of the Royal Air Force, was to strike at a series of dams that provided water and energy for factories in the Ruhr. And 617 was to use a remarkable new weapon dropped from Lancaster bombers. Known as the 'bouncing bomb' it was, in the words of Air Vice Marshal Cochrane, commanding 5 Group of which 617 Squadron was a part, 'a five-ton lump of iron resembling a large garden roller.'

617's commander, 24-year-old Wing Commander Guy Gibson, DSO, DFC and Bar, was a veteran of 170 operations and a strict disciplinarian. He had two experi-

Above: Some of the men of 617 Squadron. Thrown into battle, with little time to train together, the skill and daring they showed in breaching the Ruhr dams won them the undying admiration of the British people. Gibson is sitting in the middle of the front row. Below: A smashed Moehne Dam and a much weakened German war effort; the fruits of the famous raid. A 450ft wide section of masonry has been cut away, and water continues to gush from the breach. A few days after the attack the reservoir was less than half full and villages 15 miles below the dam were covered by floodwater. Farmland in the area was barren for many years.

DAM BUSTERS

enced flight commanders: his deputy, Squadron Leader Young, DFC, a former Oxford rowing blue and passionate yoga and bridge devotee, and Squadron Leader Maudslay, DFC, a champion athlete and old Etonian.

The 133 flying personnel gathered at RAF Scampton in Lincolnshire in late March were a mixed bunch. Apart from Gibson, Young and Maudslay, 16 had DFCs, 10 DFMs and one, Flight-Lieutenant Hopgood, had a DFC and Bar. The other 103 (including six pilots) who would fly to the dams had no decorations. Ninety of the squadron were RAF (including the extrovert, moustachioed Australian low-flying expert, Flight Lieutenant Martin), 29 came from Canada (one a large, blond American, Flight Lieutenant McCarthy), two were from New Zealand and 12 from Australia. They ranged in age from 20 to 32. Of the initial 21 crews, one was replaced for 'failing to reach the standard necessary for this operation', and one left voluntarily. However, another crew organised its own posting to 617, and kept the squadron at full complement.

617 Squadron arrived at Scampton under-strength. Flight Lieutenant Shannon came from 8 (Pathfinder) Group with an incomplete crew. Sergeants Henderson and Sumpter from 57 Squadron, hearing that 'a chap on 617' was looking for a flight engineer and bomb aimer, 'went along to give him the once over'. The meeting was mutually satisfactory and both joined Shannon. Other aircrew were transferred without option. Flight Sergeant Powell, from 57 Squadron, sorted out the ground crew of riggers, fitters, signallers and radar specialists.

On 27 March, without yet knowing the actual targets, Gibson learnt that the operation would involve an attack across water and low-level navigation over enemy territory in moonlight with a final approach to the target at 100ft at a precise speed. He also discovered that the bombload had to be released at exactly 150ft after pulling out of a dive from 2000ft. Cochrane showed Gibson models of the two larger targets, the Moehne and Eder dams, on 29 March, but swore him to secrecy. To add to Gibson's problems, he had only 10 aircraft for his 22 crews to practise with.

WING COMMANDER GUY GIBSON, VC.

There were few men better qualified than 24-year-old Wing Commander Guy Penrose Gibson to lead the 'Dam Buster' squadron in the spring of 1943. In the seven years since he joined the RAF in 1936, Gibson had proved himself a first-rate pilot, bomber captain and leader.

After stints with 83 and 29 Squadrons, flying Hampden bombers and nightfighters, Gibson transferred to 106 Squadron in March 1942. He led the unit for a year, during which time he added a Distinguished Service Order (DSO) to his Distinguished Flying Cross (DFC) and Bar. On 11 March 1943, as Gibson flew the last operation of his third tour of duty, the order for his transfer to 617 Squadron came through.

Gibson's flying experience was second to none, but the Dam Busters also needed a leader who could inspire men, and, by stamping his authority on them, build a highly-motivated fighting unit. Gibson was the perfect choice; he was widely recognised as a tough commanding officer where anything connected with flying was concerned. His office was painted in sky blue with seagulls and aeroplanes all over it, and he always kept a loaded service revolver on his desk.

The breaching of the Ruhr dams in May 1943 totally vindicated the RAF's faith in Gibson. As much as the skill of the Lancaster pilots, the ingenuity of the bouncing bomb and the detailed planning that went into the mission, it was Gibson, above all others, who showed the way. He led from the front, placed himself in the thick of the action and spared no effort in aiding his fellow pilots. The Victoria Cross he won was the nation's recognition of his central role in the Dam Busters raid.

Left: Wing Commander Guy Gibson wears standard Air Force battledress, plus fleece-lined flying boots, an officer's service cap, inflatable life jacket and, in his hand, carries a flying helmet. Rank is indicated by the slide on his shoulder straps.

THE BOUNCING BOMB

The extraordinary weapon used by 617 Squadron to breach the Ruhr dams was the brain-child of civilian engineer Barnes Wallis. Although the Air Staff was lukewarm to his initial plans, Wallis continued his experiments, and, early in 1942, proved that the Moehne Dam could be destroyed by a 'bouncing bomb' exploding 30 feet beneath the surface of the reservoir, against its retaining wall.

Wallis' research team, based near Weybridge worked round the clock to complete the bomb's design. Tests to perfect the idea involved catapulting marbles over water in a tin bath, firing projectiles across a lake and shooting small spheres along an indoor water tank. During the winter of 1942-43 a Wellington bomber, fitted with special rotating and release gear, carried out a series of trials with practice spheres at Chesil Beach near Weymouth.

A full-size weapon, however, had yet to be tested, and it was not until April 1943 that these bombs were issued to the RAF. Unfortunately the practice spheres broke on impact or veered off course, but Wallis, who had an eye for simple solutions, removed their outer-casings – the bomb then worked and the German dams were doomed.

In its final form 'Upkeep' (the weapon's codename) comprised a 9250lb cylindrical canister, 60in long and 50in in diameter.

The explosive charge, consisting of 6600lb of Torpex, was detonated by three hydrostatic pistols set to activate at 30 feet below the water or, as a fail-safe device, a self-destructive mechanism that was timed to operate 90 seconds after the bomb was launched. The Germans, who analysed a sphere recovered from a downed Lancaster, called the weapon a rotating depth charge. Whatever the accuracy of this description, Wallis' invention has gone down in history, nevertheless, as the 'bouncing bomb'.

Nevertheless, Gibson devised a series of cross-country routes over the North Sea, Scotland, the Irish Sea, Wales and England. Starting on 31 March, the exercises were never less than three hours long and the crews flew the 10 available Lancasters in rotation. Bombing exercises were carried out at Wainfleet in the Wash, air-to-air gunnery with towed targets and air-to-sea firing at floats over the North Sea. Over Scampton's runways, pilots were required to dive steeply towards a whitewashed line.

The special weapon had to be released exactly 425yds from the target

To simulate moonlight during the day, an idea of wearing dark glasses was rejected in favour of synthetic night flying equipment - amber celluloid was fitted over windows and crew members wore blue goggles. As Gibson discovered, when he almost dived into Derwent reservoir near Sheffield, judging height above water posed a major problem. Eventually, two Aldis lamps were fixed to each aircraft and adjusted to form a figure of eight (two touching circles) forward of the leading edge of the starboard wing at the attacking height of 150ft.

It now became clear, however, that the special weapon had to be released at exactly 425yds from the target, otherwise it would either sink short of the dam wall or bounce harmlessly over. Some of the dams had twin towers on top; so a wooden triangular device, with a peep-hole at its apex and two nails at the extremities of its base, was developed. A piece of wood attached underneath allowed the bomb-aimer to hold this crude sight, line it up with the target and press the bomb release when the nails and towers coincided.

The awkward shape, size and weight of the special weapon, officially termed a 'mine', led Avros to modify the Lancasters by removing their mid-upper turrets and bomb-bay doors for the operation. The displaced mid-upper gunner was redeployed permanently in the front turret, and stirrups were rigged to keep his boots out of the bomb-aimer's hair. These disembowelled Lancasters were dubbed 'gutted fish' or 'abortions' and the two 'cymbal-like contraptions' dangling beneath the fuselage to hold the mine were called 'clappers'.

Intensive training was carried out during April. It put a great strain on men and machines, but by the end of the month, Gibson reported that 617 Squadron comprised 58 officers and 481 other ranks and that over 1000 hours had been flown in training. All crews were competent to navigate at low level by map-reading at night, bomb accurately to the required specifications and fly safely at 150ft over water. Shortly afterwards, due to problems in finalising the mine, the height came down to 60ft. 617 Squadron quickly adapted to this change.

Thirty-one exercises involving 168 bombing attacks on the sight-screens at Wainfleet were flown in the first week of May. A large-scale night manoeuvre on 6 May ended chaotically due to poor radio reception in the air and Gibson decided to co-ordinate the operation in the target area himself by R/T. Clear reception was crucial and so new sets were quickly installed in the modified Lancasters.

Between 11 and 14 May, crews flew to Reculver and attacked, 'remarkably accurately', canvas towers on the promenade with full-size, practice mines. On the evening of 14 May Gibson described the full dress rehearsal as 'completely successful'. and on the next day he learnt that the attack, Operation Chastise would take place on Sunday 16 May.

There were six target dams. Gibson would lead three formations of three aircraft each over the North Sea, across the Scheldt estuary, and follow specified canals, rivers and railway junctions skirting the Ruhr, to the Moehne Dam. He was then to fly to the Eder Dam and finally the Sorpe Dam. Five other Lancasters, flying singly, would cross the Frisian Islands off Holland, as Gibson reached the coast 120 miles further south, turn over the Ijsselmeer (Zuider Zee) and join the southern route west of the Ruhr to bomb the Sorpe Dam. They faced a particular complication. The other target dams were masonry structures, which could be attacked at right angles from 60 feet at precisely 220mph with the mine bouncing over the water. The Sorpe, however, had sloping earth sides. Here the mine would not be spun, bounced or delivered at right angles. The Lancasters would fly lengthways along the crest of the dam and drop their mines directly on top.

All 19 aircraft were to fly at 100ft, trusting the aimer's map-reading and sharp eyes

These 14 aircraft were to take off from Scampton at intervals between 2128 and 2159 hours on 16 May. Five others, forming a reserve wave, would not leave until about two hours later. They were to fly separately along Gibson's route and be directed, while airborne, to any of the main targets or three others (Lister, Diemel and Ennepe) that remained intact. All 19 aircraft were to fly at 100ft over the continent, trusting that the bomb-aimer's map-reading and sharp eyes would warn of power lines, church steeples, trees and other hazards. Three light flak guns (effective vertically or horizontally up to 6,360ft) had been identified on the Moehne Dam, with three more in meadowland immediately to the north. The other dams were undefended.

Far left: In April 1943 bombing trials moved to Reculver Bay in Kent, giving the RAF the chance to test the full-size weapon and practise low-level precision attacks Caught at the moment of release, this bomb left the Lancaster at 60 feet. Tests were completed only two weeks before the date set for the operation. Left: Barnes Wallis at work on the design of the bouncing bomb. Without his genius and ability to deal with the 'brasshats' of the Air Staff the project would never have gone beyond the drawing board.

Below, clockwise from top: Approaching the target at 60 feet the Lancaster had to drop the bomb about 425 yards from the target. Two lights slung beneath the aircraft gave the exact release height, when their reflections met on the surface of the reservoir. The backspin of the bomb carried it over the nets and on to the dam, it then 'crawled' down the retaining wall and blew up at 30 feet. Judging the point of release was made possible by a simple wooden device. When the two nails at the end of its arms coincided with the towers on the dam the bomb was dropped. Lancasters, modified by the removal of the mid-upper turret and parts of the bomb-bays, were used to carry Wallis' weapon.

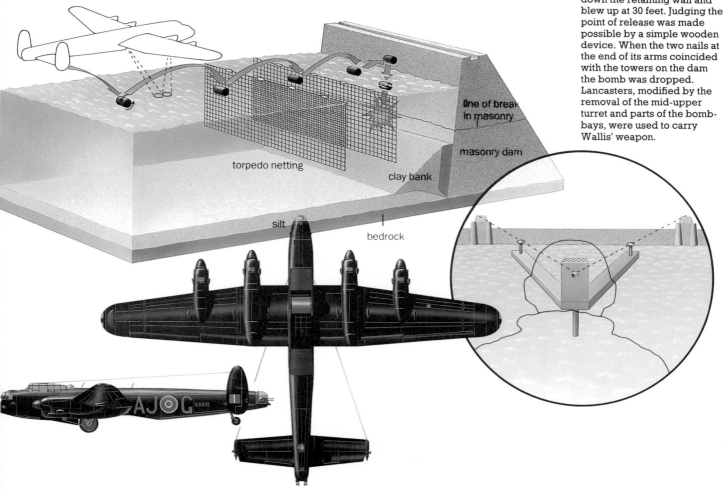

line of break in masonry

masonry dam

torpedo netting

clay bank

silt

bedrock

Gibson briefed his flight commanders, bombing leader and deputy leader on the Moehne on the Saturday evening. The rest had to wait until the day of the operation when the hangars and offices were 'very quiet, like a morgue', and according to one gunner 'the longest briefing I ever attended' took place. Details of the targets, routes, procedures and the potential disaster for enemy steel production of this 'historic' operation were explained, studied and discussed in depth. Afterwards, one gunner observed that in each Lancaster there were now 'seven men against the Reich', and a bomb-aimer recorded that everybody was in high spirits and ready to go.

The period remaining before take-off was nerve-racking. Flight Sergeant Brown's flight engineer went out to his aircraft and vainly tried to lift the mine in its retaining arms. On another mine a wireless operator, who would not return that night, defiantly chalked, 'Never has so much been expected of so few'. Young tidied his room, and others wrote letters. Hopgood prophesied that he would not come back. Flight Sergeant Townsend thought that they were 'all for the chop', and his front gunner took a bath, 'determined to die clean'. Gibson remained outwardly calm.

In the moonlight the Moehne looked 'grey and solid...heavy and unconquerable'

It was soon time to go. Getting off the grass strip with a maximum load caused the first headache. Some feared that the bumping would put the spotlights out of line and consign them all to a watery grave, others worried that the bomb might explode there and then.

Gibson's nine aircraft evaded flak until the Rhine, but one plane was lost on the edge of the Ruhr. Despite the meticulous training, reaching the target area was not easy. Martin's rear gunner noted: 'Lost Hoppy! Later picked up searchlights near Rhine – shot some out somewhere – bit off track over some

town – bags of shooting – lost Winco – arrived Moehne – Hoppy and Winco turned up.'

In the moonlight the Moehne looked 'grey and solid... squat and heavy and unconquerable'. Gibson attacked first. Flying through 'spiteful' flak and, emerging unscathed, he dropped his mine but failed to breach the dam. Hopgood went next but his plane disintegrated in a sheet of orange flame as the mine, dropped late, cleared the wall and destroyed a power station behind in a shower of blue sparks. The bomb aimer, who parachuted to safety, thought the ground-fire intense and for the gunners aiming at an aircraft, illuminated by its own spotlights, 'pretty simple duck shooting'. The mine from the third attacking aircraft veered left of the wall, but the fourth and fifth Lancasters both breached the dam. 'The spout of water [from each] was silhouetted against the moon. It rose with tremendous speed and then gently fell back. You could see the shock wave at the base of the jet.' To Gibson the flood rushing through the devastated dam 'looked like stirred porridge in the moonlight'. It was 'a fabulous sight' to Shannon. The burning wreckage of Hopgood's aircraft made Martin's rear gunner 'madder than Hell'.

Gibson, Young and the three Lancasters with mines left flew on to the Eder where early morning mist caused unexpected confusion. Shannon went

Above left: Lancaster 'G' for George, flown by Guy Gibson. The spinning device, a large V-belt powered by an electric motor, can be seen on the starboard side of the aircraft. Above: four views of the Moehne and Eder Dams before and after the attack. Repairs were not completed until the end of September 1943, and even then the water in both had to be kept below pre-raid levels.

the wrong way up the reservoir and prepared to attack another dam, before flares fired by Gibson brought him back to the correct rendezvous. A difficult, diving approach over Waldeck Castle, followed by a sharp turn to port and an extremely steep hill beyond the dam, faced him, Maudslay and Pilot Officer Knight. The first two attacked without breaking the dam, but with the last mine of the first wave Knight was successful. It was 'as if some huge fist had been jabbed at the wall and a large, almost round, black hole appeared'. 'Terribly elated', the crews turned for home, only to lose Young and Maudslay on the way. Of the first nine aircraft only five survived.

The second wave, flying to the Sorpe, also ran into trouble. Two turned back early. One was damaged by flak, another lost its mine after hitting the sea. Two others were shot down. Only the American, McCarthy, reached the dam. The approach over a hillside village was so tricky that he made 10 runs before releasing the mine. As he pulled up over another hill at the far side of the dam, he saw it was damaged but not breached. His rear gunner acidly advised him 'to get the hell down', as they were sitting ducks for nightfighters at that height. The way home was dicey especially when the off-track Lancaster crossed the heavily-defended railway junction of Hamm; but eventually McCarthy got his plane back to Scampton.

The third wave also suffered losses. Townsend experienced a 'very, very nasty flight', and years later his front gunner recalled: 'I still remember very vividly some of those power lines and pylons'. Damaged by flak, one Lancaster from this wave turned back with a mine. Two others were shot down. Of the two remaining aircraft, Brown attacked the Sorpe and, like McCarthy, experienced similar difficulty and lack of success. Townsend was sent to the Ennepe Dam, and arrived back at Scampton at 0615 on Monday morning in broad daylight. He landed downwind and bounced 'an awful number of times – it seemed like twenty-four'.

Eight Lancasters were lost on Operation Chastise. Fifty-six men failed to return, including both

Busting the German Dams
617 Squadron's flight-paths, 16 May 1943

GERMANY

ENGLAND

NORTH SEA

HOLLAND

ZUIDER ZEE

Amsterdam

Rotterdam

Münster

Dortmund-Ems Canal

London

Rhine

Weser

Dortmund

Moehne

Diemal

Essen

Sorpe

Kassel

Ruhr

ENGLISH CHANNEL

Antwerp

Ennepe

Eder

BELGIUM

Lister

FRANCE

Brussels

Cologne

Scampton

Key
First wave
Second wave
Third wave
Dam attacked
Dam not attacked

flight commanders, although three were POWs. Allowing for the two early returns and the one abortive, 50 per cent of the attacking aircraft were lost. Cochrane argued that this 'brilliantly conducted operation', through the destruction of two major German dams and devastation caused by the subsequent tidal waves, made the losses worthwhile. Nevertheless, 617 Squadron had lost almost 40 per cent of its aircrew in its first operation.

After the operation, Mess staff thought it 'a very sad sight to see the empty chairs', and for the Canadians congratulations on 'a good show' scarcely compensated for the loss of 13 colleagues. Shannon's bomb-aimer reflected on a sense of anti-climax, as 'it was all over in half a minute.' Avros gave a celebratory dinner for the crew, 34 of whom were decorated. Gibson was awarded a well-deserved VC. To Townsend's navigator, he 'set a standard of perfection. It's called leadership – how do you define it?' The C-in-C Coastal Command sent a telegram that summed up the whole squadron's achievement: 'Well done Scampton. A magnificent night's work.'

Although the raid was well-executed, and the performance of the men superb, the military value of breaching the Moehne and Eder Dams remains open to debate even to this day. Water output was restored by 27 June, and the Germans off-set the temporary loss of electricity generating power by diverting supplies from elsewhere. In these particulars at least, the raid was only a temporary inconvenience, and did little permanent damage. Over 1250 people lost their lives in the raid, but more important was the destruction of farmland, bridges and machinery that forced the Germans to rebuild part of their war industry in the area. The use of forced labour to complete repairs, and the stationing of over 10,000 troops to protect the dams was clearly a more lasting drain on resources.

617 Squadron's attack did much to raise the morale

MOMENT OF TRIUMPH

Guy Gibson, flying overhead when the Moehne was breached, had a clear view of the action, and saw the destruction caused by the flood of unleashed water:

'Nearly all the flak had now stopped and the other boys came down from the hills to have a closer look to see what had been done. There was no doubt about it at all – the Moehne Dam had been breached and the gunners on top of the dam, except for one man, had run for their lives towards the safety of the solid ground; this remaining gunner was a brave man, but one of the boys quickly extinguished his flak with a burst of well-aimed tracer. Now it was all quiet, except for the roar of the water which steamed and hissed its way from its one-hundred-and-fifty-foot head. Then we began to shout and scream and act like madmen over the R/T, for

Below left: Members of Gibson's crew telling the story of the epic raid to senior officers Harris and Cochrane (standing). An intelligence officer (left, sitting) takes the details from (left to right) Spafford, Taerum and Trevor-Roper. Below right: At a banquet held in 617 Squadron's honour, Gibson gives his own special seal of approval to the raid by signing an aerial view of the breached Moehne Dam.

of the British people, who were, in 1943, eager for news of any military success. The Dam Busters were used as a symbol of the efficiency of Bomber Command, and, through the unit's mixture of crews from foreign countries, Allied co-operation. The squadron went on to carry out other precision-bombing missions, but Wallis' bomb and the specially-converted Lancasters were never used again in such a role. After the war the remaining bombs were dumped in the Atlantic, and the specially adapted Type 464 Provisioning Lancasters were scrapped. It was a less than fitting end to the equipment that gave the squadron the means to breach the dams.

THE AUTHOR John Sweetman is currently Head of the Department of Political and Social Science at the Royal Military Academy at Sandhurst and has written *Operation Chastise, The Dams Raid: Epic or Myth.*

this was a tremendous sight, a sight which probably no man will ever see again.

'Then I looked again at the dam and at the water, while all around me the boys were doing the same. It was the most amazing sight. The whole valley was beginning to fill with fog from the stream of gushing water and down in the foggy valley we saw cars speeding along the roads in front of the great wave of water which was chasing them and going faster than they could ever hope to go. I saw their headlights burning and I saw the water overtake them, wave by wave, and then the colour of the headlights underneath the water changing from light blue to green, from green to dark purple, until there was no longer anything except the water bouncing down in great waves. The floods raced on, carrying with them as they went viaducts, railways, bridges, and everything that stood in their path. Three miles beyond the dam the remains of Hoppy's aircraft were still burning gently, a dull red glow on the ground. Hoppy had been avenged.'

617 Squadron's victory was won by the quality of its aircrew. They came from all over the world to join the RAF, and many gave their lives in its service. Left: Australians of Lancaster AJ-P. Piloted by Flight Lieutenant Martin (second from left), this aircraft was the third to drop its bomb at the Moehne Dam. The crew were awarded five medals – three DFCs, one DSO and a DFM. Below: Flight Lieutenant McCarthy (third from the right with his Canadian crew) piloted the only aircraft to reach the Sorpe Dam. A direct hit damaged the dam, and the Germans had to reduce its capacity by half. McCarthy received a DSO for the dedication he showed in flying over the target ten times before the bomb was dropped.

VIEW FROM THE MOEHNE

Karl Schütte was a member of the SS flak unit stationed in the northern tower of the Moehne Dam and he witnessed 617 Squadron's attack: 'Some machines were firing at us from the valley end and we replied, but then the gun failed – the lock was stuck. We tried desperately to remove the cause and even tried sheer force, but without success. A premature shell had damaged the housing. It was hopeless. We stood high on the tower, in front of us the lake and behind us the valley. Attacked from all sides we could not defend ourselves. We waited literally for the end.

'Then a fifth plane started its attack. Only the gun on the lower wall was still firing. The machine neared the wall at an incredible speed; they now had an easy game – I could almost touch it, and I think even today I can see the outline of the pilot. With our gun silent we did that which we had drilled so often – defence with rifles!

'Again, the lake quaked and a gigantic wave came over the wall. The wall had been breached and relentlessly the water began to run into the valley. The plane banked away.

'Because of the one plane we did shoot down, we thought we had done our best. We all felt very proud.'

The pinpoint bombing skills developed by the Australian Canberra crews of No.2 Squadron, RAAF, earned them the admiration of their allies in the Vietnam War

ON 23 APRIL 1967 the Canberra B. Mk 20 bombers of No.2 Squadron, Royal Australian Air Force (RAAF), began operations over South Vietnam. The eight aircraft, under the command of Wing Commander R.B. Aronsen, had flown in from the Australian base at Butterworth in Malaysia four days earlier. On arrival at Phan Rang, 165 miles northeast of Saigon, they came under the operational control of the USAF's 35th Tactical Fighter Wing. This unit was primarily equipped with the F-100 fighter-bomber, but it was also assigned two squadrons of B-57s (the B-57 being the USAF version of the Canberra). No.2 Squadron's first sortie, flown by Wing Commander V.J. Hill, was a 'Combat Sky Spot' radar-directed, blind bombing mission against two targets in the Mekong Delta. A further seven sorties were scheduled for 23 April, but one Canberra was forced to abort its mission and return to Phan Rang with its bombs. The Canberra's standard warload for these early operations was six 500lb bombs, four of which were carried in the

Below: A Canberra B.Mk 20 bomber of No.2 Squadron, Royal Australian Air Force, painted black for night operations and bearing the red lightning-stroke tail insignia of the squadron, receives the attentions of groundcrew at Phan Rang, the squadron's base to the northeast of Saigon. Right: An RAAF armourer unloads bombs at Phan Rang. Behind him, a steel revetment guards the ordnance depot from the bomb blast of North Vietnamese air attack. Bottom: Canberra bomber crews ready for 'Boomer' missions against the Viet Cong. The codename means 'a large male kangaroo'.

bunker and tunnel complex in Phuoc Tuy Province. This was bombed from 10,000ft altitude, after which the 7th Australian Battalion was lifted into the target area by helicopter. At that time all of No.2 Squadron's missions were 'Combat Sky Spot' blind bombing sorties, some of which were flown at night. The attack was directed from an MSQ-77 ground radar station which would accurately plot the bomber's track. The radar operator decided the correct bomb release

internal weapons' bay and two on wing-tip mountings. This ordnance was of World War II vintage, and had been withdrawn from store in Australia for shipment to Vietnam.

Soon after their arrival in South Vietnam, the RAAF Canberras went into action in support of Australian ground forces. The target was a Viet Cong (VC)

point, which varied according to the type of bombs carried, the nature of the target and the aircraft's altitude and speed. Such operations not only depended on the accuracy of the ground station's radar tracking, but also on the precision of the bomber crew's flying for its success. The Australians soon gained a reputation for getting their bombs onto the target. However, the crews found this type of mission frustrating because there was very little indication as to the effects of their bombing. They had been trained to carry out precision daylight attacks, using high-altitude level-bombing tactics. Uniquely among the attack aircraft of the Vietnam War, the RAAF's Canberras were fitted with a World War II type of bombsight in the aircraft's perspex nose cone. The USAF's standard ground-attack tactics, in contrast, relied on dive-bombing with the attack being directed by an airborne forward air controller (FAC). In the American view, the Canberras were unsuited to this mission and so they were assigned exclusively to blind bombing sorties.

'Bomb damage assessments from day strikes are immediate, satisfying and good for morale'

The RAAF airmen determined to prove that they were as capable of carrying out precision daylight attacks as they were the 'Combat Sky Spot' missions. Wing Commander Hill set to work to develop suitable procedures, enlisting the help of Wing Commander Anthony Powell, an RAAF officer on an exchange posting with a USAF forward air control unit. On 25 June the Canberras flew their first missions under the direction of a forward air controller

on an experimental basis. The USAF's Seventh Air Force agreed that No.2 Squadron could undertake daylight precision attacks as part of its normal operations from September 1967. These sorties, codenamed 'Boomer', were an immediate success. Wing Commander Aronsen reported: 'bomb damage assessments from day strikes are immediate, satisfying and good for morale... All bombs have been 100 per cent on target.' By early November these 'Boomer' sorties accounted for half the squadron's operational flying. Many missions were flown over the Australian Task Force's combat area in Phuoc Tuy Province, but the Canberras also flew in support of US Army and Army of the Republic of Vietnam (ARVN) ground forces.

Wing Commander Aronsen led one of the most noteworthy precision visual attack missions of this period. He and his navigator, Flight Lieutenant A. W. Clarke, had been assigned to a radar bombing mission in company with the Canberra crewed by Wing Commander H. A. Hughes and Flying Officer P. Grindon-Ekins on 19 November 1967. However, this attack had been cancelled after the two bombers had taken off and, rather than bring back their bombs, Aronsen requested an alternative target. He was directed northwards to Dak To, a key town in the Central Highlands region of South Vietnam, where a major battle was in progress against four regiments of the North Vietnamese Army (NVA). As this diversion would leave the two Canberras low on fuel, Aronsen requested permission to land at Pleiku after

NO.2 SQUADRON, RAAF

No.2 Squadron, RAAF, can trace its origins back to January 1917, when No.68 Squadron, Royal Flying Corps, was formed in Britain from Australian personnel. Equipped with the D.H.5 fighter, it moved to France in September 1917 and by the following January had re-equipped with the S.E.5a. It was at that time that its designation was changed to No.2 Squadron, Australian Flying Corps. No.2 Squadron ended the war with 40 air victories to its credit, and was disbanded in February 1919. Following the creation of the Royal Australian Air Force in 1921, it was proposed to form a new No.2 Squadron as part of the RAAF's No.1 Wing. The new service was, however, greatly hampered by a shortage of suitable aircraft, and progress was slow. Nonetheless, by the outbreak of World War II No.2 Squadron, a general reconnaissance unit, was operating Ansons, and by the time that Japan entered the war it had re-equipped with Hudsons. Based at Darwin, the squadron went into action against advancing Japanese forces early in 1942. It carried out numerous bombing attacks against shipping and land targets, as well as long-range reconnaissance missions, braving the risk of interception by greatly superior Japanese fighters. Later in the war it converted onto Beauforts and by the spring of 1944 it was operating Mitchells. After World War II the squadron flew Liberators and Lincolns, before equipping with Canberras in 1954. Four years later it moved to Butterworth, Malaya, at the start of a 13-year continuous overseas deployment – a record for an RAAF squadron.

BOOMER ATTACK

the attack. Arriving over Dak To, the Australian crews were briefed by a forward air controller. Great precision was called for, as the target was a group of North Vietnamese troops dug in on an 8000ft ridge who were engaging friendly forces with mortar and heavy machine-gun fire. The FAC marked the target with white phosphorus rockets and the Canberras bombed accurately. This attack effectively silenced the North Vietnamese fire, which had been inflicting heavy casualties on friendly troops. On 27 November Aronsen returned to Dak To and carried out an accurate attack on a pinpoint target in mountainous terrain. Low cloud forced him to come down to low level before releasing his bombs and the Canberra came under anti-aircraft fire. The aircraft was not hit and Aronsen returned safely to base.

The Dak To missions came at the end of Wing Commander Aronsen's period of command. He had taken over the squadron in November 1966 at Butterworth and supervised its move to South Vietnam and its successful introduction into combat. A veteran of World War II, Aronsen had served with No. 10 Squadron, RAAF, which was based in Britain with Sunderland flying boats. He had also flown Lincoln bombers with No. 1 Squadron, RAAF, during the Malayan Emergency. His successor, Wing Commander David Evans, inherited a squadron which had already established an enviable reputation for

No. 2 Squadron, RAAF
South Vietnam, 1967-71

efficiency with the Americans. He reported:
'FACs have frequently expressed surprise at the accuracy of our bombing. Furthermore, our ability to deliver bombs singly, in pairs or in sticks of variable length, and our endurance capability in the target area are only now realised. The present accuracy is obtained by extremely accurate flying... and a close and constant supervision by squadron executive officers. When a bombing error in excess of 60ft is reported the crew is debriefed in detail in order to determine the cause of error. If it does not seem to be crew error, then the whole aircraft bombing system is

checked meticulously, even though it may appear to be completely serviceable. In this way the most minute errors in the bombing system have been discovered and corrected at the earliest possible stage.'

By the end of 1967 No.2 Squadron had flown a total of 1995 bombing sorties over South Vietnam, during which 3300 individual targets had been attacked.

During the first three months of 1968, No.2 Squadron's Canberras were heavily engaged in air support operations around the besieged outpost of Khe Sanh and in countering the Tet Offensive. On 30 January four Canberras, operating in pairs, bombed enemy bunkers around Khe Sanh, while other crews were assigned targets at Quang Tri. Two days later, the Canberras ranged over three of South Vietnam's four military regions in search of targets. On 2 February four aircraft were despatched to the Long Binh and Bien Hoa area to support the troops of the Australian Task Force. During the following two days the squadron reverted to high-level 'Combat Sky Spot' radar-bombing missions in the Khe Sanh region. A

equal part with the aircrews in achieving these results. Aircraft serviceability at 96 per cent was near perfect, but to obtain such results work had to carry on around the clock, with the maintenance men divided into two shifts. Apart from routine servicing, numerous modifications of the Canberra became necessary in the light of combat experience and these were undertaken by the squadron's ground-crew. For example, armour plating was fitted to increase protection from ground fire and the aircraft's camouflage paint had to be replaced by darker colours to suit local conditions. The Canberra's good endurance compared to that of the USAF's fighter-bombers gave it a greater operational flexibility. Wing Commander Evans pointed out that, 'on many occasions fighter aircraft had to be diverted from targets because of low cloud or poor visibility.' But the Canberra was frequently able to bomb below the cloud, or to 'hold' until the weather improved so that the original target could be bombed. The ability to 'hold' also allowed the Canberra to take advantage of the ever-changing tactical situation.

total of 63 500lb bombs was dropped as part of Operation Niagara – a massive application of aerial firepower in support of the beleaguered garrison, which included 'Arc Light' missions by B-52s. The last Canberra missions in this area were flown on 4 and 5 April at the time when the siege was finally lifted. The Australian airmen also operated over the former Vietnamese capital city of Hue during the bitter fighting to recapture it from NVA and VC forces. Other missions were flown in support of the US Army's 25th Division to the west of Saigon, and attacks were made on the enemy's sanctuaries along the Cambodian border.

The squadron's operations at this time were an impressive effort by a unit with only eight aircraft on strength. The Australians' reputation for bombing accuracy was also maintained and in 1968 the RAAF Canberras were credited with 16 per cent of all bomb damage inflicted by the 35th Tactical Fighter Wing's aircraft, while their share of the total sorties flown was only between four and six per cent. The men of the squadron's Maintenance Flight played an

Top left: A Canberra jettisons its 500lb bombs on a 'Boomer' daylight precision attack. Centre left: Bomb-bursts straddle a target area in South Vietnam. Left: Navigators of No.2 Squadron study a map of the country over which they are to fly on a mission from Phan Rang. Top: Wing Commander Anthony Powell, who served with the squadron as a forward air controller (FAC) in Vietnam. Inset above: Wing Commander David Evans, who succeeded Wing Commander R.B. Aronsen as commander of No.2 Squadron in November 1967. Above: A No.2 Squadron Canberra, armed and on its way to the enemy.

In November 1968 Evans handed over command of the squadron to Wing Commander John Whitehead. Evans' last mission was flown on 17 November over the Mekong Delta area. Descending to 1500ft to bomb (the average bombing height at this time being 3000ft) the Canberra was hit by ground fire and its port elevator holed. Evans did not realise that his aircraft was damaged until it was pointed out to him after landing. In accordance with a tradition inherited from the USAF, the wing commander was hosed down by the fire truck to mark the successful end of his tour of operations. In the following March his work was officially recognised by an award of the Distinguished Service Order.

The squadron's main area of operations during 1969 was the Mekong Delta. The flat terrain meant that an accurate estimate of the target's altitude (only a few feet above sea-level) could be fed into the Canberra's bombsight, thus further increasing its precision. In July the squadron's share of the 35th Tactical Fighter Wing's overall bombing results was assessed at 58.8 per cent. Typical of sorties flown at

this time was a mission over the Delta on 30 August. South Vietnamese troops had made contact with the NVA along a canal bank 55 miles southwest of Can Tho. They put in an urgent request for air support and an RAAF Canberra was diverted from its pre-planned mission to assist them. Conditions were far from ideal, as friendly forces were in close proximity to the North Vietnamese and cloud cover forced the aircraft to bomb from low altitude. Nonetheless, the Canberra carried out an accurate attack and the bodies of 19 North Vietnamese troops were later found in the target area.

The process of 'Vietnamization' brought some problems for No.2 Squadron, mainly because the Vietnamese Air Force FACs were not aware of the Canberra's special characteristics. Wing Commander Whitehead commented that:

'In some cases sortie cancellations were due to the failure of FACs to appreciate the low-level bombing capability of the Canberra. In general, FACs are attuned only to the capabilities of fighter aircraft and do not realise that the Canberra can operate to finer tolerances in poor weather conditions.'

In September 1969 faults were discovered in the Canberras' tailplanes, necessitating the grounding of the aircraft until replacements could be fitted. The unforeseen problem did not lead to the loss of an aircraft, but no fewer than 54 scheduled sorties had to be cancelled. Another difficulty encountered at the time was damage to aircraft caused by the explosion of their own bombs on the ground. The minimum safe bombing height had been set at 1000ft, but in an attempt to overcome the problem it was raised to 1200ft. Even after this change, aircraft continued to suffer damage from this cause, and on one such occasion it was established that the bombs had been released from 2000ft. It was then realised that the reason for the damage was the switch from the 500lb bomb to the US 750lb bomb, stocks of the former weapon having been exhausted. As the 750lb bomb was both more streamlined and more powerful than the older weapon, a greater margin of height clearance had to be allowed for the releasing aircraft.

Top: Wing Commander John Downing and his navigator, Flight Lieutenant Allen Pinches (below top), who ejected after being hit by a SAM and were rescued by a USAF 'dust-off' helicopter. Above: The personnel of No.2 Squadron pose in front of a Canberra B.Mk 20 before leaving for Australia in June 1971. Above right: Flying Officers D. Smith and P. Murphy, who flew the squadron's last strike.

Accordingly, the minimum safe bombing height was raised to 2400ft above ground level and no further bomb damage was suffered by the Canberras.

The Canberras' range of operational roles was further expanded in the spring of 1970 when they began to fly interdiction missions over Military Region I, immediately to the south of the Demilitarized Zone. Their objective was to cut the supply route through the A Shau Valley, which linked the main arteries of the Ho Chi Minh Trail with the NVA and VC forces operating in Military Region I. The autumn monsoon season brought in its train low cloud, mist and rain, which so hampered visibility that the Canberras generally reverted to radar-guided bombing missions. It was on one such sortie, on 3 November 1970, that No.2 Squadron suffered its first operational loss of the Vietnam War. Operating under the call sign 'Magpie 91', a Canberra flown by Flying Officer Michael Herbert, with Pilot Officer Robert Carver as navigator, was carrying out a 'Combat Sky Spot' mission in the Da Nang area. The bombs were released from an altitude of 22,000ft and the pilot then reported that he was turning onto a heading of 120 degrees. Nothing further was heard from Magpie 91 and the aircraft's wreckage was never found, despite an intensive search for it. Its fate remains a mystery, as no evidence was found to account for its loss.

With the launching of Operation Lam Son 719 into Laos on 29 January 1971, No.2 Squadron was committed to a further period of intense air support operations. It was found that the Canberras were particularly adept at coping with the difficult operational conditions caused by low cloud over mountainous terrain. But it was during these operations that the squadron suffered its second operational loss. On 14 March, Wing Commander John Downing and his navigator, Flight Lieutenant Allen Pinches, were flying just south of the Demilitarized Zone when their Canberra was hit by a surface-to-air missile. Downing had time to broadcast a 'May Day' distress call

before he and Pinches were forced to eject. Both men were injured, but managed to find cover in the jungle to avoid capture by the enemy. They spent an anxious and uncomfortable night, but on the following day were able to contact a rescue helicopter on their survival radios and were lifted to safety.

Wing Commander Downing's injuries forced him to hand over the command of the squadron to Wing Commander Tom Thorpe. Thorpe, who like Aronsen had flown Lincolns during the Malayan Emergency, was to be No.2 Squadron's last commanding officer in Vietnam. It had been decided to withdraw the Canberras by May 1971 and, meanwhile, as a result of the loss of Downing's Canberra, No.2 Squadron's aircraft were no longer required to operate in the area near the Demilitarized Zone, where they were at risk from surface-to-air missiles.

Although the enemy's bunkers were only 200yds from friendly troops, the Canberra was cleared to bomb

This restriction did not signify any let-up in the pace of operations, however, although the squadron's aircraft strength was by then reduced to six Canberras. On 7 April, Flight Lieutenant Stan Fenton and his navigator, Flying Officer Peter Murphy, carried out a highly effective attack on NVA and VC forces that were assaulting the US Army's Fire Base 6 near the Laotian and Cambodian borders. Although the enemy's bunkers were only 200yds from friendly troops, the Canberra was cleared to bomb. Its attack was right on target and the pressure on the defenders was immediately eased. On 31 May, the squadron's last day of operations, nine sorties were flown. One of them was undertaken by Wing Commander Thorpe, but the honour of dropping the RAAF's last bomb of the Vietnam War went to Flying Officer D. Smith. Four days later, the Canberras took off from Phan Rang for the last time and set course for Darwin. In just over four years of operations in Vietnam they had carried out 11,963 sorties and earned a reputation for bombing accuracy that was second to none.

THE AUTHOR Anthony Robinson was formerly on the staff of the RAF Museum, Hendon, and is now a freelance military aviation writer. His books include *American Air Power* and *Aerial Warfare*.

THE ROYAL AUSTRALIAN AIR FORCE IN VIETNAM

Australia's involvement in the Southeast Asia conflict began in 1962, when a team of Army advisers was sent to South Vietnam. In August 1964, the RAAF committed a flight of Caribou transport aircraft to the combat theatre and this began to operate from Vung Tau under the control of the USAF's 315th Air Commando Wing. Designated the 'RAAF Transport Flight Vietnam', the unit had completed 17,702 sorties by 1 June 1966, when it became No.35 Squadron. Its operational tasks included the transportation of cargo, mail and passengers (both military and civilian); medical evacuation; and paratroop dropping, including Australian SAS troops. Nicknamed 'Wallaby Airlines', the Caribou unit was the last RAAF squadron to be withdrawn from South Vietnam, ceasing operations in February 1972. In seven and a half years the Caribous flew 79,739 sorties.

As Vietnam was the helicopter's war, it was inevitable that the RAAF would commit a helicopter squadron in support of the Australian Army. No.9 Squadron, equipped with the Bell UH-1 Iroquois, arrived at Vung Tau in June 1966 and began operations the following month. In addition to troop lift and routine resupply missions, they carried out 'dust off' sorties to rescue wounded troops – often under enemy fire – and clandestine missions with the Australian SAS.

When operations ceased in November 1971, the squadron had flown 223,487 sorties. The total number of RAAF sorties flown by No. 2, 9 and 35 Squadrons in Vietnam was 315,189. RAAF casualties were 70 in all, including four killed, two missing and 30 wounded in combat.

Left: The English Electric Canberra B.Mk 20 was built under licence in Australia by Commonwealth Aircraft, and a total of 48 was delivered.

BOMBERS OVER HANOI

The 43rd Strategic Wing, one of the premier United States bomber units during the war in Vietnam, could trace its history back to World War II when, as the 43rd Bombardment Group, it operated in the southwest Pacific as part of the Fifth Air Force. Initially equipped with B-17 Flying Fortresses, it later went over to flying B-24 Liberators.

The group took part in the Battle of the Bismarck Sea in March 1943 and, operating from the island of Ie Shima in July 1945, flew bombing missions over the Japanese mainland.

After the end of the war, the group was returned to the United States, where it was reactivated as a B-29 Superfortress unit and assigned to Strategic Air Command. During reorganisational changes in the early 1950s, the unit was retitled the 43rd Bombardment Wing. Successively re-equipped with B-50s, B-47 Stratojets and B-58 Hustlers, the unit remained in the US until the spring of 1970, when it was deactivated. The unit then reappeared as the 43rd Strategic Wing at Andersen Air Force Base on the island of Guam and was responsible for controlling Strategic Air Command's B-52 operations against North Vietnam.

During the Vietnam War, the wing, commanded by Colonel James R. McCarthy, comprised some 50 B-52D bombers. The Stratofortresses were organised into two bomb squadrons: the 60th under Lieutenant-Colonel Charles R. Maynard and the 63rd commanded by Lieutenant-Colonel David D. Rines. *Above: The badge of the 43rd Strategic Wing.*

During the 11 days of the Linebacker II operations, American B-52 bombers dropped more than 20,000 tons of bombs on North Vietnam

ON 16 December 1972 Admiral Thomas H. Moorer, the chairman of the US Joint Chiefs-of-Staff, directed the C-in-Cs of Pacific Command and Strategic Air Command to launch:

'A three-day maximum effort, repeat maximum

BOMBS ON TARGET

effort, of B-52 tacair [tactical air] strikes in the Hanoi/Haiphong areas. Object is maximum destruction of selected military targets. Be prepared to extend operations past three days. All B-52 aircraft will carry maximum ordnance. Exercise precaution to minimise risk of civilian casualties.'

Two days later the first bombing mission of the Linebacker II campaign was flown against the heartland of North Vietnam, initiating an 11-day air campaign that was to devastate many strategically important targets and force a reluctant North Vietnamese government to resume peace negotiations.

The primary instrument of this air offensive was the eight-engined B-52 Stratofortress strategic bomber. During February 1972 the B-52 force had been strengthened in response to the North Vietnamese build-up prior to the spring invasion of the South and,

at the start of the Linebacker II operations, more than 200 of these bombers were committed to the war in Southeast Asia. One B-52 unit, the 307th Strategic Wing, operated from U-Tapao in Thailand, while Andersen Air Force Base (AFB) on the island of Guam housed the B-52Ds of the 43rd Strategic Wing, under the command of Colonel James R. McCarthy, and the B-52Gs of the 72nd Strategic Wing.

Guam, nicknamed 'the Rock' by the B-52 crews, was some 2650 miles from Hanoi and the bombers had to carry out long overwater flights to and from their objectives. Moreover, tactical considerations often made a direct approach to the target area inadvisable, thus lengthening the flight times even further: a 12-hour sortie was routine and some bombers were airborne for over 18 hours. In-flight refuelling was essential for the bombers operating from Guam, especially for the older B-52Ds of the 43rd Strategic Wing. This was provided by KC-135A tanker aircraft based on Okinawa, which usually rendezvoused with the bombers north of Luzon in the Philippines to provide them with fuel.

Numerous other support aircraft operated over

STRATOFORTRESS AT WAR

Created because of the United States' need for a long-range strategic bomber able to carry a nuclear payload, the B-52 Stratofortress was the brainchild of a team from Boeing who produced the basic design in October 1948. A pair of prototypes was soon ready and the first proving flight, regarded as being extremely successful, took place on 15 April 1952.

Boeing then began a nationwide production programme with several firms providing parts for the new bomber.

After further evaluation, the B-52B version was cleared for duty in June 1955, but nagging problems with several basic features led to the aircraft being grounded for widespread modification.

Despite these improvements, the B-52 was involved in two mid-flight accidents in the late 1960s and was gradually redeployed in a more conventional role.

During the Vietnam War, B-52s were primarily used to strike at the enemy's industrial centres or to support ground operations. Used in this role, for the first time, a new version of the Stratofortress was produced.

In late 1965, the USAF ordered a programme of modifications to the B-52D to carry a larger payload. Later known as the Big Belly initiative, the plans left the aircraft's exterior untouched, but modified its bomb-bays. The Stratofortress was still powered by eight Pratt and Whitney jet engines that could generate a maximum speed of 551 knots at over 6000m and its range stayed at 5581km.

However, the six-man crew were able to deliver a greater weight of bombs.

Below: Vital to the success of Linebacker II, KC-135 tankers provided an in-flight refuelling service for the B-52s.

Right: A Boeing B-52 takes on much-needed fuel from a KC-135 Stratotanker during the gruelling flight from Guam to its target area over North Vietnam.

North Vietnam during the B-52 strikes, attacking surface-to-air missile (SAM) sites and anti-aircraft emplacements, carrying out electronic counter-measures (ECMs), providing fighter escort and, if necessary, search and rescue. For example, on 26 December 1972, an attacking force of 120 B-52s was supported by 113 USAF, US Navy and US Marine Corps escort, electronic warfare and attack aircraft.

By comparison with the B-52Gs of the 72nd Strategic Wing, the 43rd Strategic Wing's B-52Ds were less powerful, had an inferior range and, in some respects, carried less advanced equipment. However, to offset these disadvantages, they did carry the greatest conventional bomb load of any Stratofortress variant.

The age of the B-52D presented problems for the aircraft maintenance technicians as well as the aircrews. At the peak of the Linebacker II campaign, some 5000 men of the 303rd Consolidated Aircraft Maintenance Wing were responsible for the servicing of 155 B-52s, spread over some five miles of parking ramps on Andersen AFB. It was an enor-

mous job. For example, armament specialists on Guam loaded some 58,000 bombs aboard the B-52s during Linebacker II; a physically demanding and potentially dangerous job carried out in 12-hour shifts, seven days a week. When their work was done, the maintenance men could expect little relaxation. Andersen AFB was badly overcrowded and most personnel had to live under canvas. Yet the work of the men on the ground earned the gratitude and respect of all the aircrews. This was succinctly expressed by a sign on the base, which read, 'Our mission is BOMBS ON TARGET – It takes us all'.

A total of 34 strategic targets were attacked during the Linebacker II offensive, all of them within a 60-mile radius of Hanoi and over 60 per cent within 25 miles of the city centre. The North Vietnamese capital, codenamed Bullseye by the Americans, together with the nearby important seaport of Haiphong, were heavily defended by SAMs, interceptor aircraft and anti-aircraft batteries. The SAMs proved to be the greatest threat, with some 200 SA-2 launchers in the area. MiG-21s operated only spor-

Aside from the usual 24 bombs mounted on external points, the B-52D carried some 10,000kg more bombs than early versions.

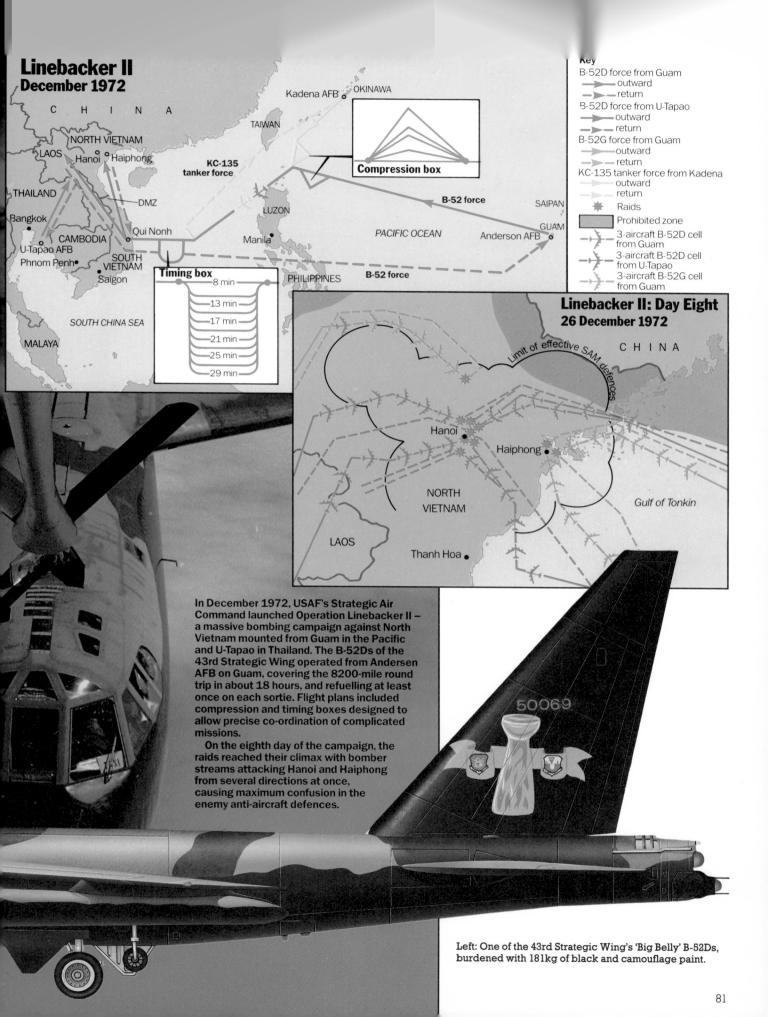

Linebacker II
December 1972

CHINA

Kadena AFB OKINAWA

TAIWAN

NORTH VIETNAM

LAOS

Hanoi Haiphong

KC-135
tanker force

THAILAND

DMZ

Bangkok

LUZON

SAIPAN

Qui Nonh

CAMBODIA

U-Tapao AFB

PACIFIC OCEAN

GUAM

Manila

Anderson AFB

Phnom Penh

SOUTH
VIETNAM

Saigon

PHILIPPINES

B-52 force

B-52 force

Timing box

SOUTH CHINA SEA

8 min

MALAYA

13 min

17 min

21 min

25 min

29 min

Compression box

Key
- B-52D force from Guam
  - → outward
  - --▶ return
- B-52D force from U-Tapao
  - → outward
  - --▶ return
- B-52G force from Guam
  - → outward
  - --▶ return
- KC-135 tanker force from Kadena
  - → outward
  - --▶ return
- ✳ Raids
- ▓ Prohibited zone
- 3-aircraft B-52D cell from Guam
- 3-aircraft B-52D cell from U-Tapao
- 3-aircraft B-52G cell from Guam

Linebacker II: Day Eight
26 December 1972

Limit of effective SAM defences

CHINA

Hanoi

Haiphong

NORTH
VIETNAM

Gulf of Tonkin

LAOS

Thanh Hoa

In December 1972, USAF's Strategic Air Command launched Operation Linebacker II – a massive bombing campaign against North Vietnam mounted from Guam in the Pacific and U-Tapao in Thailand. The B-52Ds of the 43rd Strategic Wing operated from Andersen AFB on Guam, covering the 8200-mile round trip in about 18 hours, and refuelling at least once on each sortie. Flight plans included compression and timing boxes designed to allow precise co-ordination of complicated missions.

On the eighth day of the campaign, the raids reached their climax with bomber streams attacking Hanoi and Haiphong from several directions at once, causing maximum confusion in the enemy anti-aircraft defences.

50069

Left: One of the 43rd Strategic Wing's 'Big Belly' B-52Ds, burdened with 181kg of black and camouflage paint.

adically against the B-52s, and anti-aircraft fire wa
restricted to that from radar-directed 100m
weapons.

The B-52s always attacked under cover of dar
ness, in order to make the defenders' task as difficu
as possible. Bombing was carried out using data from
the aircraft's all-weather attack radar and weapons
aiming computer, and it proved to be extremel
accurate. The basic tactical formation was the three
aircraft cell, which was identified by a colour code
name such as Cobalt, Rust, Maroon or Amber; the
combined effect of ECM jamming from three bom

bers in formation was considerably more effective than that of an individual B-52. However, as McCarthy testified, it took a good deal of courage for a pilot to maintain close formation over the target, 'because the miss distance that the system is designed to give you makes it virtually impossible to tell if the SAM is going to fly right up your nose, or miss.'

The opening mission of Linebacker II was flown by a total of 129 B-52s, 33 of them from the 43rd Strategic Wing, on the night of 18 December. The bombers flew in three waves, with four to five hours between each, and approached the Hanoi area from the northwest. After reaching their initial point (IP), they made a straight run to the target with no evasive manoeuvring for a period of some four minutes. After dropping their bombs, they turned away and headed out of the target area to the west and northwest. Similar tactics were followed during the following two missions. As the last B-52s landed back at Andersen AFB, the first bombers assigned to the next night's mission were leaving the ground. Two of the 72nd Strategic Wing's B-52Gs and a B-52D from the 307th Strategic Wing, had been lost, but the 43rd Strategic Wing escaped with only two bombers badly damaged.

On 19 December McCarthy acted as the Airborne Mission Commander, at the head of 93 B-52s. He strongly believed that wing commanders should lead from the front:

'We, as high-ranking officers, had a lot of information that the enemy would dearly have loved to get and, normally speaking, we should never have been allowed to fly. But we discussed it and

Operating out of Andersen Air Force Base on Guam, the 43rd Strategic Wing demanded large back-up facilities to keep flying. Far left above and centre: Armament specialists of the 303rd Consolidated Aircraft Maintenance Wing bomb-up a pair of B-52s. Co-ordinating the diverse elements of a Linebacker II mission required great skill from all those involved. Crews had to be ready to move with little warning (bottom left) and then wait for their turn to take off (below). Bottom right: A heavily laden B-52 claws its way aloft. The dense smoke trails indicate that the bomber's water-injection system is being used to gain extra thrust.

decided that the value of the information was not as important as the morale factor which our flying would have.'

The target for the 21 B-52s in Wave I was the Kinh No railway yards and storage area. Lieutenant-Colonel Allison was the radar navigator in Captain Charles Core's Rose 3 (Rose cell was the third to reach the target). As his bomber neared Hanoi, the crew saw numerous SAM launches ahead. Allison later recalled:

'None of the missiles at that time was a serious threat to our cell. I attribute that almost entirely to the heavy salvoes directed at the two cells ahead of us, which perhaps emptied the launchers and had some of the guidance radars looking away from us. I gladly accepted the limited glory which this afforded us, because it thus allowed us to do what we had gone to do – clobber Kinh No. My crosshairs were dead on the aiming point and Charlie Core had the steering indicator exactly centred when I called, "Bombs Away".'

McCarthy in the leading bomber, White 1, had an even closer view of the SAMs:

'As one was fired on the ground, an area about the size of a city block would be lit up by the flash. As the missile broke through the clouds, the large lighted area was replaced by a ring of silver fire that appeared to be the size of a basketball. This was the exhaust of the rocket motor that would grow brighter as the missile approached the aircraft. Three of the SAMs exploded at our altitude, but in this case were too far away to cause any damage. Two others passed close to the aircraft, but exploded above us.'

eft: Flying in tight
ormation, B-52s carry out a
aylight raid against Hanoi.
he results, as illustrated by
burning oil storage facility
below) and a shattered
ailway yard (bottom), were
equently devastating.

Surprisingly, in view of the strength of the defences, no B-52s were lost that night. This immunity was attributed to the close formations maintained by each cell, relying on ECM jamming rather than evasive manoeuvring to defeat the SAMs. However, on the following night the North Vietnamese defences reacted especially strongly, launching approximately 220 SAMs against the American bombers. This resulted in the loss of four B-52Gs, two B-52Ds and a third D damaged. One of the missing bombers, Straw 2, was the first 43rd Strategic Wing aircraft to go down in the campaign.

For the following two nights, the 307th Strategic Wing at U-Tapao flew all offensive sorties against North Vietnam. On 23 December, they were joined by 12 bombers from the 43rd Strategic Wing in attacks on the Lang Dang railway yards and three SAM sites. Again, on 24 December, all bomber sorties against the North were mounted from U-Tapao; no mission was flown on Christmas Day.

All three B-52 wings contributed to a maximum-effort mission by 120 bombers on 26 December. The intention was to saturate the defences by concentrating the entire attack within the space of 15 minutes. These tactics would make great demands on the piloting and navigational skills of the B-52 crews, especially since there was no opportunity to practise them beforehand. The 43rd Strategic Wing contributed 33 B-52Ds to the force, including the lead aircraft, captained by Major Bill Stocker, which carried McCarthy as Airborne Mission Commander. Stocker recalled the pre-flight build-up, 'In the minute or so before we took off, I was treated to the sight of one of the most awesome armadas ever assembled. As far as we could see there were B-52s lined up nose-to-tail'. En route to the target, the Guam-based bombers encountered

a problem which threatened to wreck the entire mission. Part of the supporting tanker force was delayed for 20 minutes by an emergency at Kadena airbase on Okinawa. However, the bombers affected by this delay managed to make up time and the attack went in on schedule.

McCarthy later recalled the action over the target; including the ferocity of the enemy's ground fire:

'About 100 seconds prior to bombs away, the cockpit lit up like it was daylight. The light came from the rocket exhaust of a SAM that had come up right under the nose. The electronic warfare officer had reported an extremely strong signal and he was right. It's hard to judge miss distances at night, but that one looked like it missed us by less than 50ft. The proximity fuze should have detonated the warhead, but it didn't. After 26 SAMs, I quit counting. They were coming up too fast to count. It appeared in the cockpit as if they were now barraging SAMs to make the lead element of the wave turn from its intended course.

'At bombs away, it looked like we were right in the middle of a fireworks factory that was in the process of blowing up. The radio was completely saturated with SAM calls and MiG warnings. As the bomb doors closed, several SAMs exploded. Others could be seen arcing over and starting a descent, then detonating. If the proximity fuze didn't find a target, SA-2s were set to self-destruct at the end of a pre-determined time interval.

'Our computer's bombs-away signal went to the bomb bay right on the time hack. Despite the SAMs and the 100-knot headwinds, the nav team had dropped their bombs on target at the exact second called for in the order.'

Two American bombers were lost on 26 December and on the following night's mission, a repeat of the earlier raid on a smaller scale, with 60 B-52s despatched, another two B-52s went down. This was to be the last success for the North Vietnamese defences. Two further raids were flown on 28 and 29 December, but without loss to the B-52s. The crews reported that fewer SAMs were fired and that their guidance was often erratic. It was deduced that the enemy's command-and-control network was breaking down and that his ammunition stocks were low.

The North's powerful air defences had virtually ceased to function

A ceasefire agreement followed swiftly after the ending of Linebacker II, but B-52 operations in Southeast Asia continued, with attacks on Cambodia and Laos until 15 August 1973. The cost of the 'Eleven-Day Air War' had been high, with 15 B-52s lost and 33 of their crew members killed or missing in action. However, this represented only four per cent of the sorties to the high-risk Hanoi-Haiphong area. The North Vietnamese in the area had suffered serious damage from the bombing, with 80 per cent of their electrical power and 25 per cent of their petroleum stocks destroyed. Moreover, the North's powerful air defences had virtually ceased to function. In the opinion of the British counter-insurgency expert, Sir Robert Thompson, it was the Linebacker II campaign which forced the North Vietnamese back to the negotiating table.

THE AUTHOR Anthony Robinson was formerly on the staff of the RAF Museum, Hendon, and is now a freelance military aviation writer. He has edited the books *Aerial Warfare* and the *Dictionary of Aviation*.

TANK BUSTERS

In June 1941 Hitler turned on the Soviet Union, unleashing the dive bombers of Stukageschwader 2 'Immelmann' in a furious Blitzkrieg against the Red Army

Below: Hans-Ulrich Rudel, commander and undisputed Stuka ace of StG 2. Main picture: A Ju 87B-2 of StG 2 in May 1941 during the battle for Crete. Bottom right: StG 2 in action on the Eastern Front in August 1941, against a railway bridge.

AT PRECISELY 0315 hours on 22 June 1941, the might of the Wehrmacht was unleashed against the Soviet Union. As armoured columns and infantry stormed towards their initial objectives, the air was filled with the menacing scream of Junkers Ju 87 Stuka dive-bombers swooping down on their targets. The Luftwaffe had assembled some 334 Stukas for Operation Barbarossa, the codename for Hitler's Blitzkrieg in the east, and their mission was to pulverise the enemy's strongpoints, and smash concentrations of tanks and infantry.

Chief among the dive-bomber units was Stukageschwader 2 (StG 2) 'Immelmann'. Named after Max Immelmann, a fighter ace of World War I, StG 2 contained some of the finest ground-attack pilots in he Luftwaffe. The Geschwader's virtuoso performer, destined to destroy over 500 tanks before the end of the war, was Hans-Ulrich Rudel.

With the opening of the war on the Eastern Front, the Ju 87 Stuka again came into its own after the crippling losses suffered at the hands of the RAF. Soviet fighter opposition was minimal and the pace of operations was hectic, with flying from dawn until dusk, and individual pilots routinely carrying out four or more sorties every day. Rudel, then an Oberleutnant with StG 2's 1 Staffel, recalled this period:

'Our targets are always the same: tanks, motor vehicles, bridges, fieldworks and AA sites. On and off, our objectives are the enemy's railway communications or an armoured train when the Soviets bring one up to support their artillery. All resistance in front of our spearheads has to be broken so as to increase the speed and impetus of our advance.'

During the first weeks of the war in the Soviet Union, it became apparent to the pilots of StG 2 that enemy tanks were difficult targets to destroy by air attack. On 25 June 1941 all three Gruppen of StG 2 had carried out a series of dive-bombing missions against a concentration of about 60 tanks south of Grodno. Despite the scale of the attacks, it was later discovered that only one tank had been destroyed in the onslaught. The clear need for specialised anti-armour weapons resulted in a number of developments, including 30mm, 37mm and 75mm cannon firing solid-shot armour-piercing rounds; cluster bomb dispensers which scattered SD-4 hollow-charge bomblets, and, in the closing stages of the war, rocket projectiles. The Ju 87G tank-destroyer version of the Stuka was armed with the 37mm Flak 18

(or BK37) cannon. Two of these weapons were carried underwing, mounted outboard of the undercarriage legs. Each cannon was fitted with a six-round magazine of armour-piercing shells, the 1.36kg shell being a wolfram-cored explosive round with good penetrative qualities.

In order to establish whether the Ju 87G and various other tank-destroyer aircraft could perform successfully under operational conditions, the *Versuchsverband fur Panzerkampfung* (Tank-fighting Experimental Unit) was formed at Bryansk in February 1942 under the command of Oberstleutnant Otto Weiss. Many of this unit's pilots were sceptical of the Flak 18's ability to cope with the 45mm frontal armour of the Soviet T-34 tank, and even more dubious about its performance against the KV-1's 75mm protection. However, one airman, the redoubtable Hauptmann Rudel, who had been seconded from StG 2 for the trials, saw in the cannon's excellent ballistics an opportunity to defeat the Soviet tanks. He recorded:

'What impresses me is the possibility of being able to shoot with an accuracy of within 20 to 30cm. If this is attainable, one should be able to hit the vulnerable parts of the tank, provided one could get within close enough range – that is my conviction. From models, we learn how to identify the various types of Russian tank and are taught where the most vulnerable parts are located: engine, petrol tank, ammunition chamber.'

The Ju 87G tank destroyer first saw action on 18 March 1943, flying from Bryansk, and in May Rudel moved south to the Crimea to test the new aircraft on the Kuban front. It was soon apparent that both enemy fighters and flak defences could pose serious

StG 2

The Luftwaffe's most successful unit deployed in the anti-tank or Panzerknacker role was Stukageschwader 2 (StG 2). StG 2 could trace its origins to the Luftwaffe's first dive-bomber unit, formed at Schwerin in 1935. Although StG 2 undertook operational evaluation of the Ju 87A during the Spanish Civil War, the unit's first real test came in September 1939, when two Gruppen took part in the invasion of Poland.

In the following spring, StG 2 was involved in the offensive against the Low Countries and France as part of the Luftwaffe's VIII Fliegerkorps. By the start of the Battle of Britain, the unit had been brought up to full strength with three Gruppen. Losses during the air battle against the RAF were so heavy that the Luftwaffe withdrew its Stuka units from frontline service. In the right circumstances, however, the Stuka was still a potent weapon. StG 2 played a major role in the invasion of Greece and the fighting in the Mediterranean. The unit was responsible for sinking the cruiser HMS *Gloucester* and the destroyers HMS *Kelly*, HMS *Greyhound* and HMS *Kashmir* during the assault on Crete in 1941. The Geschwader was then transferred to the Eastern Front in time for Operation Barbarossa, and fought against the Soviet army until 1945.

threats to the Ju 87G, which was even slower and less manoeuvrable than the Ju 87D dive-bomber. Over Krymskaya, Rudel encountered Soviet Spitfire Mark Vs for the first time. This was an indication of the improved technical quality of the fighter opposition and, to make matters worse, Soviet-built Lavochkin La-5FNs and Yakovlev Yak-9s were reaching the fighter regiments in increasing numbers. Yet, the training of Soviet pilots remained generally poor and Rudel commented on 'the bad morale of the majority of Red fighter pilots; only a few crack units are the exception to the rule'. Anti-aircraft fire was a different matter, however, and Rudel considered it necessary for the Ju 87Gs to be escorted by bomb-armed Ju 87Ds to deal with flak emplacements.

Left: Their bomb racks empty, a pair of Ju 87s return from a mission. Left below: Groundcrew maintain one of the underwing 37mm cannon on a Ju 87G. Specifically designed for the anti-tank role, this aircraft wreaked havoc with the Soviet armoured forces. Bottom: A Ju 87 is bombed-up prior to a mission on the Eastern Front.

THE STUKA

The Junkers Ju 87 Stuka was conceived in 1933 as a ground-support aircraft to pave the way for Blitzkrieg style attacks. After extensive trials, the Ju 87 was ordered into production in 1936. The first Stukas to see action fought with the Condor Legion during the Spanish Civil War, where they gained a reputation for accurate bombing.

By mid-1939 full-time production was underway and the Ju 87B series began to equip several Luftwaffe units. This series was powered by a 1200hp Jumo 211Da engine, giving the Stuka a top speed of 383km/h. Defensive armament comprised two fixed forward-firing 7.9mm machine guns and a single MG 15 machine gun in the rear cockpit; a maximum bombload of 500kg could be carried.

Despite its successes in Spain and the early stages of World War II, the Stuka suffered heavily in the Battle of Britain against fighter opposition. In response to these losses, the Ju 87 was deployed in theatres where opposition was minimal.

During the war on the Eastern Front, two models, the Ju 87D and G, were widely used against Soviet ground forces.

The Ju 87D entered service in late 1941 and differed from previous series in having better armour, more defensive armament and an increased bombload.

The Ju 87G was specifically designed to carry out anti-tank missions; based on the D-series design, it carried two 37mm cannon.

With the operational trials of the Ju 87G satisfactorily concluded, the aircraft was ready to take its place in the Luftwaffe's order of battle on the eve of Operation Zitadelle, the great German offensive against the Kursk salient. Three Stukageschwader, equipped with Ju 87D dive-bombers, were committed to this battle, namely StG 1, StG 2 and StG 77, making a total of nine Gruppen. The Ju 87Gs were formed into two Panzer Jäger Staffeln, which were attached to StG 1 and StG 2. Later in the year, the tank destroyer units were formally constituted as a tenth Staffel, attached to each of the Stukageschwader. The Staffel joining the Immelmann Geschwader being designated 10(Pz)/StG 2.

The basic tactical formation adopted by the Stuka units was a three-aircraft 'V' formation known as the 'Kette'. A Staffel was made up of nine or 12 Ju 87s, and a Gruppe comprised three Staffeln, plus a headquarters flight manned by the Gruppenkommandeur and his staff. The Kommodore of StG 2 was 36-year-old Oberstleutnant Dr. Ernst Kupfer.

The Luftwaffe had assembled some 1800 aircraft for what was to be their last major offensive on the Eastern Front. In addition to strong bomber and fighter contingents, the ground-attack element of this force comprised the three Stukageschwader, Schlachtgeschwader 1 (equipped with Focke Wulf Fw 190s and Henschel Hs 129 tank destroyers) four additional Hs 129 Staffeln, and a Panzer Jäger Staffel flying Messerschmitt Bf 110s. Realising that the Soviet army was well-prepared for an attack on the Kursk salient, the German High Command relied on air-power to force a path for the Wehrmacht's tanks through the enemy's armoured units and field fortifications. The tank destroyers were to operate over the battlefield, while the Ju 87Ds also attacked Soviet communications.

According to one witness, the opening day of the battle, 5 July, 'dawned bright and warm, a typical languid summer's day in central Russia.' The Stukas were heavily engaged from the outset, with every unit flying five or six missions during the course of the day. Rudel, at the head of StG 2's Panzer Jäger Staffel, was impressed: 'Great tank battles rage below us...a picture such as we have rarely had the chance of seeing since 1941.' He was soon in the thick of it:

'In the first attack four tanks explode under the hammer blows of my cannon; by the evening the total rises to 12. We are all seized with a kind of passion for the chase. After the first day, the mechanics have their hands full, for the aircraft have been heavily damaged by flak. The life of such an aircraft will always be limited.

'The succeeding days and battles complete the picture, and further successes are not denied us. While the cannon-carrying aircraft go in to attack, a part of the bomber formation deals with the ground defences; the rest circle at a fairly low level, like a broody hen round her chicks, in order to protect the anti-tank aircraft from interception by enemy fighters. Little by little, I discover all the tricks. Skill is often the result of getting hurt. We lose aircraft in weakly defended areas because we are cruising in the middle of an artillery duel. The airspace in the line of the artillery's trajectories must be avoided. After some time, the Soviets manage fairly successfully to cope with our air attacks against their tanks. If it is at all possible, they move up their AA guns with the leading tanks.'

Although the Soviet fighter regiments attempted to intervene over the battlefield, they were unable to break through the Luftwaffe's fighter screen. Huge air battles developed and, on 5 July alone, the Jagdgeschwader of Fliegerkorps VIII claimed 432 air victories. Because of heavy losses, the Soviet armies were consequently forced to rely on anti-aircraft fire to deal with the Luftwaffe's ground-attack aircraft. This was often very effective, as the German aircraft were operating at low level and well within range of even light anti-aircraft weapons. On 8 July, the Staffelkapitän of 9/StG 2, Hauptmann Bernhard Wutka, was hit by return fire from a Soviet tank and crashed to his death. Later in the month, Oberleutnant Willi Hörner, the commander of StG 2's 7 Staffel, who had been awarded the Knight's Cross only two months before, was lost in action. His Ju 87D was hit by flak northeast of Orel and came down between the lines with its pilot dead at the controls.

Rudel recorded the attacks by Soviet aircraft on StG 2's bases:

'Russian aircraft raid our airfield in the Orel sector every night. There are slit trenches alongside our tents and we are supposed to take cover in them as soon as the raiders appear. Some of us, however, sleep through the raids because a good night's rest is indispensible if we are to be fit to go out again the next day. In any case Ivan generally keeps up his bombing all night.'

These nuisance raids were usually carried out by antiquated Polikarpov U-2 biplanes, operating at low level and armed with fragmentation bombs. They scored one success on 17 July, when the Kommandeur of III/StG 2, Hauptmann Walter Krauss, was killed during a night raid. His place was taken by Rudel, who in the following month flew his 1200th combat sortie. Rudel's regular radio-operator/gunner, Oberfeldwebel Erwin Hentschel, who was awarded the Knight's Cross at the end of the year, had himself completed 1000 missions.

By 23 July it was clear that the German offensive at Kursk had failed and that the initiative had passed to the Soviet forces. A month later, advancing Soviet troops entered Kharkov and from then on the Wehrmacht could only fight a series of delaying actions on the Eastern Front. One of the lessons of Kursk for the Luftwaffe was that its ground-support forces were

The Eastern Front, 1943

2nd Pz Army
Bryansk

SOVIET UNION

Orel

9th Army

Kursk

Voronezh

4th Pz Army

Kharkov

Don

Poltava

Dnepropetrovsk

Donets

Stalino

Zaporozhye

Rostov

Dneiper

SEA OF AZOV

CRIMEA

Krasnodar

Key
— Front line, March – July 1943
➤ German offensive, July 1943 (Operation Zitadelle)
➤ Soviet counter-offensive, July – August 1943

In the summer of 1943 the German Panzer armies in the southernmost section of the Eastern Front launched Operation Zitadelle, the attack on the Soviet salient around Kursk. Spearheading the German offensive were the newly-deployed tank-busting Ju 87Gs of Stukageschwader 2.

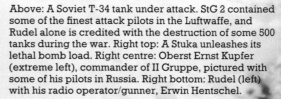

Above: A Soviet T-34 tank under attack. StG 2 contained some of the finest attack pilots in the Luftwaffe, and Rudel alone is credited with the destruction of some 500 tanks during the war. Right top: A Stuka unleashes its lethal bomb load. Right centre: Oberst Ernst Kupfer (extreme left), commander of II Gruppe, pictured with some of his pilots in Russia. Right bottom: Rudel (left) with his radio operator/gunner, Erwin Hentschel.

HANS-ULRICH RUDEL

Born on 2 May 1916 in Silesia, Hans-Ulrich Rudel was destined to become the most outstanding ground-attack pilot of World War II. In 1938, two years after joining the Luftwaffe at the age of 20, he was posted to Stukageschwader 168. Surprisingly, Rudel was considered to be a poor pilot and was re-assigned to observer duties. Rudel took part in the Polish Campaign, earning the Iron Cross, Second Class. In 1940 he returned to a Stuka unit, but doubts about his abilities persisted and he saw no action until the invasion of the Soviet Union in 1941. Assigned to StG 2, Rudel soon showed himself to be the best dive-bomber pilot on the Eastern Front. By February 1943 he had completed 1000 sorties, and by the following October had destroyed 100 tanks. Rudel was appointed commander of StG 2's Third Gruppe in March 1944 and six months later became the leader of the whole Geschwader. Despite losing part of one leg in February 1945, Rudel returned to his unit and fought until the end of the war. His estimated final tally was impressive: in 2530 missions, he destroyed at least 519 tanks, sank one battleship, one cruiser, one destroyer and 70 assault craft, and destroyed more than 800 vehicles, 150 self-propelled guns and four armoured trains. His air victories included nine planes shot down. He himself was shot down 30 times and was wounded five.

91

Below: Ju 87s of StG 2 prepare to take off. Left: A Ju 87 dives into action. Clearly visible beneath the wings are the two 37mm tank-busting cannon.

inadequate to meet the needs of the Russian theatre, even though individual units had performed well. Moreover, most of the aircraft types assigned to this role were obsolescent and in need of replacement.

In October 1943, the Stukageschwader were re-designated as Schlachtgeschwader, and by mid-1944 most of them had been re-equipped with the Fw 190. The exception to the general rule, apart from a number of specialised Panzer Jäger Staffeln, was III/StG 2, which continued to operate a mixture of Ju 87D and Ju 87G Stukas until the end of the war in Europe. The Fw 190s of II/StG2, under the command of Major Kurt Kennel, were often called on to provide fighter cover for the slow and unwieldy Stukas.

It was largely due to Rudel's personal preference for the Ju 87 that III/StG 2 did not convert onto the Fw 190. In August 1944 he was appointed Geschwader Kommodore and command of III Gruppe passed to Hauptmann Kurt Lau, a veteran of the 1941 campaign in Greece. Thereafter, Rudel flew both the Ju 87 and Fw 190. The mixed nature of his Geschwader's equipment was in some ways an advantage, and during the defence of Budapest in late 1944, Rudel recorded that the unit became 'maids of all work; we are dive bombers, attack aircraft, fighters and re-connaissance aircraft'. Nonetheless, he was well aware of the Stuka's shortcomings, as his account of an anti-tank mission against the Soviet bridgehead over the Oder in February 1945 makes clear:

'Before coming into the attack, I climb to 800m as the flak cannot reach me at this altitude. From [this height] I scream down in a steep dive, weaving violently. When I am close to the tank I straighten up for an instant, to fire and then streak away at low level over the tank, using the same evasive manoeuvres, until I reach a point out of range of the flak when I am able to climb again. Such attacks are of course out of the question for my comrades for the simple reason that they do not have my experience.'

It was only because of the courage of Rudel and his pilots that the Ju 87 remained an effective combat aircraft until the end of the war. The men of StG 2 are remembered to this day: the proud title of the 'Immelmann Geschwader' is perpetuated by the reconnaissance wing Aufklarungsgeschwader 51 of today's West German air force.

THE AUTHOR Anthony Robinson was formerly on the staff of the RAF Museum, Hendon, and is now a freelance military aviation writer. His books include *American Air Power* and *Aerial Warfare*.

Major Hans-Ulrich Rudel, Stukageschwader 2, Russia 1944

Major Rudel wears a two-piece flying suit (known as the 'Invasion Suit') with ample pockets for maps and survival equipment, topped by a *Fliegermütze* (side cap). His shoulder straps denote the rank of Major, the yellow underlay signifying the flying branch. At the throat he wears the Knight's Cross with Swords and Oak-leaves.

GRAND SLAM

Barnes Wallis developed new monster bombs that gave 617 Squadron an awesome strike-power during 1944 and 1945

EARLY IN June 1944, a delivery of 'lethal, shark-like, sleek' bombs with offset tail-fins arrived at Woodhall Spa, 617 Squadron's operational station. Tallboy, designed by Barnes Wallis to penetrate deep into the earth and explode beneath a target, was ready for action.

Within three days of the Allied landings in Normandy, 19 Lancasters of 617 Squadron demonstrated the bomb's power at the Saumur tunnel east of Nantes, through which the main railway line ran from southwest France into Normandy. At 0200 hours on 9 June, Wing Commander Leonard Cheshire dived his Mosquito from 5000 to a mere 100ft and dropped red markers in the mouth of the tunnel. From the following bombers, one Tallboy pierced the roof, others fell alongside and more destroyed the cutting. The squadron justifiably received a 'special commendation' for 'a magnificent effort'.

Previous page: A Lancaster unloads a Tallboy 'earthquake' bomb. Designed by Barnes Wallis, Tallboy and Grand Slam detonated deep beneath the earth, creating shock waves that literally shook the target to pieces. These bombs left craters over 100ft in diameter, as can be seen in the aerial photo (bottom) taken after the attack on the Saumur railway tunnel.

Six days later Tallboy was used to combat the dangerous E-boat threat in the English Channel. An attack was planned for sunset, when enemy ships gathered in Le Havre harbour before launching their nightly operations, and the Mosquitoes were thus called upon to mark with smoke in daylight for the first time. Diving through intense flak, Cheshire's aircraft was severely damaged and very nearly shot down. However, the accompanying Lancasters were able to devastate the E-boats, smash many of their protective pens and breach the harbour wall. The following day, 15 June, a similar attack was made at Boulogne, and together these two operations sank or damaged over 100 enemy craft.

Meanwhile the first V-1 had fallen on England, and 42 launching sites were soon identified in the Pas de Calais. Tallboy seemed the ideal riposte. Due to bad weather it was not until 19 June that Cheshire could lead 617 in daylight to 'a constructional works' near Watten, where he and Squadron Leader David Shannon marked for the Lancasters to bomb from 10,000ft. The Tallboys disappeared into the ground and, after a short while, the earth mushroomed. 'God help the Jerries!', muttered Cheshire's navigator, watching the awesome scene of destruction below.

Cheshire's hundredth operation was unique. At Marquise-Mimoyesque, the Germans had sunk three shafts deep into a hillside in which huge guns were being prepared to fire 600 tons of explosive a day into London. From above, the three camouflaged shell exits measured about 30 by 20yds. So accurate was 617 Squadron's attack that all three tunnels were heavily damaged and the V-3 was never fired. On Cheshire's return, Air Vice-Marshal Cochrane said: 'A hundred's a good number to stop at,' and he was grounded, along with the last three pilots from the Dams Raid still with the squadron, Squadron Leaders Shannon, Munro and McCarthy.

Cheshire was succeeded as squadron commander by J.B. 'Willy' Tait, a 26-year-old taciturn Welshman addicted to a large pipe, who soon distinguished himself in further Tallboy attacks on V-weapon sites and stores during the closing weeks of July 1944. At Wizernes on 17 July, realising that his smoke markers could not be seen in poor visibility, he circled low over the target and ordered the Lancasters above to aim at him. But they could not even identify his plane clearly and returned home with their bombs, while Tait limped back in a Mustang perforated by flak.

In August, Allied troops overran the V-sites and 617 Squadron found itself switched to operations against U-boat and E-boat pens. At Brest, for instance, two large holes were torn in a 16ft-thick roof and at La Pallice 12 Tallboys hit U-boat pens measuring only 240 by 120yds. Later, a shortage of Tallboys compelled 617 to use 1000lb and 2000lb bombs to attack the old battleship *Gueydon* at anchor three miles upstream, to prevent the enemy moving it to block the entrance to Brest harbour.

Not all of the squadron's activities were south of the Channel, for early in September Cochrane announced: 'Tait, you're going to sink the *Tirpitz*.' This formidable German battleship was positioned in Alten Fjord, north Norway, ready to menace the Arctic convoys or break out into the Atlantic as *Bismarck* had done. Protected by the steep sides of her anchorage, strong main and secondary armament, armoured plating on sides and decks, and by smoke apparatus deployed on ground alongside, above the ship and in 20 commandeered fishing

vessels around it, *Tirpitz* lay beyond the range of shore-based aircraft in Britain.

Thus on the evening of 11 September 1944, 38 Lancasters of 617 and 9 Squadrons (carrying 26 Tallboy and 12 special anti-ship 'Johnny Walker' mines), an RAF film-unit aircraft, two Coastal Command Liberators and a photo-reconnaissance Mosquito took off from Lossiemouth in Scotland under the command of Group Captain C.C. McCullen, with Tait leading 617. They were to fly direct to Russia, then bomb *Tirpitz* from an unexpected easterly direction and return to Russia before flying home. One Lancaster soon turned back, the rest found the landing area near Archangel swathed in low mist with navigation made more difficult by indifferent maps. An added complication was that the wrong call-sign had been issued to wireless operators, but eventually all but six aircraft landed on airfields. The others put down in swamps, forest and rough fields. During the next 24 hours the Russians mounted a massive rescue operation and frantic repairs were carried out by RAF

Far left, above: Surrounded by massive water-filled craters, a 100yd section of the Bielefeld viaduct lies in ruins after the Grand Slam and Tallboy attack by 617 Squadron in March 1945. **Far left, below:** A 617 Lancaster crew poses beside a Grand Slam before setting out on a mission. **Main picture:** The up-turned hull of the mighty German battleship *Tirpitz,* victim of two direct hits with the 12,000lb Tallboy.

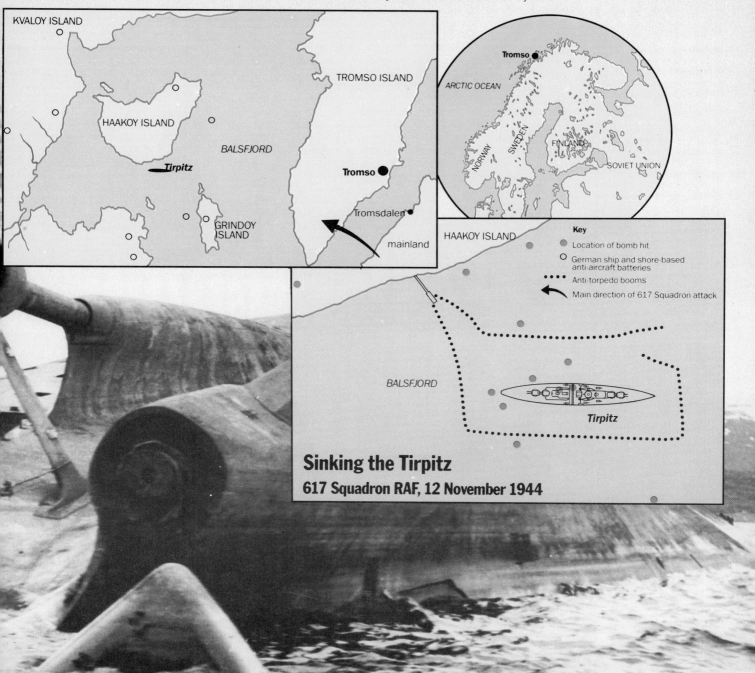

KVALOY ISLAND

TROMSO ISLAND

HAAKOY ISLAND

BALSFJORD

Tirpitz

GRINDOY ISLAND

Tromso

Tromsdalen

mainland

Tromso

ARCTIC OCEAN

NORWAY

SWEDEN

FINLAND

SOVIET UNION

HAAKOY ISLAND

Key
- Location of bomb hit
- German ship and shore-based anti-aircraft batteries
- Anti-torpedo booms
- Main direction of 617 Squadron attack

BALSFJORD

Tirpitz

Sinking the Tirpitz
617 Squadron RAF, 12 November 1944

THE EARTHQUAKE BOMBS

At the outbreak of World War II the civilian engineer Barnes Wallis designed the 'earthquake bomb', a weapon that destroyed not by its explosive impact but through a seismic shock wave created by its explosion locked deep underground. The idea received no effective support at first, however, and Wallis went on to develop the 'bouncing bomb' which destroyed the dams in 1943.

The first true earthquake bomb was code-named Tallboy, designed by Wallis and finished in March 1944.

It was a scaled-down version of the '10-tonner', 21½ft long with a 38in diameter and weighing 12,000lb. A streamlined, sinister object, its highly resistant blue-black steel casing could be made by only two foundries in Britain. Unlike conventional heavy bombs, it was specifically designed for accurate flight and deep penetration.

Dropped from 20,000ft it passed the speed of sound on its descent, sank 80ft into the earth and produced a crater 80ft deep and 100ft across. One Tallboy used against the *Tirpitz* burst through the forecastle and peeled back the armoured upper deck like the lid of a sardine tin.

The apotheosis of the earthquake bombs was Grand Slam, similar in design to Tallboy, 25½ft long and weighing 22,000lb, of which 15,400lb was explosive. Grand Slam was the biggest bomb of the war, and only the Lancaster was able to carry it. If dropped from 40,000ft it could penetrate to 135ft and it created such a tremor that buildings and stone structures nearby were literally shaken into rubble. Above: The Bomb Aimers' Wing Badge.

maintenance crews from the Liberators.

Eventually at 0630 hours on 15 September, 27 Lancasters (21 with Tallboys, six with Johnny Walkers) and the film-unit aircraft took off. They aimed to attack *Tirpitz* at 1100 from a maximum of 18,000ft, having dived to the bombing height when 60 miles away to beat the smoke screen expected to gather in eight minutes. All went well. In clear skies, *Tirpitz* was slow to put up the smoke screen. Half a dozen

Tallboys were dropped before 'plumes of white drawing together across the still water and mingling with soot from the guns' obscured the battleship. Light flak proved ineffective against the high-flying Lancasters, heavy flak 'moderate' and 'inaccurate', but the flashes provided a useful aiming point. Seventeen Tallboys were dropped, and several crews reported that at least one hit *Tirpitz*, 'with one or two near misses'. Every attacking aircraft (including four still with Tallboy) returned safely to Yagodnik in Russia and eventually Scotland.

In mid-October the damaged *Tirpitz* was moved south to Tromso, where additional anti-aircraft vessels were anchored close by and fighters stationed within reach. The 'solitary dinosaur', in the words of C-in-C Bomber Command Sir Arthur Harris, remained a grave potential threat. But it now lay within range of Lossiemouth. To outflank enemy radar, it was decided to approach once more from the east using the cover of mountain ranges until the last possible moment and making a round trip of approximately 2250 miles. The attacking Lancasters would be fitted with more powerful Merlin 28 engines, carry extra Wellington overload tanks and a Mosquito drop tank, dispense with the mid-upper turret (as on the Dams Raid) and strip out all non-essential

equipment, including the front guns. At 0300 hours on 29 October 37 Lancasters (including a film-unit aircraft) took off in darkness and pouring rain and darkness and, without mishap, commenced their bombing runs at 0900. *Tirpitz* was unprepared, but as the Lancasters closed on it low cloud came in from the sea to blanket the target. Some crews made five runs and still could not bomb. Only one near-miss was claimed; and one Lancaster holed by flak made an emergency landing in Sweden.

By the end of November, the Arctic winter would have come to deny daylight until the following spring; time was therefore short. In spite of the fact that the Germans had been alerted to the possibility of a landward attack against Tromso, at 0200 hours on 12 November 30 Lancasters of 617 and 9 Squadrons, again accompanied by a film-unit plane, left Lossiemouth for the third time in two months. Following the same plan as that of 29 October, the Lancasters breasted the last ridge and saw 'a huge vessel, black and squat' lying at anchor like a giant spider in a web of anti-torpedo netting. Incredibly, in perfect visibility, there was no smoke screen; and although the flak was intense the Tallboys were dropped accurately. After bombing, Tait circled back to watch anxiously as his pilots went in, worried that the threatened fighters would appear. Why they never materialised remains a mystery. Two Tallboys struck *Tirpitz*, causing a magazine to explode and tear a gash in its side, so that the battleship 'capsized with little of her bottom showing above the surface'. No longer would it dominate naval strategic thinking in home waters.

Between the first and second *Tirpitz* operations, 617 Squadron once more attacked a dam. It was feared that the Germans would open the floodgates of the Kembs dam close to the Swiss frontier, as American forces crossed the Rhine near Belfort. If the dam could be breached before the crossing, such a disaster would be averted.

Left: Bomb away! A Grand Slam drops from the modified underbelly of a 617 Squadron Lancaster. Clearly visible, hanging below the aircraft, is the sturdy retaining chain used to keep the massive bomb in place during the outward flight. Below left: The 'earthquake' bombs were very effective against 'hard' targets such as U-boat and E-boat pens, when they crashed through thick layers of heavy concrete before detonating. Below, main picture: Lancasters en route for Hitler's personal mountain stronghold, the Eagle's Nest. Below right: A Lancaster goes in to attack the Eagle's Nest. This was 617's last operation.

The complex plan required a high force of seven Lancasters approaching from the west to bomb at 8000ft, while Mustangs concentrated on strafing flak positions and six Lancasters led by Tait attacked from the east at low level, one at a time dropping Tallboys fitted with delayed-action fuzes to lie embedded at the base of the dam. The 617 Lancasters took off on the afternoon of 7 October, met escorting Mustangs over Kent and crossed France in beautiful sunshine. Skirting the Swiss frontier one Lancaster was damaged by warning anti-aircraft fire, but the high force and the Mustangs attacked on time. However, coming in low, Tait still had to cope with active flak. His bomb vanished under the water close to the dam wall and, circling back, he saw two of his Lancasters shot down. As the survivors made their way home, the delayed-action fuzes worked and the dam collapsed.

Tait flew one more operation after the final *Tirpitz* attack, then he too was grounded. In December 1944, Johnny Fauquier, an experienced, stocky Canadian, 10 years older than most of his crews, became Commanding Officer of 617. On the last day of the year he led a night attack on the cruisers *Emden* and *Köln* in Oslo fjord, damaging the former. But poor weather restricted the squadron to one operation in January 1945 – against U-boat pens at Bergen. Enemy fighters mauled the Lancasters, causing one to ditch on the homeward flight. Saved by an Air Sea Rescue launch, the pilot's only printable comment was: 'Bloody cold in that dinghy.'

While Tallboy proved its worth, work had progressed on Barnes Wallis's 10-ton bomb – his original idea advanced four years earlier. Hence on 14 March 1945, 14 617 Lancasters attacked Bielefeld viaduct, which provided a vital rail link to the Ruhr. Thirteen carried Tallboys. The fourteenth, piloted by Squadron Leader G.C. Calder, had no mid-upper gunner, no wireless operator and no bomb-bay doors. But it did have a strengthened fuselage, powerful Merlin 24 engines – and a Grand Slam bomb. Calder was lucky to be on the operation. Fauquier's Lancaster (also with Grand Slam) developed engine trouble during pre-flight checks and Calder, in the reserve aircraft, turned a Nelsonian blind eye to his CO's gesticulating figure bent on using his plane. At the viaduct Calder reported 'a very near miss' from a height of nearly 12,000ft – much lower than Wallis ideally wanted. But it worked. The viaduct had been wrecked over a distance of 100yds and would carry no more traffic. Newspapers dubbed Grand Slam 'our V-bomb' and 'Two-ton Tess', and Wallis declared the result 'exquisite...marvellous bombing'. Thereafter he hung a framed copy of the reconnaissance photo in his study.

617 now used Grand Slam and Tallboy against railway bridges and viaducts, achieving 'outstanding accuracy of bombing' in the closing phase of the war. Then, on 16 April, Fauquier took 18 Lancasters to attack the German pocket battleship *Lützow* in her Baltic anchorage. In the face of German fighters and fierce predicted flak they bombed and left the vessel on the sea-bed with only its superstructure still above water. There followed 617's last operation of the war, an attack on Hitler's Eagle's Nest near Berchtesgaden, on 25 April 1945.

Plans to use the squadron in the Far East during 1946 evaporated after the two atomic bombs had been dropped and Japan surrendered. Leonard Cheshire acted as official observer for the second of these raids. So he survived the war, as did Tait and Fauquier. Wing Commander Guy Gibson, the first CO, had been killed in September 1944. Martin, once 617 Squadron's temporary commander, further distinguished himself, as Gibson had, as a night-fighter pilot and eventually became an air marshal.

THE AUTHOR John Sweetman is a specialist in airpower history and has written *Operation Chastise, The Dams Raid: Epic or Myth*.

MARINE AVIATION

The first US marine to undergo flight training qualified in 1912, but when the US entered World War I in 1917, marine aviation amounted to no more than 39 men. The unit was quickly expanded, however, and in July 1918 the 1st Marine Aviation Force arrived in France. Though without its own aircraft until September, four marine squadrons served with British and French units and carried out a total of 57 raids. By the armistice, Marine Corps aviation had grown to 2462 men and 340 aircraft. Between the wars the units participated in Caribbean counter-insurgency operations, and new techniques of dive-bombing and ground support were tried in combat.

At the onset of World War II, marine aviation had only 251 aircraft and 708 pilots. When the two brigades of marines were reorganised into divisions in February 1941, their air support groups were redesignated 1st and 2nd Marine Aircraft Wings (MAWs). By January 1945 the number of pilots had risen to 10,412, an additional three MAWs had been formed, and the total number of squadrons had reached 132.

One criticism often levelled at US marine aviation in World War II was that frequently it could not fulfil its primary role, that of covering the marines' amphibious assaults. The raids were often beyond the range of the marines' land-based aircraft, but, rather than insist on carrier facilities, many aviation leaders preferred to seek opportunities for aerial combat.

Above: The badge of VMF-214, 'The Black Sheep'.

US Marine pilots of VMF-214, 'The Black Sheep', in Vought F4U Corsairs, proved more than a match for the Japanese over the Solomons

THE CULMINATION of the bitterly fought Solomons campaign in the Pacific, which had begun on Guadalcanal island in August 1942, was the elimination of Rabaul as a major Japanese base. From this strategically important port on the northeastern tip of New Britain, the Japanese had planned to dominate the Solomon Islands to the south, New Guinea to the west and ultimately the Australian mainland. In November 1943 the Japanese were still maintaining substantial air forces in the area, with a total of 373 aircraft based on four airfields. Their neutralisation was the responsibility of Major-General Ralph J. Mitchell, USMC, who as the ComAirSols (Commander, Aircraft, Solomons) controlled a mixed force of fighter, bomber and support aircraft drawn from the USAAF, US Navy, US Marine Corps and Royal New Zealand Air Force. Spearheading the Allied fighter offensive against Rabaul was Marine Fighter Squadron 214 (VMF-214), 'The Black Sheep', commanded by Major Gregory Boyington who was to end the war as the leading US Marine Corps fighter ace.

VMF-214 had originally been commissioned on July 1942 at Marine Corps Air Station Ewa, Hawaii with a nucleus of experienced pilots from Midway. In February 1943 it arrived at Espiritu Santo in the New Hebrides and its Grumman F4F Wildcat fighters moved forward to Guadalcanal during the following month. On 7 April the squadron was part of a force of 76 American fighters that intercepted a raid by 6

SOLOMONS AIR BATTLE

Aichi D3A 'Val' dive-bombers of the Imperial Japanese Navy, escorted by 110 Mitsubishi A6M 'Zero' fighters. VMF-214 claimed 10 enemy aircraft destroyed. In June the Wildcats were replaced by Chance Vought F4U Corsairs and on 18 July four of VMF-214's F4Us, led by their then commanding officer, Major William H. Pace, intercepted and shot down three Mitsubishi G3M 'Nell' bombers which were attacking the seaplane tender USS *Chincoteague*. One of the squadron's best pilots at this time was Lieutenant Alvin Jensen, who ended the war with seven air victories. On 28 August, Jensen became separated from his flight in a tropical storm. Finding himself over the Japanese airfield of Kahili, he strafed the aircraft lining the runway to such good effect that later photographic reconnaissance confirmed 24 of them had been destroyed. For this considerable feat of arms Jensen received the Navy Cross.

Jensen's action came at the end of VMF-214's second tour of operations and, as the commanding officer, Major Pace, had

Above: Chance Vought F4U Corsair fighter-bombers warm up on their landing strip in the Solomons. The Corsair (in flight below left) was one of several powerful American fighters introduced into the Pacific theatre to challenge the Mitsubishi A6M Zero-Sen (below right), an aircraft which enjoyed a reputation of invincibility until the air combats over Guadalcanal. To redress the balance the Japanese then uprated the Zero's engine, but the consequent reduction in fuel capacity and range was a serious disadvantage in the Solomons campaign, and by February 1944 most of the Japanese air units in the area had been withdrawn.

been killed in action earlier in the month, it was decided to disperse the squadron's personnel to other units. VMF-214 became a squadron on paper only. However, this period of 'suspended animation' came to an end early in September when the unit was re-organised under Boyington's leadership with 48 pilots drawn from replacement pools. As a result of these unconventional origins, the unit was dubbed 'The Black Sheep', although the pilots' original choice had been 'Boyington's Bastards'. The latter name was considered unsuitable for publication in the American press, but it nonetheless led to the incorporation of a bar sinister in VMF-214's badge. The Black Sheep's 30-year-old commander was nicknamed 'Pappy' or 'Gramps', although he was not, in fact, the oldest member of the squadron. Robert Sherrod, the historian of Marine Corps Aviation in World War II, described Boyington as:

'a brash, swashbuckling pilot whose belligerent career had included a term with the Flying Tigers in China (where he was credited with shooting down six Japanese planes). Boyington was not only a natural pilot, but he was also a skilful leader...'

Captain John M. Foster of VMF-222, who served alongside Boyington in the Solomons, saw him rather differently:

'He had the sturdy body of the wrestler and the keen mind of the scholar with the spirit and tenacity of the bulldog. Every time I saw Boyington I always seemed to think of a bulldog. Perhaps

THE F4U CORSAIR

During World War II a total of 2140 enemy aircraft fell victim to the Vought F4U Corsair fighter, and with a ratio of 11 enemy planes destroyed to every Corsair lost, it was probably the best US combat plane of the war.

Though designed as a carrier-based fighter, the Corsair was rejected by the US Navy as its long nose restricted visibility and its undercarriage was liable to cause the aircraft to bounce on touchdown. The Marine Corps, on the other hand, was delighted with the plane and it was first brought into service in February 1943. The Corsair's combat debut in the South Pacific was a great success, and within six months all eight Marine fighter squadrons in the area had been equipped with F4Us.

In early 1944 the US Navy began to operate night-fighters from carriers, the problems of landing them having been solved, but it was not until January 1945 that carrier-based F4Us were flown by day.

Powered by a 2000hp Pratt and Whitney R-2800-8 engine, the Corsair had a maximum speed of 415mph at 20,000ft, and a normal range of 1015 miles. Variants of the F4U carried different armaments: for example, the F4U-1 had six 0.5in Browning machine guns while the F4U-1D fighter-bomber had provision for underwing bombs or rockets.

it was the set of his jaw. Perhaps it was the legend he had built around himself.'

The squadron pilots ranged in age from 21 to 31 years, and a number of them were already combat veterans. Boyington's executive officer, Major Stanley R. Bailey, 'in fresh starched khaki with rank insignia on his collar and on his hat, which few of us bothered to wear', was certainly not typical of the Marine pilots in the Solomons, whose unkempt appearance reminded one new arrival to the base of the 'sourdoughs of Alaska'. From the beginning, Boyington had assessed a small group of his men as 'born pilots'. They included Captain Paul A. 'Moon' Mullin, who ended the war with six-and-a-half kills (the fraction indicating a shared victory); the swarthy and gypsy-like Captain Christopher Magee, with nine kills, who was nicknamed 'Bandana Maggie', Captain Donald H. 'Moe' Fisher, who often flew as the CO's wingman and claimed six victories; and Major John F. Bolt Jnr, who scored six victories in World War II and added another six to them over Korea, flying F-86 Sabres with the USAF's 51st Fighter-Interceptor Wing.

The newly re-formed VMF-214 began to operate its F4U Corsairs from the Russell Islands, but soon moved forward to Munda. The immediate objective was the Japanese garrison on Bougainville, the northernmost island of the Solomons group, but this was simply a stepping stone to the major target of Rabaul. The Black Sheep flew their first mission, a

bomber escort to Ballale, on 16 September. The formation was engaged by about 40 Zeros, a force which outnumbered the VMF-214 Corsairs by two to one. Nonetheless, the Marine pilots emerged as the victors, claiming 11 Japanese fighters shot down and a further eight probable kills, for the loss of only one Corsair and its pilot. Boyington led the scoring, with a total of five confirmed victories. One of his victims exploded 'right in front of my face, [so] that I didn't know which way to turn to miss the pieces.' Captain Robert T. Ewing failed to return from the mission. His fighter was last seen by Boyington flying at low level and under attack from two Japanese fighters, its cockpit canopy and fuselage sides smeared with oil. Boyington drove off the attackers, shooting one of them down, but could not then find the crippled Corsair.

During four weeks of combat VMF-214 claimed a total of 47 enemy aircraft shot down in the Bougainville area. On 4 October Boyington was leading the squadron over the Japanese airfield at Kahili, when he was requested by radio 'in perfect English' to report his height and position. This proved to be a ruse by Japanese ground-controllers, as Boyington suspected, but he was equal to the situation. He replied giving his true position, but gave his height as 20,000ft when in fact it was 25,000ft. He was rewarded by 'about the most beautiful sight a fighter pilot can dream of': a formation of some 30 Zeros climbing beneath his aircraft. The Black Sheep dived onto

Background: A parade of 1st Marine Air Wing aircraft at Bougainville. Left: VMF-214 personnel stoically help themselves in 'Dysentery Chowhall'. Below left: The Corsair was designed to accommodate one of the largest propellers in the world. Bottom: Air crew dash out to their waiting Corsairs after briefing.

Pilot, United States Marine Corps, Pacific 1943

The lightweight attire of this pilot serving in the equatorial Pacific contrasts sharply with the heavy and bulky clothing of personnel in the European theatre. Over light khaki flying overalls he carries an inflatable life vest. Basic equipment hung on the belt includes a field-dressing pouch on his right side, a pouch containing two automatic pistol magazines worn at the front, and a water-bottle carrier. The flying helmet is of leather, although fabric helmets were also common, and the goggles worn over it are tinted against glare.

them from out of the sun and Boyington claimed three victories in a combat which lasted for just 30 seconds.

Some of the larger air battles which VMF-214 fought at this time were worthy subjects for the cinema screen, or so Boyington thought:

'You could see planes going around in circles, half-circles, you could see Zeros, Corsairs, Zeros, all firing at each other; you could see the red balls from the tracers, just like Roman candles going every which way in the sky. The battles would cover an area from about 3000ft above the water to about 20,000ft, and equally as wide.'

In late October VMF-214 withdrew from Munda to Espiritu Santo and then on to Sydney, Australia, for a much-needed period of rest and recreation. 'It was all like discovering a new life,' one Marine pilot recalled of his period of 'R & R' in Sydney. 'The hot baths, luxurious theatres, good food, soft beds with pillows and the friendly beautiful girls – all proved just about more than we could take in such a concentrated dose.' On Munda the pilots lived under canvas in an area which turned into a sea of mud after every tropical downpour. They were tormented by flies and malaria-carrying mosquitoes, frequently attacked by Japanese nightbombers, and the food was in short supply and of such bad quality that the landing strip's mess hall was known as 'Dysentery Chowhall'.

The Black Sheep returned to the Solomons in late October 1943 and moved to the forward base of Vella Lavella to prepare for the air assault on Rabaul. The ComAirSols, General Mitchell, selected Boyington as the tactical leader of his fighter forces. However, the first sweep over Rabaul on 17 December was not an unqualified success. A total of 31 Marine F4U

Corsairs, 22 Navy Grumman F6F Hellcats and 23 Curtiss P-40 Kittyhawks of Nos. 14 and 16 Squadrons of the Royal New Zealand Air Force saw only sporadic action with the defending Japanese fighters. The New Zealanders, flying at low level, claimed five enemy aircraft destroyed, but they lost three of their own pilots including their wing leader, Wing Commander T. Freeman. VMF-214's only victories went to Lieutenant D.J. Moore, who fought with seven Japanese fighters and shot down two of them.

Boyington set to work to analyse the causes of this poor performance. He concluded that a formation of 76 fighters was far too large to be efficiently managed in the air and that a sweep by between 36 and 48 aircraft would be quite adequate to deal with any opposition. He also thought that such missions ought to be restricted to fighters with the same performance characteristics. One of the problems during the sweep on 17 December had been that the RNZAF Kittyhawks had reached the Rabaul area before the high cover squadrons were in position. Given the

Right: Members of VMF-214 pose on the inverted gull wings of a Corsair. The excellent combat record and unconventional origins of the 'Black Sheep' did much to engender a fierce pride within the unit. **Below right:** Major Stanley Bailey, Boyington's executive officer in VMF-214, with Mid-Nite, the squadron's woolly mascot.

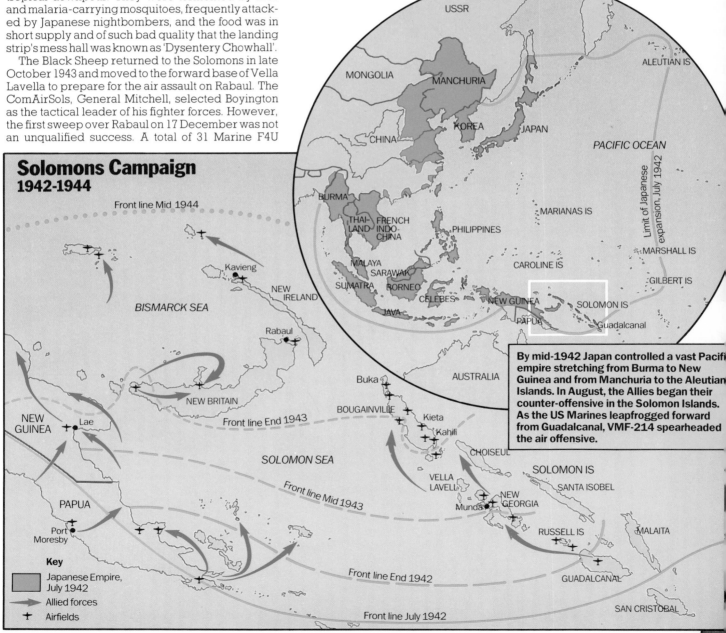

Solomons Campaign
1942-1944

Front line Mid 1944

Kavieng

BISMARCK SEA

NEW IRELAND

Rabaul

NEW BRITAIN

Buka

Front line End 1943

BOUGAINVILLE

Kieta

Kahili

NEW GUINEA

Lae

SOLOMON SEA

Front line Mid 1943

CHOISEUL

VELLA LAVELLA

SOLOMON IS

SANTA ISOBEL

PAPUA

Port Moresby

Munda

NEW GEORGIA

RUSSELL IS

MALAITA

Front line End 1942

GUADALCANAL

Key

☐ Japanese Empire, July 1942

→ Allied forces

✛ Airfields

Front line July 1942

SAN CRISTOBAL

USSR

MONGOLIA

MANCHURIA

ALEUTIAN IS

CHINA

KOREA

JAPAN

PACIFIC OCEAN

BURMA

THAI-LAND

FRENCH INDO-CHINA

PHILIPPINES

MARIANAS IS

Limit of Japanese expansion, July 1942

MARSHALL IS

MALAYA

SARAWAK

CAROLINE IS

GILBERT IS

SUMATRA

BORNEO

CELEBES

NEW GUINEA

SOLOMON IS

JAVA

PAPUA

Guadalcanal

By mid-1942 Japan controlled a vast Pacific empire stretching from Burma to New Guinea and from Manchuria to the Aleutian Islands. In August, the Allies began their counter-offensive in the Solomon Islands. As the US Marines leapfrogged forward from Guadalcanal, VMF-214 spearheaded the air offensive.

AUSTRALIA

limited range of their aircraft, the RNZAF pilots had had no option. Nonetheless, Boyington reasoned, a smaller formation would not have taken so long to form up, and Corsairs or Hellcats would have had sufficient fuel reserves to allow them to wait for their high-cover squadrons. Boyington was a thoughtful student of air tactics and not all of his ideas were orthodox. For example, Captain John Foster remembers him saying:

'I don't expect any wingman to follow me in a fight.... In fact a man can take care of himself if he has the altitude advantage to start with. Of course, if the Japs have the advantage, a wingman is the best form of life insurance you have.'

On 23 December Boyington's tactics were put to the test. A fighter sweep by 48 Corsairs was planned to follow shortly after an escorted bomber strike on

Rabaul. The Marine pilots found 40 Japanese fighters still airborne and accounted for no fewer than 30 of them. The Black Sheep claimed 12 of these kills, with Boyington shooting down four. He later recalled:

'We caught a dozen or so [Zeros] that had been heckling our bombers, B-24s. The Nips dove away and ran for home, Rabaul, for they must have been short of gasoline. They had been fighting some distance from their base, with no extra fuel because they wore no belly tanks. They had not expected us to follow, but we were not escort planes and didn't have to stay with our bombers.

'Nosing over after one of these homebound Nips, I closed the distance between us gradually, keeping directly behind his tail, first 1000yds, then 500[ft], finally closing in directly behind to 50ft. Knowing the little rascal couldn't have any idea he was being followed, I was going to make certain this one didn't get away. Never before had I been so deliberate and cold about what I was doing. He was on his way home, but already I knew he would not get there....

'One short burst was all that was needed. With this short burst flames flew from the cockpit, a yellow chute opened and down the pilot glided into the Pacific. I saw the splash.

'Using my diving speed with additional power, I climbed, and as I climbed I could see off to my right two more enemy planes heading for Rabaul. One was throwing smoke. I closed in on the wounded plane, and it dove. His mate pulled off to one side to manoeuvre against me, but I let the smoker have it – one burst that set the plane on fire – and again the pilot baled out. His mate then dove

MAJOR GREGORY-BOYINGTON

Gregory Boyington joined the US Marine Corps in 1935 and trained as a pilot. He resigned his commission in 1941 to join the American Volunteer Group (AVG), otherwise known as the 'Flying Tigers', in China. As a member of the AVG's 1st Pursuit Squadron he took part in the defence of Rangoon in Burma. Returning to the US in July 1942 with six air victories to his credit, Boyington rejoined the US Marine Corps. In September 1943 he was appointed Commanding Officer of VMF-214 and led the unit in action until 3 January 1944, when he was shot down and made prisoner of war. During his service with VMF-214 he claimed 22 personal victories, which, when added to his six claimed with the AVG, made him the top-scoring Marine pilot.

Boyington suffered considerable hardships as a prisoner of the Japanese, but he survived to receive the Medal of Honor that he had been awarded on 12 April 1944. Surprisingly, it was the first decoration that this 'superb airman and determined fighter against overwhelming odds' had received from his country, although he was later awarded the Navy Cross. Boyington retired from the Marine Corps after World War II with the rank of colonel.
Left: Major Boyington in the cockpit of his Corsair.

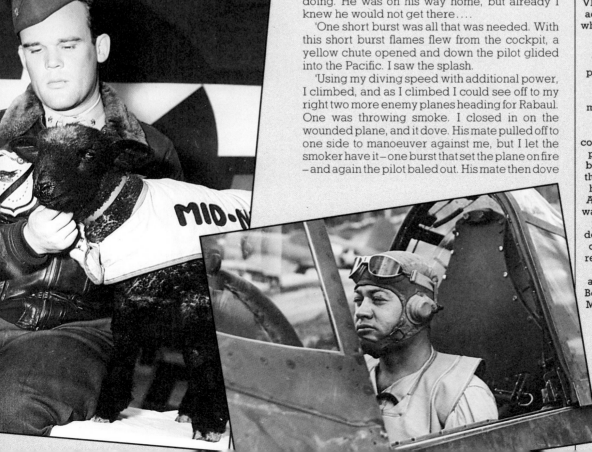

Below: Pilots are briefed by Gregory Boyington. Bottom: Corsairs of VMF-214, one with the squadron's insignia clearly visible, muster for a strike at an airbase on Okinawa during the closing stages of the war with Japan.

in from above and to the side upon my own tail to get me, but it was simple to nose down and dive away....'

Between 17 December 1943 and 1 January 1944 a total of 147 Japanese aircraft were claimed as shot down over Rabaul. Japanese records indicate that the actual losses were probably 64 aircraft, but nonetheless the Solomons-based fighters had gained a significant victory. Boyington's tactical leadership had been vindicated, but he found himself under considerable pressure. His kills on 23 December had raised his score to 24 victories, just two below the total of Major Joseph Foss, the leading Marine ace. On 27 December Boyington scored his 25th victory and on 3 January two VMF-214 pilots reported witnessing his 26th kill over Rabaul. However, their commanding officer and his wingman, Captain George Ashmun, failed to return from that mission. After the war, Boyington was repatriated from a PoW camp in Japan and was able to report a further two victories gained on 3 January making him the top-scoring Marine Corps ace.

VMF-214's combat tour in the Solomons ended five days after Boyington was lost. The squadron then returned to the United States for carrier training and re-entered combat in March 1945, embarked aboard the USS *Franklin* off the coast of Japan. Its CO was Major Bailey, Boyington's former executive officer, but the other pilots were, in Robert Sherrod's words, 'new sheep, barely sooty'. In the event their combat tour was to last for only two days, as on 19 March *Franklin* was bombed and so badly damaged that she was barely able to limp back to port. The Black Sheep ended World War II as the seventh-highest scoring Marine fighter squadron with 127 victories, all but 30 of which had been gained during Boyington's period of command. In August 1950 VMF-214, still flying Corsairs, was one of the first Marine Corps squadrons to see action in the Korean War. By the mid-1960s when the unit's Douglas A-4 Skyhawks were committed to the Vietnam War, the Black Sheep had been redesignated a Marine attack squadron (VMA) and the unit today continues in that role, operating the A-4M version of the Skyhawk.

THE AUTHOR Anthony Robinson was formerly on the staff of the RAF Museum, Hendon and is now a freelance military aviation writer. He has edited the books *Aerial Warfare* and the *Dictionary of Aviation*.

HITLER'S JETS

KAMPF-GESCHWADER 76

The origins of Kampfgeschwader 76 (KG 76) date back to April 1935, when the three Gruppen of Kampfgeschwader 155 were established at Giebelstadt, Ansbach and Schwäbisch Hall in southern Germany and equipped with Dornier 17s. In May 1939 the unit, established at 94 bombers, was redesignated Kampfgeschwader 76.

KG 76 took part in the campaigns in Poland, and during the Battle of Britain its three Gruppen, one equipped with Junkers 88s and two with Do 17s, took part in several major attacks and suffered heavy losses in both aircraft and crews. Following the end of the large-scale daylight battles, KG 76 took part in the night Blitz on targets in the British Isles.

By the time of the German invasion of the Soviet Union in June 1941, all three Gruppen had re-equipped with Ju 88s and they were heavily committed from the outset, suffering further heavy losses during that long and gruelling campaign. During 1942 and 1943, the 1st and 2nd Gruppen were in the Mediterranean where, operating from bases on Crete and in Italy, they opposed the Allied landings on Sicily, and Salerno and Anzio on the Italian mainland. At the end of 1943 the 1st Gruppe moved to northern Germany to take part in the 'Baby Blitz' against England early in 1944. On 7 June 1944, the day after the Normandy invasion, all three Gruppen of KG 76 were withdrawn from operations and began re-equipping with the Arado 234 jet bomber. The Geschwader resumed operations in December 1944 and continued flying until the armistice in May 1945, when it surrendered to British ground forces entering Schleswig Holstein.

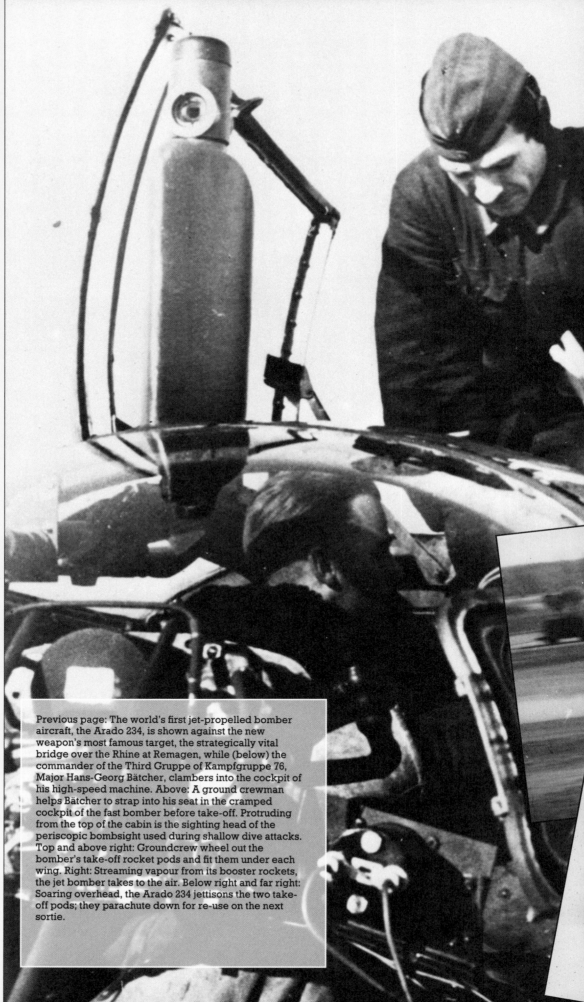

Previous page: The world's first jet-propelled bomber aircraft, the Arado 234, is shown against the new weapon's most famous target, the strategically vital bridge over the Rhine at Remagen, while (below) the commander of the Third Gruppe of Kampfgruppe 76, Major Hans-Georg Bätcher, clambers into the cockpit of his high-speed machine. Above: A ground crewman helps Bätcher to strap into his seat in the cramped cockpit of the fast bomber before take-off. Protruding from the top of the cabin is the sighting head of the periscopic bombsight used during shallow dive attacks. Top and above right: Groundcrew wheel out the bomber's take-off rocket pods and fit them under each wing. Right: Streaming vapour from its booster rockets, the jet bomber takes to the air. Below right and far right: Soaring overhead, the Arado 234 jettisons the two take-off pods; they parachute down for re-use on the next sortie.

In late 1944, a new weapon was seen in the skies over Europe – the world's first jet bomber, flown by the pilots of Kampfgeschwader 76

IN AUGUST 1944, the battle-hardened aircrews of the Third Gruppe of Kampfgeschwader 76 (KG 76), one of the most experienced bomber units in the Luftwaffe, took delivery of the first jet-propelled bomber aircraft in the history of aviation. A few months previously, Germany's revolutionary new jet interceptor, the Messerschmitt Me 262, had begun operational service, and in July Kampfgeschwader 51 had begun flying ground-attack missions over France in modified Me 262s. The weapon now being delivered to the Third Gruppe, however, was custom-made for the high-speed bombing role.

The new bomber was the Arado Ar 234 Blitz (Lightning). In August the Gruppe received three of the aircraft and began working up at the Arado works airfield at Alt Lönnewitz. Aircrew training was provided by KG 76 members who had received conversion training on the Arado at the test establishment at Rechlin, and the groundcrews assisted on the production lines and watched the bombers being readied for flight tests in order to gain first-hand experience of the weapon's new technology.

Reichsmarschall Göring ordered that KG 76 should bring the Arado 234 into action as soon as possible

On 1 September the Third Gruppe (comprising the 7th, 8th and 9th Staffeln) moved to Burg, near Magdeburg, and training continued; by the end of the month the unit possessed seven aircraft. Reichsmarschall Göring ordered that KG 76 should bring the Ar 234 into action as soon as possible, but the need to modify aircraft as they came off the production line slowed deliveries. Therefore, rather than wait for the entire Gruppe to re-equip with the new type, it was decided to concentrate on getting just one of the Staffeln operational as soon as possible. By mid-December 1944, the 9th Staffel had received its full complement of 16 Ar 234s and was declared ready for operations.

There can be no doubting the exceptional quality of the Third Gruppe of Kampfgeschwader 76 at that time. The Gruppe's commander, Major Hans-Georg Bätcher, was one of the most famous German bomber pilots; he held the Knight's Cross with Oakleaves, one of his nation's highest decorations, and had some 650 operational missions to his credit. Hauptmann Diether Lukesch, commander of the 9th Staffel, also held the Knight's Cross with Oakleaves and had flown 372 operational bombing missions. Hauptmann Regler had flown 279 missions; five other pilots on the unit had flown more than 100 missions, no man had flown less than 10 missions and every pilot wore the Iron Cross.

On 17 December the 9th Staffel began moving to its operational base at Handorf near Münster in western Germany, taking 10 jet bombers with full modifications. By 21 December the move was complete and the Staffel prepared to go into action in support of German troops heavily engaged in Hitler's last offensive, the thrust into the Ardennes. During the next two days bad weather prevented operations, but the ground staff of the 9th Staffel put the time to good use by getting all the aircraft ready for action when the weather cleared, and improving the ground organisation and technical services at their new base.

The first operational mission with the new bombers took place on the next day, Christmas Eve. At 1014 hours Lukesch led a nine-aircraft force from Handorf, each bomber carrying a single 1100lb bomb under its fuselage. Their targets were the rail yards and a factory complex at Liège. Once airborne, the bombers climbed to 13,000ft and, with little to fear from enemy fighters so long as they maintained high speed, flew in loose trail without attempting to assemble into formation. Thirty-five minutes after getting airborne the attack began, with aircraft bombing singly in shallow dives and releasing their bombs at altitudes around 6500ft. Afterwards, the pilots levelled out and headed straight back to Handorf without trying to regain altitude. The German pilots observed defensive patrols of Spitfires and Republic P-47 Thunderbolts in the area

of the target, but none made any serious attempt to intercept the jet bombers. As he was pulling away from the target, Lukesch passed close to a Spitfire which chanced to be in his path. The British pilot, who had no way of knowing that the only weapon on board was the German pilot's pistol, turned sharply and dived clear of the Arado. All the jet bombers returned to Handorf and landed safely except for that flown by Unterfeldwebel Winguth, which suffered minor damage when its undercarriage collapsed on landing; the pilot was not injured.

During a similar operation that afternoon, Lukesch led eight Arados to attack the same target, and again all returned safely. That evening the remaining six of the Staffel's Arados arrived from Burg, after modification to bring them to full operational standard.

On the next day, Christmas, the 9th Staffel flew two eight-aircraft operations against Liège. As he was returning from the first mission, Leutnant Alfred Franks came under attack from a Hawker Tempest

Right: Although KG 76 used the Arado 234 primarily as a jet bomber, it was also used in the reconnaissance role. Here, the film magazines are being removed from the rear fuselage after a photo-reconnaissance mission. Below: The Arado hurtles in to land. Below left: Staff officers discuss a mission with Major Bätcher (second from right) and Hauptmann Diether Lukesch (right).

Right: The Arado 234B-2 jet-propelled bomber.

flown by Pilot Officer R. Verran of No.80 Squadron. The British pilot's cannon shells inflicted severe damage to the jet bomber and forced it to crash land in Holland. Returning from the same mission, Oberfeldwebel Dierks' aircraft suffered slight damage on landing. During the afternoon mission Oberleutnant Friedrich Fendrich had a tyre burst on landing and the nose of his aircraft was damaged. In all three cases, however, the pilots escaped without injury.

On 26 December the 9th Staffel mounted two attacks on American troop positions near Bastogne. Operations continued at a similar rate during the days that followed, whenever the weather permitted. Although the jet bombers carried Lotfe tachometric bombsights, which enabled the pilots to aim their bombs during horizontal flight at high altitude, Diether Lukesch did not favour this form of attack and never used it during any operational mission he led. He told the author:

'During such an attack the pilot could not see behind, and there was a continual worry about being surprised by an enemy fighter; a fighter diving from 1000 or 2000m [3250ft or 6500ft] above could easily reach our speed, especially if we were carrying bombs. Also, flying a straight course for so long would have made things easy for the enemy flak. The only justification for the high-altitude attack would have been to get extra range; but the targets we bombed were all close enough to our base for us to reach them flying at medium altitude.'

During the early morning darkness on 1 January 1945 Diether Lukesch led the first-ever jet night-bombing mission – though the bombs were intended to deceive the enemy and any damage they caused was incidental. The force of four aircraft took off from Handorf and climbed to high altitude, then flew a circular route which took them over Rotterdam, Antwerp, Brussels, Liège and back to their base. The pilots' task was to conduct a weather reconnaissance over Belgium and Holland in preparation for Operation Bodenplatte, a massed attack on Allied airfields in both those countries which the Luftwaffe planned to mount at first light. The Arados released bombs in the general areas of Brussels and Liège to conceal the true purpose of their mission.

Later, on the morning of New Year's Day, the remaining Arados of the 9th Staffel played a more normal part in Operation Bodenplatte, when Oberleutnant Artur Stark led six of the jet bombers in an attack on the airfield at Gilze Rijen in Holland, which was being used by the Royal Air Force.

For the rest of January the wintry weather imposed a brake on air operations, and the Staffel was able to

THE ARADO 234

Conceived originally as a single-seat, high-speed jet reconnaissance aircraft, design work on the Arado 234 began in 1941. The prototype made its maiden flight in June 1943, by which time production was well advanced on an initial batch of 20 Arado 234 reconnaissance planes. The new jet immediately caught the eye of Colonel Dieter Peltz, Luftwaffe Inspector of Bombers, and, following his representations, a bomber version was built and ordered into large-scale production at the company's plant at Alt Lönnewitz in Saxony.

The design of the Ar 234 B-2 Blitz featured two 1980lb thrust Jumo 004 jet engines, which gave the aircraft a maximum speed of 461mph when carrying a 1100lb bomb. Armament usually consisted of one 1100lb bomb or cluster-bomb container under the fuselage or two 550lb bombs carried under the engine nacelles. Some of the bombers were fitted with the self-defence armament of two 20mm cannon firing rearwards from fixed mountings in the fuselage. With a normal operational weight of 20,870lb, two booster rockets were employed for take-off.

The jet bomber was kept in production under increasingly difficult circumstances until March 1945 when, after 210 had been built, the approach of Soviet ground units forced the evacuation and destruction of the Arado factories in Saxony.

mount attacks on only four other days after Boden-platte: on the 2nd, against Liège; on the 14th, against Bastogne; on the 20th, against Antwerp; and on the 24th, when Diether Lukesch led a four-aircraft attack which scored hits on port installations at Antwerp.

Meanwhile, the 7th and 8th Staffeln of III KG 76 had been working up for operations with the new jet bomber at Briest near Berlin; in the third week of January these units were declared ready for combat, thus bringing the Third Gruppe to full operational status. On the morning of 23 January, 18 Arados from the 7th and 8th Staffeln left Briest for their operational base at Achmer near Osnabrück. By this stage of the war the all-pervading Allied air supremacy reached to the furthest corners of Germany, a fact demonstrated to the jet-bomber pilots with disconcerting suddenness. As the Arados circled their new base before landing they were pounced on by Spitfires of No. 126 (Canadian) Wing. Pilots from No. 401 and 411 Squadrons later claimed to have shot down three 'Messerschmitt 262s' and inflicted damage on six others, but it is clear that the victims were Arado 234s. German records confirm that three of the jet bombers were shot down and two pilots killed, and two aircraft seriously damaged.

During February 1945 the shortage of fuel throughout the Luftwaffe began to bite, and even though it had top priority, Kampfgeschwader 76 had restrictions placed on its operations. Fewer attacks were flown than before, though with more Arado 234s now available the attacking forces became larger. On 8 February the unit mounted a seven-aircraft attack on targets around Brussels; on the 16th it put in two 16-aircraft attacks on enemy troop positions near Cleve; on the 21st the Gruppe mounted what was to be its greatest number of sorties in a single day: 21 Arados in the morning against British forces advancing in the area near Cleve, followed by a 16-aircraft attack in the afternoon on targets in the same area. The next day the Third Gruppe flew 23 sorties against British troop positions near Aachen.

They found themselves embroiled in a series of high-speed engagements and four bombers were shot down

On 25 February the Gruppe flew another 18 Arado sorties against the British forces near Aachen. A pair of Tempests intercepted one of the jet bombers near the target and inflicted damage, but the Arado returned safely. And on the approach to Achmer a pair of Mustangs from the 364th Fighter Group, USAAF, pounced on another of the jet bombers and shot it down, killing the pilot.

On 7 March American forces breached the last German natural defensive obstacle in the west by capturing the Ludendorff bridge over the Rhine at Remagen. Göring designated the bridge a target of the highest priority, but for a week, air attacks on the bridge were hindered by low cloud, and attempts by KG 76 resulted in little effective damage. On 14 March, however, the cloud gave way to blue skies – which were promptly filled by Allied fighters patroll-

ing the areas around Achmer and Remagen. When 11 Arados attempted to attack the bridge they found themselves embroiled in a series of high-speed engagements and four bombers were shot down. The bridge finally collapsed 10 days after its capture, but by then the Allied bridgehead on the east bank of the Rhine was well established and nothing could prevent the flow of traffic eastwards.

Following the attacks on Remagen, the Third Gruppe resumed its normal attacks on enemy troop positions and vehicles whenever the weather permitted. But now, with Allied ground forces advancing into Germany from both the east and the west, the remaining Luftwaffe flying units had to move frequently to avoid being overrun, and they found themselves being squeezed into the narrowing strips of land that remained under German control. Early in April the Gruppe moved to Kaltenkirchen near Hamburg, and continued operating from there.

The unit mounted several attacks in support of German forces fighting desperately to defend the capital

When the Allies identified the bases being used by German jet aircraft, those bases under attack from the air, and on 7 April that fate overtook the airfield at Kaltenkirchen. A force of 143 B-17s of the US Eighth Army Air Force bombed the airfield and caused extensive cratering. Repairs were begun immediately, however, and within two days the airfield was back in use and the Arados resumed operations.

On 20 April – ironically Adolf Hitler's birthday – there came yet another clear pointer to the pilots of KG 76 that the collapse of German military power was imminent. On that day the unit received orders to attack Soviet troops south of Berlin: the Arado 234s at Kaltenkirchen were now within striking distance of enemy forces moving forward on both the eastern and western fronts. During the days that followed, the unit mounted several attacks in support of German forces fighting desperately to defend the capital. The last recorded operation by KG 76 was on the afternoon of 3 May, when Feldwebel Drews of the 8th Staffel attacked troops near Bremerhaven.

When the ceasefire was announced on 8 May, the surviving jet bombers of Kampfgeschwader 76 were on the airfields at Schleswig, Leck and Hennstedt in Schleswig Holstein. Under the terms of the armistice the aircraft were grounded, and on the following day the unit formally surrendered itself to British troops moving into the area. The Geschwader's history as one of the finest units in the Luftwaffe was at an end.

During its time with the Arado 234 the Third Gruppe of Kampfgeschwader 76 had some of the best bomber pilots in the Luftwaffe and it was equipped with the most advanced bomber type in the world. Yet even on its most active day the Gruppe mounted only 37 jet-bomber sorties and delivered about 18 tons of bombs on designated targets; by that stage of the war the huge American and British forces of strategic and tactical bombers were delivering more than 20 times that tonnage against each of the 10 or more targets they attacked each day. Against that background, there was nothing the small force of German jet bombers could do to reverse the already established course of the war.

Left: Overrun by the US Third Army in April 1945, the airfield at Manching in Bavaria yields a haul of battle-scarred Luftwaffe aircraft, including two Junkers 88s, a Bücker 181D Bestmann trainer, and an Arado 234B. Left above: The jet bomber's technology was of great interest to the Allies: here, a captured Ar 234 in RAF markings is evaluated.

THE AUTHOR Alfred Price served as an aircrew officer in the RAF for 15 years, specialising in aircraft weapons and tactics. He has written extensively on aerial warfare.

Above: The badge of
No. 616 Squadron.

THE RAF'S FIRST JET SQUADRON

No. 616 (South Yorkshire) Squadron of the Auxiliary Air Force was formed in Doncaster on 1 November 1938, as a bomber unit flying Hawker Hinds. In October 1939, now re-designated a fighter squadron, the unit moved to Leconfield, Yorkshire, where it re-equipped with Spitfire Mk 1s. Operating from airfields in Norfolk and London, No. 616 entered action in 1940 and distinguished itself during the Battle of Britain, destroying 30 enemy aircraft.

In 1942, flying from Kirton, Lincolnshire, No. 616 flew the high-altitude Spitfire Mk VI in defensive patrols against enemy reconnaissance aircraft. In September 1943 the squadron received Mk VIIs and continued in its high-altitude interception role. In 1944, operating from Culmhead, Somerset, the squadron switched to escort duties, its Spitfires accompanying British bombers that were attacking communications in France and the Low Countries as part of the bombing programme leading up to D-day.

In July 1944 No. 616 Squadron moved to Manston, Kent, to concentrate on developing the Royal Air Force's first jet fighter – the Gloster Meteor F.Mk 1. In January 1945 the squadron moved to Colerne, Wiltshire, with a detachment based at Melsbroek, Brussels. The squadron was disbanded on 29 August 1945 at Lübeck, in northern Germany.

It reformed as the South Yorkshire Squadron in July 1946, flying Meteor F. Mk 3s and later Mk 8s. The squadron was finally disbanded at Finningley in 1957.

When swarms of V-1 flying bombs appeared over England, Hitler's newest weapon was met by the Meteor pilots of No.616 Squadron

FLIGHT OF THE METEOR

When swarms of V-1 flying bombs appeared over England, Hitler's newest weapon was met by the Meteor pilots of No.616 Squadron

ON 6 JUNE 1944, Allied forces went ashore in Normandy in the greatest amphibious operation in the history of warfare. Overhead, British and American fighter squadrons maintained constant patrols over the beachheads, ensuring complete Allied air supremacy. Two years earlier, when Allied forces had made their disastrous landings at Dieppe on 19 August 1942, it had been a different story – the Luftwaffe had been airborne in strength, and whirling dogfights had spread out across the Channel. But now, as the Allies consolidated their bridgehead, their combined air forces were the unrivalled masters of the sky.

As they patrolled the Normandy beachheads in their Spitfires, the pilots of No. 616 Squadron were unaware of the revolutionary role they were soon to play against Germany's newest weapon – the V-1 flying bomb. Earlier that year, the squadron had escorted Allied medium bombers engaged in a series of attacks on V-1 bomb sites along the Pas de Calais. The Germans planned to launch a massive

V-1 offensive – codenamed Operation Rumpelkammer – once production had reached a certain level, and the carefully camouflaged flying-bomb sites were therefore kept under constant air attack.

However, the first V-1 was launched against London on the night of 12 June 1944, and it was soon apparent that this deadly offensive could not be curtailed until the missile sites were overrun by Allied ground forces. With the latter still fighting hard to retain their foothold in Normandy, it would be several weeks before this objective could be achieved.

Since the spring of 1944, the officers' mess of No. 616 Squadron had been full of rumours that the unit was to be re-equipped, yet most of the pilots believed that their new charges would be Spitfire Mk XIVs. In June, this belief was strengthened when two of these aircraft flew into No. 616's base at Culmhead, Somerset. A few days later, there was fresh speculation when Squadron Leader Andrew McDowall, together with five of the unit's pilots, was sent on detachment to Farnborough. Not until McDowall and his colleagues arrived did they learn what awaited them – a conversion course to Gloster Meteor F.Mk 1 fighters, the first jet aircraft allocated to the Royal Air Force (RAF). Once the six officers had become accustomed to not having a propeller in front of them, the Meteor proved a delightful aircraft to fly. Indeed, on arrival back at Culmhead in early July, they were so enthusiastic about the virtues of the new fighter that their eagerness for re-equipment quickly spread throughout the squadron.

No. 616 Squadron's first Meteor, EE219, arrived at Culmhead on 12 July 1944 – the German V-1 offensive against Britain began in earnest that same day. During the next two weeks a further 11 Meteors were flown in from Farnborough and the task of converting the squadron's pilots onto the radical new aircraft continued. Without exception, the pilots echoed McDowall's praise of the jet fighter.

On 21 July the squadron's Spitfires, accompanied by two Meteors, flew to Manston airfield, Kent, where they were joined two days later by five more of the jet aircraft. The pilots of the RAF's first jet flight were the newly-promoted Wing Commander McDowall, Wing Commander Wilson, Squadron Leader Watts, Flying Officer Roger, Flying Officer McKenzie, Flying Officer Clark, Flying Officer Dean and Warrant Officer Wilkes.

On 27 July, No. 616 was ordered to carry out its first 'diver' patrol – the codename for sorties against the V-1 flying bomb. However, the week that followed was full of frustration and disappointment, with none of the pilots sighting any enemy missiles. In order to increase the time on patrol, it was decided to decrease the distance between the squadron base and the approach path of the flying bomb by moving the Meteors to a dispersal aerodrome near Ashford, in Kent.

The first real break came on the evening of 4 August, when Flying Officer Dean sighted a V-1 only minutes after taking off from Ashford. The enemy

In February 1941 No. 616 Squadron joined the Tangmere Wing, commanded by Wing Commander Douglas Bader (far left bottom). The sqaudron immediately went onto the offensive, flying Spitfires in fighter sweeps and bomber escort flights over northern France. However, the development of the Gloster Meteor (left) transformed No. 616's combat duties. The V-1 flying bomb (far left) cruised across the channel at 585 miles per hour – beyond the reach of most Allied fighters – and the squadron was therefore assigned 'diver' patrols to counter this new and formidable threat.

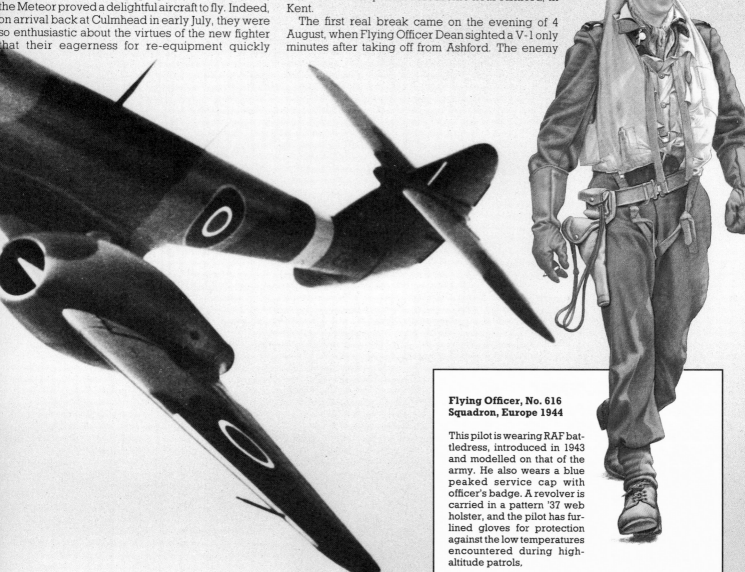

Flying Officer, No. 616 Squadron, Europe 1944

This pilot is wearing RAF battledress, introduced in 1943 and modelled on that of the army. He also wears a blue peaked service cap with officer's badge. A revolver is carried in a pattern '37 web holster, and the pilot has fur-lined gloves for protection against the low temperatures encountered during high-altitude patrols,

aircraft was some distance ahead and a few thousand feet lower down, and Dean eased his Meteor over into a gentle dive. As the speed built up to more than 385 miles per hour, the distance between the two aircraft narrowed swiftly. Dean soon recognised the unmistakeable silhouette of the flying bomb – the fat fuselage with its nose packed with a ton of high explosive, the short stubby wings and the long, pulse jet engine exuding spurts of flame from its exhaust. Dean curved in behind the V-1 until its orange jet exhaust was lined up squarely in his sights, and then gently throttled back. He had read the combat reports of Spitfire and Tempest pilots who had almost been destroyed by the enormous explosive power of the V-1 when their cannon shells had touched off the missile's warhead.

Dean pressed the firing button. A short burst of shells roared out from the Meteor's cannon and then the guns jammed. The flying bomb streaked on, apparently undamaged. Determined not to let his enemy escape, Dean throttled forward and brought his aircraft alongside the flying bomb. Racing over the countryside at 385 miles per hour, Dean and his adversary were only five minutes' flying-time from London. The Meteor pilot knew that he had to act now – while the bomb was still over open country. A sudden flash of inspiration decided Dean on his course of action, and, juggling with the controls, he edged his aircraft closer to the speeding bomb. With infinite care and ice-cool nerves, he slid his wing tip

As the only Allied jet aircraft to reach combat status during the war, the Meteor (below) was assured of a place in aviation history. The pilots of No. 616 quickly mastered their new charges, increasing their flight endurance to 90 minutes by the end of August 1944. In addition, the Meteor's engines proved very reliable. It was estimated that the squadron's groundcrew (below right) halved the maintenance time that had previously been required on the Spitfire's single Griffon engine. Bottom left: Wing Commander Andrew McDowall, who commanded No. 616 Squadron from July 1944 to May 1945.

under that of the V-1 and slowly pushed the control column over to the left. The Meteor shuddered violently as the two wing tips made contact. Dean tensed, half expecting the shock to detonate the bomb. Instead, the V-1's wing lifted higher and higher until the bomb flicked over sharply onto its back and dived earthwards. Dean watched his adversary as it hurtled down, pulse jet still going flat out. Seconds later it exploded harmlessly in open country.

Soaked in sweat, Dean set course for base. He had become the first British jet pilot to destroy an enemy aircraft and the Meteor, which was to remain the backbone of Royal Air Force Fighter Command for more than 10 years, had been blooded in combat. On landing back at Ashford, Dean learned that another pilot, Flying Officer J.K. Roger, had also attacked and destroyed a flying bomb minutes after his own

victory. Roger's cannon had worked satisfactorily, and the V-1 had dived into the ground and exploded near Tenterton.

Following these early successes, the frequency of the diver patrols was stepped up considerably. Using a relay system, the squadron had two Meteors airborne throughout the day, flying patrols of 30 minutes duration. By 10 August, Dean had destroyed two more V-1s, completing his hat-trick, and the squadron's score mounted steadily. The most fruitful days were 16 and 17 August, when the Meteor pilots destroyed five flying bombs. On 31 August, when the V-1 sites were finally overrun, the squadron's score stood at 13 destroyed. Although this was only a fraction of the number of missiles destroyed by the British air defences, it nevertheless demonstrated the Meteor's capability in action against small high-speed targets.

For the remainder of 1944, No. 616 Squadron participated in air exercises jointly co-ordinated by the RAF and the United States Army Air Force (USAAF). Their objective was to develop new defensive tactics against the German Messerschmitt 262 jet fighters that were attacking Allied bomber formations over Europe. These enemy fighters had a speed advantage of 100 miles per hour over the Spitfires, Mustangs and Thunderbolts of the Allies and, unless a new set of tactics could be devised, they would present a serious threat to Allied air supremacy over Western Europe.

In October, to provide the American pilots with

GLOSTER METEOR

In late 1939, the Ministry of Supply initiated the 'Rampage' programme, with the intention of introducing a jet-propelled single-seat day fighter into service within three years. Design began in January 1940, with the DG206/G prototype making its first flight at Cranwell, Lincolnshire, on 5 March 1943. The F.Mk 1 was armed with four 20mm Hispano cannon in the nose, and was powered by two Rolls-Royce/Welland engines developing a 1700lb-thrust. Maximum speed of the Mk I was 415 miles per hour, and the aircraft had a service ceiling of 40,000ft.

The second, and final, variant of the Meteor to see service in World War II was the F.Mk 3 (bottom left). This had a larger fuel capacity and improved performance. Two late production models of the Mk 3 were used for low-altitude speed trials, and, on 7 November 1945, one of these established a new world record speed of 606 miles per hour. The last 195 Mk 3s were powered by the 3500lb-thrust Derwent 5 engine. The Derwent 5, when combined with a strengthened airframe led to the Meteor Mk 4, with improved take-off and landing speeds. The Meteor Mk 4 saw service with many air forces, including the Belgian, Danish, Egyptian and French.

The Meteor Mk 5 was a reconnaissance fighter, fitted with a nose camera and two vertical cameras located aft of the fuselage fuel tank.

The most prolific variant of the Gloster Meteor was the F.Mk 8, with a lengthened fuselage and re-designed tail unit. Extra equipment included a gyro gunsight and a Martin-Baker ejector seat. Fifteen variants of the Meteor were built, and the last operational sortie by an RAF Meteor was flown by an NF.Mk 14 night-fighter at Tengah, Singapore, in September 1961. Total Meteor production was 3875 aircraft.

EE 234

Right: Flight-Lieutenant Leslie Watts, photographed here before his promotion to the rank of squadron leader. Watts flew Spitfires with No. 616 Squadron until 1944, and the courage, skill and tenacity he exhibited were recognised by the award of the Distinguished Flying Cross Watts was among the first of the squadron's pilots to receive conversion training on the Meteor and, after years of flying tailwheel aircraft, the only real problem lay in accustoming the pilots to the jet's tricycle undercarriage.

Below right: Groundcrew refuel a Meteor jet fighter in preparation for action. The establishment of a Meteor flight at Manston airfield was carried out in conditions of strict secrecy, with a tight security cordon being thrown around the airfield. Far right: Pilots from No. 616 Squadron take time off to pose for a group picture beneath a mock signpost.

some experience in action against jet fighters, a programme of air exercises was scheduled for the 10th to the 17th, with four Meteors pitted against elements from the Eighth Army Air Force's 65th Fighter Wing and 2nd Bombardment Division. Commanding the detachment from No. 616 Squadron was Wing Commander McDowall, who arrived at Debden, south of Cambridge, on 8 October in order to work out the details of the programme with Brigadier-General Jesse Orton, the commanding officer of the 2nd Bombardment Division. The three other Meteor pilots in McDowall's detachment arrived at Debden the following day. On 10 October a formation of 120 B-24 Liberators and B-17 Flying Fortresses of the 2nd Bombardment Division took off from their respective bases in East Anglia. Making rendezvous with their fighter escort of P-47 Thunderbolts and P-51 Mustangs 9000ft over Peterborough, the formation set out in four tight boxes over the exercise route – flying from Peterborough to Colchester, back to Peterborough, and finally turning northwest towards East Anglia.

During the flight, the Meteors made a series of high-speed 'attacks', closing in from various angles and passing through the formation before the fighter escorts had time to react. These hit-and-run tactics paralleled those employed by the Messerschmitt 262 pilots and proved extremely effective. The only way to catch the fleeting jets was to step up the fighter escort at least 5000ft above the bombers, enabling the Mustang and Thunderbolt pilots to build up speed by diving in pursuit of the Meteors. Although this method required split-second timing, by the end of the week the American fighter pilots were achieving an increasing percentage of successful passes.

On 18 December 1944, No. 616 Squadron received its first two Meteor F.Mk 3s, EE231 and EE232, with three more arriving during the course of the next month. In January 1945, following a move to Colerne in Wiltshire, the squadron exchanged all its remaining Mk 1s for F.Mk 3s. Also in January, a flight of No. 616's Meteors flew to Belgium to join No. 84 Group of the RAF 2nd Tactical Air Force based at Melsbroek, near Brussels.

The pilots of the Meteor flight had viewed their move to the continent as an indication that they were soon to see action in a defensive capacity against Me 262s. However, they were to be sadly disappointed and the next few weeks were remarkable only for their lack of activity. Due to the risk of the Meteors falling into enemy hands, pilots were given strict instructions not to fly over enemy territory. Instead, they were assigned to fly standing patrols over Nijmegen and other Allied air bases in the vicinity. In an attempt to vary the monotony of this routine, the pilots set themselves a number of unofficial competitions to see, for example, which of them could record the fastest scramble time or climb to altitude.

Throttling forward into the attack, Cooper executed a single firing pass

The remainder of No. 616 Squadron arrived in Belgium on 31 March, and early in April the Air Ministry authorised the jet fighters to undertake a more offensive role. Although the Meteors made a number of short forays into enemy territory, they failed to make contact with the Luftwaffe and it was decided to employ them on armed reconnaissance and ground-attack missions. On 17 April, Flight-Lieutenant Cooper became the first Meteor pilot to fire his guns in anger over enemy territory when, during an armed reconnaissance patrol, he sighted a large enemy truck near Ijmuiden. Throttling forward into the attack, Cooper executed a single firing pass that sent the vehicle careering off the road, bursting into flames seconds later.

Meanwhile, a second Meteor squadron had formed in the United Kingdom. This was No. 504 (County of Nottingham) Squadron Auxiliary Air Force, and, after a short working-up period on the new aircraft, it was declared operational and sent to the continent in July 1945.

For No. 616 Squadron, the last weeks of the war in Europe were marked by feverish activity. The squadron moved from airfield to airfield in the wake of the Allied advance, carrying out its reconnaissance and attack sorties under considerable enemy pressure. On 24 April, Wing Commander McDowall led a formation of four Meteors on a daring attack on an enemy airfield at Nordholz, in western Germany. Diving out of the sun from 8000ft, McDowall destroyed a Junkers 88 on the ground during a single firing pass, and sent several cannon shells rocketing through another vehicle. Flying Officer Wilson attacked two petrol bowsers, setting them on fire,

The pioneering work of the Meteor continued after the end of the war. On 7 September 1946 Group Captain E.M. Donaldson of the RAF High Speed Flight used a Mk 4 to set a new world speed record of 616mph. But, by the end of 1947, the Meteor was outdated compared with other Allied fighters such as the United States Air Force's Lockheed P-80 Shooting Star; cuts in the aeronautical research budged had preventd the RAF from developing a successor to the Meteor. To compensate for this, the Mk 8 was introduced in 1949. Although Gloster produced a variant of the Mk 8 designed for ground-attack, the RAF assigned the Meteor an air-combat role, and it continued to serve in this capacity until replaced by the Hawker Hunter in 1954. Although the Meteor Mk 8 (below) was no longer a front-line fighter, it continued to do valuable work for the RAF in a subsidiary role. The last Meteor was delivered to the RAF on 26 May 1954, and during the last 1950s many were converted for the target towing task.

and raked airfield installations with his remaining shells. Flying Officer Moon strafed a dozen railway trucks on the airfield perimeter and destroyed an anti-aircraft post. The fourth pilot, Flying Officer Clegg, attacked a large vehicle full of German troops who, astonishingly, waved and cheered as the Meteor bore down on them – no doubt mistaking it for a Messerschmitt 262. They were still waving when Clegg opened fire.

Up until this time, the squadron had suffered no casualties while flying Meteors. It was an unblemished record that remained intact until 29 April, when two Meteors, flown by Squadron Leader Watts and Flight Sergeant Cartmell, took off on an offensive patrol. The aircraft entered cloud in close formation, and minutes later Allied troops on the ground witnessed a large explosion followed by debris fluttering down from the skies. Neither Watts nor Cartmell were seen again.

Although the Meteor pilots still hoped for an opportunity to test their aircraft in combat against the cream of the Luftwaffe's fighters, it was clear by the beginning of May that their wishes would remain unfulfilled. Coming at the end of a week of intensive ground-attack mission tasking, 4 May 1945 was destined to be the squadron's final day of operations. During the day's activity, the pilots destroyed one enemy locomotive and damaged another, knocked out 10 vehicles and two half-tracks, in addition to strafing a number of installations. At 1700 hours, the squadron received a signal that all offensive operations over Germany were to be suspended. Four days later came the unconditional surrender of Germany.

Disappointed as they were at not having been able to engage the Luftwafe in combat, the ground-attack missions of No. 616 Squadron had set the pattern for future Meteor operations in combat. Six years later the Meteor, flown by the pilots of No. 77 Squadron, Royal Australian Air Force, was once again to prove its worth as a ground-attack aircraft – this time against a different enemy in Korea.

THE AUTHOR Robert Jackson is a freelance aviation writer who has contributed a number of articles to military publications. He is the author of the book *The Royal Air Force in Action*.

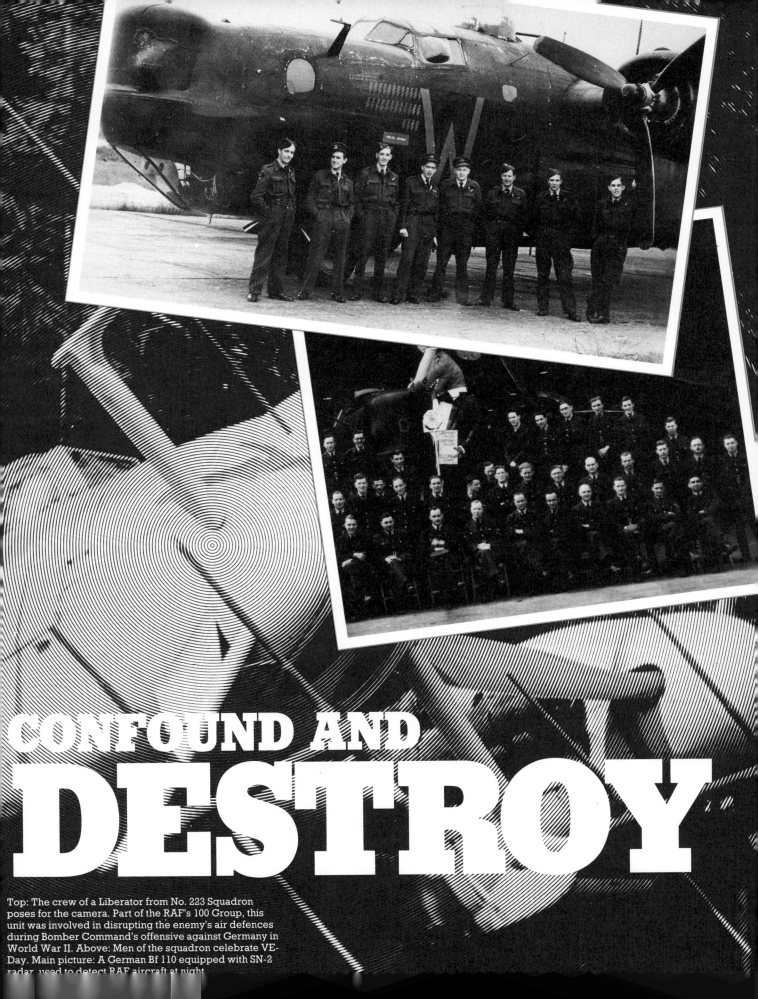

CONFOUND AND DESTROY

Top: The crew of a Liberator from No. 223 Squadron poses for the camera. Part of the RAF's 100 Group, this unit was involved in disrupting the enemy's air defences during Bomber Command's offensive against Germany in World War II. Above: Men of the squadron celebrate VE-Day. Main picture: A German Bf 110 equipped with SN-2 radar, used to detect RAF aircraft at night.

NO.100 (BOMBER SUPPORT) GROUP

Although the RAF had been aware of the importance of disrupting the enemy's air defence network since the early stages of World War II, it was not until 1943 that specific plans for the creation of an electronic counter-measures force, capable of 'spoofing' the Luftwaffe's nightfighters and radar, were discussed. The new formation, known as No.100 Group, was formally established on 8 November 1943 and an officer experienced in electronic warfare, Air Vice-Marshal E.B. Addison, was appointed to its command.

Over the following months Addison set about establishing his headquarters at Bylaugh Hall in Norfolk. It was not until the early summer of 1944, however, that 100 Group became fully operational.

Its jamming force comprised four squadrons of heavy bombers: No.171 with Halifaxes; No.199 with Stirlings and later, Halifaxes; No.214 with B-17 Flying Fortresses; No.223 with Liberators. Another unit, No.192 Squadron, flying Halifaxes, Wellingtons and Mosquitoes fitted with special receiving equipment, provided electronic intelligence support. The group's fighter force consisted of seven squadrons: Nos. 23, 85, 141, 157, 169, 239 and 515, all flying Mosquitoes.

Most of 100 Group's war effort was directed against the enemy's industrial centres. Its jamming, spoofing and intruding activities lasted until the end of the war. The group, however, did not survive for long, and in December 1945 it was officially disbanded. Above: 100 Group's badge.

The RAF's 100 Group played a deadly game of cat-and-mouse with the German anti-aircraft defences of the Third Reich

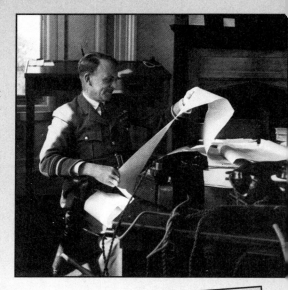

ON A PITCH-BLACK night in March 1945, Sergeant Kenneth Stone and the other crew members of a Liberator belonging to the RAF's No.223 Squadron, walked across the runway of Oulton airfield in Norfolk to board their aircraft. Ahead lay a strength-sapping flight into the heart of Hitler's Third Reich; it was a journey which was likely to bring them face to face with the cream of the Luftwaffe's nightfighter force.

The Liberator, however, did not carry bombs, but a host of electronic counter-measures which had been specifically designed to confuse the men who ran the German air-defence network. Stone's unit was one of four squadrons of bombers in No.100 Group which had been activated to protect Bomber Command's aircraft during their campaign against

the enemy's war industries. Missions were always fraught with danger: the group's aircraft often flew in advance of the main bomber formations and had to face the full force of the Luftwaffe's defences. Inevitably, this type of work called for a special type of man, an individualist able to operate sophisticated jamming equipment.

Although No.100 Group's successes in World War II owed much to the quality of its aircrews and the elegance of its electronic equipment, the outcome of a particular raid depended on its aircraft meeting the needs of Bomber Command. One of the finest examples of co-operation took place on 20/21 March 1945, when 100 Group supported two raids against vital industrial targets deep inside German territory: a force of 235 heavy bombers attacked the synthetic-oil refineries at Bohlen near Leipzig, and another formation struck at the refineries at Hemmingstedt near Hamburg. No.100 Group's counter-measures were used to deceive the German nightfighters as to the strength, direction and targets of the RAF's bombers.

Bomber Command's first action of that night, however, was a large-scale 'nuisance raid' on Berlin by 35 Mosquitoes of its Pathfinder force, launched at 1714 hours. As this raid was taking place, Mosquitoes from Nos.23 and 515 Squadrons fanned out over

Left: 100 Group's commander, Air Vice-Marshal Addison, in his office at Bylaugh Hall. Left centre: A B-17G of No. 214 Squadron equipped with Jostle IV, used to jam the enemy fighters' control frequencies. Left bottom: A Jostle IV transmitter in the bomb-bay of a B-17. An improvement on earlier jamming systems, it was introduced into service in mid-1944. Below: An ABC (Airborne Cigar) set inside a B-17. ABC was designed to interfere with transmissions between Luftwaffe ground stations and nightfighters. Bottom: Rear view of a B-17 showing antennae for 'Monica', used to warn the crew of a rear attack, and ABC.

Germany, making for the enemy's nightfighter bases. Once in position, they circled overhead, ready to pounce on any aircraft taking off or coming in to land.

Just after 0100 hours on the 21st, the main force heading for Bohlen crossed the French coast and headed southeast, keeping over Allied-held territory for as long as possible. At this juncture, another force, consisting of 64 Lancasters and Halifaxes flown by trainee crews, split off and headed towards the German border near Strasbourg to carry out a diversionary attack.

From a line just inside Allied territory, seven pairs of Halifaxes began jamming with Mandrel

No.100 Group's electronic trickery was brought into play a few moments later: from a line 80 miles long, just inside Allied territory, seven pairs of Halifaxes from Nos.171 and 199 Squadrons began jamming with Mandrel, a device used to screen the approach of the RAF's bombers from the enemy's ground radar. Behind the wall of jamming, the Bohlen attack force split into two groups: 41 Lancasters headed off to the northeast, as the main force continued on a more direct route to the target.

Meanwhile, flying south of the Mandrel screen and outside its cover, the trainee bomber crews continued their deceptive raid towards the German border in full view of the defences. Their ruse was an unqualified success: German nightfighters were moving into position to meet their threatened incursion when, at 0255, they turned round and headed for home.

A few minutes later, the two Bohlen attack forces, flying well to the north, burst through the Mandrel jamming screen and crossed into German territory. Twenty miles ahead, elements of No.100 Group continued their deceptions: four Halifaxes of No.171 Squadron and seven Liberators from No.223 Squadron dropped a dense cloud of Window to conceal the full strength of the attacking bombers. Sergeant Stone of No.223 Squadron, remembered what it was like to fly on Window and Target Support operations:

'Window spoof raids were carried out by a few aircraft dropping metalised foil to simulate a large force of aircraft on the enemy radar. The operation was very precisely worked out; there would be a rendezvous point in a safe area and timing was critical to within two minutes. If a crew arrived later than this it had to abort the mission because one aircraft was a sure give-away on radar. All aircraft had to go in together and

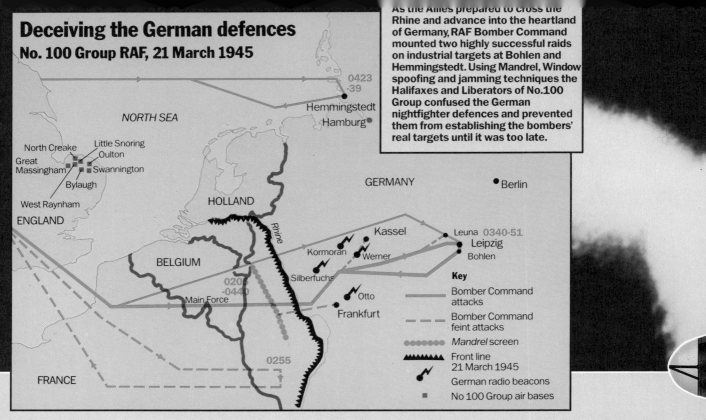

Deceiving the German defences
No. 100 Group RAF, 21 March 1945

NORTH SEA

0423 -39
Hemmingstedt
Hamburg

North Creake
Little Snoring
Oulton
Great Massingham
Swannington
Bylaugh
West Raynham

ENGLAND
HOLLAND

BELGIUM

Rhine

Main Force
0205 -0440

FRANCE

0255

GERMANY
Berlin

Kassel
Kormoran
Werner
Silberfuchs
Leuna 0340-51
Leipzig
Bohlen

Otto
Frankfurt

Key
━━━ Bomber Command attacks
╍╍╍ Bomber Command feint attacks
•••• *Mandrel* screen
▲▲▲ Front line 21 March 1945
⚡ German radio beacons
■ No 100 Group air bases

As the Allies prepared to cross the Rhine and advance into the heartland of Germany, RAF Bomber Command mounted two highly successful raids on industrial targets at Bohlen and Hemmingstedt. Using Mandrel, Window spoofing and jamming techniques the Halifaxes and Liberators of No.100 Group confused the German nightfighter defences and prevented them from establishing the bombers' real targets until it was too late.

SPOOFING

No.100 Group was created to launch a two-pronged attack on the Luftwaffe's air defence system: first, by jamming or 'spoofing' the enemy's radio and radar systems to make it difficult for their nightfighters to attack the RAF's bombers and, secondly, to despatch nightfighters to seek out and destroy their German counterparts. It was in recognition of these dual roles that 100 Group received its official motto: 'Confound and Destroy'.

When the group became operational in the summer of 1944, its jamming force consisted of heavy bombers fitted with a menagerie of recently developed electronic equipment: 'Mandrel' and 'Carpet' to jam German ground radars; 'Piperack' to jam nightfighter radars; 'Jostle' to put out a raucous wail on the enemy's fighter radio channels; and 'Window' to create hundreds of fake targets to distract the defenders.

Mandrel blotted out the enemy's early-warning radar system by 'noise jamming'. The screen usually involved between 10 and 16 bombers orbiting in pairs at 15-mile intervals along a line just clear of enemy territory. Each aircraft radiated electronic jamming from several Mandrel sets with the aim of blotting out a wide section of the enemy's radar system to conceal the movement of bomber formations flying behind the screen. In some cases where no raid was planned, a Mandrel screen was activated to force German nightfighters into the air and waste their limited reserves of fuel.

Although Mandrel was effective in the short term, it could only operate within a narrow waveband and, when the Luftwaffe began to

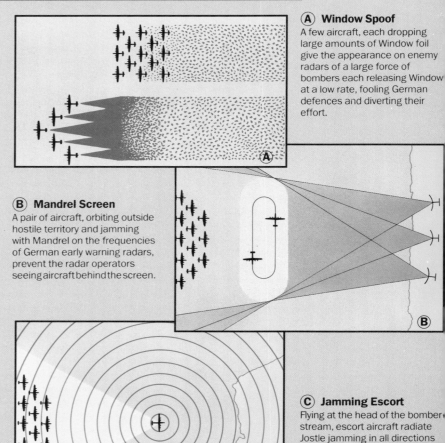

A Window Spoof
A few aircraft, each dropping large amounts of Window foil give the appearance on enemy radars of a large force of bombers each releasing Window at a low rate, fooling German defences and diverting their effort.

B Mandrel Screen
A pair of aircraft, orbiting outside hostile territory and jamming with Mandrel on the frequencies of German early warning radars, prevent the radar operators seeing aircraft behind the screen.

C Jamming Escort
Flying at the head of the bomber stream, escort aircraft radiate Jostle jamming in all directions on the enemy fighter control radio channels, and Piperack jamming rearwards on the enemy night fighter radar frequencies.

dispense Window at a regular pace. The aircraft flew a "corkscrew" course to disperse the Window more effectively and give an illusion of a larger force than was actually present. Generally six spoofers would be shown up on radar as 300+ plots. A spoof target was generally selected which either committed the defences in that area and left the genuine target free, or at worst split the defences and rendered a proportion of them useless. There were two methods of ending this type of spoof. Either we continued to the spoof target and dropped target markers there; or we stopped Windowing short of the target and dived away at a great rate of knots.

'The target support operations were of the "diciest" for the bomber support aircraft, and were therefore shared out amongst the crews in rotation. The general principle was to cover the

Left: One of the Luftwaffe's Bf 110 nightfighters explodes in a blinding flash after being hit by fire from one of No. 100 Group's Mosquitoes. Below: A Halifax bomber fitted with ABC antennae.

work with radars able to use a greater range of frequencies, its value was diminished. Enemy nightfighters were also able to home in on Mandrel transmissions by using their own radar, forcing 100 Group to restrict its use to a two-minute burst every two minutes.

Carpet was used in a target support role. When bombers reached their target, 100 Group's aircraft orbited over the defences and jammed the frequencies of the Luftwaffe's flak-control radars.

To cover RAF formations on their way to and from their targets, the Group's Fortresses, Liberators and Halifaxes flew with the bombers radiating Jostle and Piperack jamming. Jostle plotted out the frequencies used by the enemy's ground stations to communicate with their nightfighters. Weighing 600lb, it was the most powerful airborne jamming equipment designed during the war. Piperack was a jamming transmitter designed to blind the SN-2 radar used by the enemy's nightfighters to hunt their prey.

The Window spoof comprised five or more aircraft flying line abreast, with each releasing large quantities of metal foil which gave the impression on enemy radar of a large bomber force.

In addition to their normal radar, No. 100 Group's Mosquito nightfighters carried 'Perfectos' and 'Serrate', homing equipment to help them locate enemy interceptors. Perfectos triggered the German aircrafts' identification sets and their reply signals provided the Mosquito crews with the range and bearing of the enemy aircraft. Serrate permitted the Mosquito crews to home on the emissions from their counterparts' radar equipment.

target from five minutes before the initial marking began until five minutes after the bombing stopped. The big hazard was having to hang around while the bomber boys ran in, bombed, and got the Hell out of it! Fifteen minutes seemed a long long time suspended over the inferno below. The support aircraft generally flew some 2000 to 4000 feet above the bomber stream and jammed the flak and searchlight radars, the nightfighter R/T frequencies, the nightfighter radars – in other words diverting the defensive forces away from the bombers during the most critical period.'

The group's spoof tactics were entirely successful: the German fighter-controller for the Central Rhine defence area, Major Rüppel, operating from a massive concrete bunker at Dortmund, seriously underestimated the true weight of the RAF's raid, believing each force consisted of approximately 30 aircraft. Only when reports began to come in from ground observation posts did it become clear that the more southerly formation was far larger than had been thought – no amount of electronic jamming could conceal the mighty roar of 800 aircraft engines. By this stage, Rüppel had over 89 nightfighters in the air, orbiting over holding beacons until he could clarify the situation.

At first, it appeared that the RAF's main target was the city of Kassel. Indeed, available information suggested that this was the case: shortly after entering Germany, the main RAF raiding force had turned to the northeast, and eight minutes later observers at Kassel had reported signs of an imminent attack. Again, 100 Group's spoof measures were having a decisive impact. At 0308 hours Pathfinder flares, dropped by a dozen Mosquitoes, had alerted the German defences and scores of their nightfighters were ordered to the city. But this was no full-scale onslaught by the RAF, merely another feint backed by 100 Group's Liberators and Halifaxes dropping Window. However, a German nightfighter caught

DEFENDING THE REICH

Until the appointment of Josef Kammhuber to the position of General of Night Fighters in October 1940, Germany's air defences consisted of nothing more than a haphazard mix of flak batteries and searchlights. During the winter of 1940/41, however, Kammhuber set about extending the defences across northern Germany and the Low Countries by establishing a line between 50 and 100 miles inland, and by building positions around major industrial targets. The introduction of radar into front-line service enabled the Luftwaffe to further strengthen their defences and build the 'Kammhuber Line'. The line made use of the Himmelbett radar system and was based on a chain of radar-guided fighter 'boxes'. Each box, a defensive zone, was equipped with a Freya radar set, to give early warning of Allied bomber attacks, and Würzburg radars which were used to fix the location of the raiders and guide nightfighters to their target. Late in 1942, the system was improved by the introduction of Lichtenstein radar which could guide nightfighters to within two miles of their target. Although the line did have some value, it was clear that by 1943 it was being swamped by the scale of the Allied bomber offensive. In November 1943, new measures were introduced: nightfighters were scrambled to circle a beacon as soon as the course of a bomber formation was known, and then ground controllers guided them onto the target.

The nightfighters were provided with SN-2 radar, an up-dated version of Lichtenstein, that was impervious to Window jamming. Later, aircraft were fitted with 'Naxos', a device able to home in on a British bombing device, known as H2S.

Despite organisational and technical advances, however, the night defences of Germany never received adequate funding and, although the Luftwaffe often inflicted severe losses on the British, it never seized the initiative from the RAF.

and destroyed one Liberator from No. 223 Squadron but this loss was avenged when a Mosquito of No. 85 Squadron intercepted a Bf 110.

The pilot, Flight Lieutenant Chapman, afterwards reported:

'At 0255 hours on route to escort bomber force just after passing Hamm, we obtained a Perfectos [homing device] contact at 12 miles range. Mosquito closed to one mile on Perfectos but was unable to contact on Mark X [nightfighter radar] and decided that the contact was well below. Lost height and D/F'd [took a bearing] on to the target at seven miles range. Closed to six miles and obtained AI [radar] contact.

'The target was climbing straight ahead. Mosquito closed rapidly and identified as Bf 110. Opened fire from 600 feet, using half-ring deflection with a three-second burst. Enemy aircraft exploded in port engine and debris blew off. Crashed about 30 miles northwest of Kassel.'

Left: Underview of a Halifax fitted with Mandrel, used to spoof the Luftwaffe's system of early-warning radars by 'noise jamming'. Below: One of No. 192 Squadron's Halifaxes carrying a host of equipment for intelligence gathering. Bottom, left and centre: Serrate antenna and receiver in the nose and cockpit of a Mosquito. The device was used to home on emissions from the radars of the enemy's nightfighters. Bottom right: A Mark X radar set, used for airborne interceptions, inside a Mosquito NF30 nightfighter.

An hour later, during the same patrol, Chapman and his navigator, Flight Sergeant Stockley, attacked and downed an He 219 nightfighter south of Weimar.

During Chapman's first air battle, the main raiding force, flying some 25 miles south of Kassel, had turned onto an easterly heading for Bohlen. The Kassel feint held the bulk of the enemy's nightfighters in the area for nearly half an hour, and it was not until 0330 hours that Rüppel ordered his confused forces in pursuit. However, he continued to be misled. Six minutes after redirecting his nightfighters, he gave the probable target as Leipzig, the city nearest Bohlen, but by this stage the vanguard of the RAF bomber force was within 30 miles of the real target.

No. 100 Group continued its deception measures: just short of Bohlen, six Flying Fortresses and Halifaxes laid out a second Window trail, this time to the important but untargeted oil complex at Leuna, 20 miles northwest of Bohlen. Leuna was directly in the

path of the enemy's nightfighters, and Window and target markers delayed them further.

The 211 Lancasters assigned to the Bohlen attack reached their objective and carried out a concentrated 11-minute attack; all released Window in the target area. Five Fortresses and a Liberator from 100 Group, which had given jamming cover on the flight in, now provided jamming support over the oil refinery. Their efforts totally confounded the attempts of the German nightfighters to get to grips with the bomber force, and it was not until 0410 hours, as the last of the raiders was leaving Bohlen, that the first interceptors made contact with them. Their

radar operators, however, encountered severe jamming and had great difficulty in finding their prey amongst the clouds of Window.

To add to the defenders' problems as the RAF withdrew, the Halifaxes which had made up the Mandrel screen now broke away and ran a false trail of Window to Frankfurt. When they reached the city, the Halifaxes also dropped target markers as though in preparation for a large-scale attack.

At this point, however, Bomber Command's operations for the night were only half complete. While the enemy's attention was concentrated over central Germany, the force of Lancasters bound for Hemmingstedt were making their way at low altitude and in radio silence to their target. Shortly before reaching the refinery, the bombers rose above the radar horizon and began climbing to their attack altitude of 15,000 feet. Each aircraft released Window to mislead the enemy into believing that the raid was another diversion.

The sole loss was a Lancaster, which fell to a marauding nightfighter near Hemmingstedt

At precisely 0423 hours the attack on the refinery complex began, supported by jamming from a Fortress and a Liberator from No. 100 Group. Because of the bombers' low-altitude approach and the clever use of Window, the enemy trackers failed to appreciate the strength of the RAF's force until it was too late. Indeed, the bombers were well on their way home before the first radar plots of 'weak formations' were reported by the German radar officers in the target area. The sole loss was a Lancaster, which fell to a marauding nightfighter near Hemmingstedt. Most of the enemy's fighter force had been ordered to Bremen to intercept 27 Mosquitoes of Bomber Command's Pathfinder force which had appeared in the area six minutes before the Lancasters.

Thanks to the spoofery of No. 100 Group's aircraft, the raids struck a major blow against Hitler's war effort: the Bohlen and Hemmingstedt refineries were hit hard and neither resumed production before the war ended. The action cost the RAF 11 bombers, plus a Liberator and a Fortress of 100 Group. Eight of the losses were attributed to nightfighters, one to flak, two others were lost in a mid-air collision, and the circumstances of the other two losses were never established. However, the RAF had inflicted losses on the Luftwaffe's nightfighters: bomber crews claimed two kills and 100 Group's Mosquitoes destroyed two other raiders. With the arrival of the group's fighters, the enemy's nightfighters could no longer cruise at leisure in the skies over Germany, looking for bombers to bring down. The cumulative effect of the group's operations was the erosion of the German nightfighter menace.

Although the RAF's bomber support force was only in existence for a little over two years, it stamped an indelible mark on night operations and pioneered techniques which are now recognised as one of the most important aspects of modern aerial warfare. It is a fitting tribute to one of the RAF's least known formations to see service in World War II.

THE AUTHOR Alfred Price served as an aircrew officer in the RAF for 15 years, specialising in electronic warfare, aircraft weapons and air fighting tactics. He has written extensively on aerial warfare, and amongst his published works is *Instruments of Darkness*.

AGGRESSORS

The 527th Aggressor Squadron can trace its descent from the 312th Bombardment Squadron (Light), which was activated in February 1942 as part of the 86th Bomb Group flying Douglas A-20 twin-engined bombers. In September 1942 the squadron's role was changed to dive-bombing and it took its North American A-36A Invaders into action in July 1943, operating with the Twelfth Air Force in the Mediterranean theatre. In August 1943 it became the 527th Fighter-Bomber Squadron, and on 30 May 1944 was redesignated the 527th Fighter Squadron. The unit received Curtiss P-40 Warhawks early in 1944, but six months later re-equipped with the more modern Republic P-47 Thunderbolt.

In February 1946 the unit returned to the United States and was deactivated during the following month. The unit was re-activated in August 1946, as part of the 86th Bomb Group with which it had flown during World War II. Based in Germany, the squadron flew P-47 Thunderbolts until early 1950. It then received its first jets, Republic F-84 Thunderjets, and was redesignated the 527th Fighter-Bomber Squadron. Three years later it converted onto the North American F-86 Sabre, becoming a day-fighter squadron, but in February 1956 it was again deactivated. Twenty years later the unit re-appeared as the 527th Tactical Fighter Training Aggressor Squadron at RAF Alconbury, and its designation was simplified to the 527th Aggressor Squadron in 1983.

Above: The badge of the 527th Aggressor Squadron.

Simulating Soviet Air tactics in realistic combat exercises, the 527th Aggressor Squadron trains NATO pilots to 'know their enemy'

IT IS DAY 3 of Exercise Red Star 86-2. Pilots of the USAF 527th Aggressor Squadron Red Force and their opponents, F-15 Eagle pilots of the 525th Tactical Fighter Squadron 'The Bulldogs' – from Bitburg's 36th Tactical Fighter-Wing Blue Force, assemble for a ten o'clock briefing at RAF Alconbury, Cambridge. As the Aggressors' Intelligence Officer, Captain Mike Elliott, outlines the general situation, it becomes clear that the fortunes of war have shifted in favour of the Blue forces. The Red offensive has been halted and so Blue's fighters, the F-15 Eagles, will today have the job of escorting an attack by F-111F 'Aardvarks' into Red territory. For the previous two days, the Eagles have been the defenders, attempting to break through the Aggressors' fighter cover to reach the strike aircraft. 'Enemy' losses have been heavy, but the Blue fighters are warned that they are likely to face stiff opposition. They can expect to engage in dissimilar air combat with a greater number of 'Gomers' (Aggressor jargon for enemy fighters – a legacy of the Vietnam War) than previously encountered. In fact, eight of the Aggressors' F-5E Tiger IIs will represent Red's air defence forces for this mission. Four F-15 Eagles will be required to protect a similar number of Aardvarks.

The blackboard exhorts the pilots: 'Have fun, do good, but don't hit anybody'

The Aggressors' mission leader, Captain Walt Burns, then takes over the briefing. He runs through the weather forecast for the exercise area over the North Sea, and reminds the pilots to check NOTAMs (notices to airmen) for any activities that may affect them. The fight will be on when the Eagle pilots are ready. With 16 aircraft manoeuvring in a relatively small area, safety is a major consideration. The blackboard exhorts the pilots: 'Have fun, do good, but don't hit anybody.' The point is driven home by Burns, who advises: 'If you lose "SA" (situation awareness), don't press it, but break off.' In multi-aircraft engagements it is not uncommon for even an experienced pilot to become momentarily confused. He should be aware of the dangers and, instead of carrying on with the fight, leave the area and regain his orientation before re-engaging. Burns also appeals for calm on the radio from both sides. If any pilot wants to end the fight, all he needs to do is to call 'Knock it off' and this will signal the end of the engagement. 'Bring 'em all back alive, OK' is Burns' final advice. The Eagle pilots then file out of the briefing room, leaving the Aggressors to discuss their detailed tactics. All that the Bulldogs know is that their opponents will be using standard Soviet ground control of interception (GCI) procedures.

The scene is thus set for one of the more complex training missions in the Aggressors' instructional syllabus. For, underlying the mmystique of the Aggressor squadrons – the fighters painted in Soviet-style camouflage, the red-star bedecked flying helmets and hammer and sickle emblems on crew room walls – is the serious business of teaching American and NATO pilots how to master their Warsaw Pact counterparts in air combat. The origins

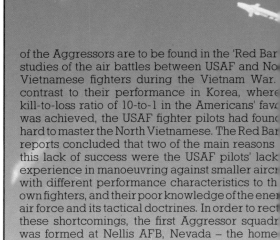

of the Aggressors are to be found in the 'Red Bar studies of the air battles between USAF and No Vietnamese fighters during the Vietnam War. contrast to their performance in Korea, where kill-to-loss ratio of 10-to-1 in the Americans' fav was achieved, the USAF fighter pilots had found hard to master the North Vietnamese. The Red Bar reports concluded that two of the main reasons this lack of success were the USAF pilots' lack experience in manoeuvring against smaller aircr with different performance characteristics to th own fighters, and their poor knowledge of the ener air force and its tactical doctrines. In order to rect these shortcomings, the first Aggressor squadr was formed at Nellis AFB, Nevada – the home USAF fighter pilot training.

Commanded by Lieutenant-Colonel 'Doc' B roughs, the 527th Aggressor Squadron has an esta lished strength of 18 Northrop F-5Es. This fighter i well-liked aircraft, which can accurately simula the current Soviet threat from MiG-23 Floggers a MiG-21 Fishbeds. Its small size is an advantage combat, making it difficult for an opponent to sp and the fighter turns and fights well at low spee

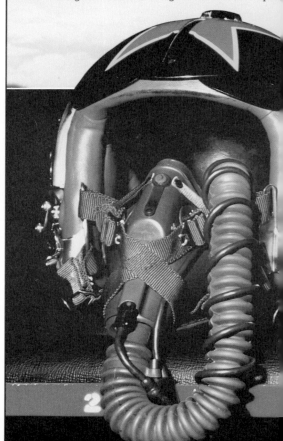

By simulating the performance capability of the MiG-23 and the tactical doctrines of the Soviet pilots, the Aggressors prepare F-15 Eagle pilots for the role of wresting air superiority from the enemy. The Aggressors also engage in dissimilar-air-combat training with ground-attack aircraft. Armed with AIM-9J Sidewinder missiles, an Aggressor Squadron F-5E (above) shadows the pilot of an F-16 Fighting Falcon (right) into the 'combat zone'. Below: Aggressor flying helmets, with the Soviet red star.

LET THE BEAR
BEWARE

Working with the squadron's own GCI controllers, who, like the pilots, are experts in Soviet tactical procedures, the F-5Es can give a good fight, in the opinion of Major Dan Griffin, the squadron's assistant operations officer. However, he believes that a new Aggressor aircraft with better radar and weaponry is now needed to simulate the latest generation of Soviet fighters (the MiG-29 Fulcrum and Su-27 Flanker). Moreover, after 10 years in service at Alconbury, the F-5E airframes are beginning to show their age. The F-20A Tigershark, designed by Northrop as a successor to the F-5E, would be well suited to undertake the Aggressor role. However, it now seems unlikely that the F-20A will go into production and it may be that the F-5Es will be refurbished and fitted with new avionics in order to extend their combat lives. In the event of war, the squadron would form part of the United Kingdom's air defences and Griffin is confident that, with the help of GCI, the F-5Es would do a good job in the point-defence role.

The emphasis is on developing effective fluid tactics, with due regard for teamwork

The F-5E's greatest asset as an Aggressor aircraft is the fact that its low wing loading gives it a very different performance to that of such fighters as the F-15 Eagle or F-4 Phantom, which have high thrust-to-weight ratios and high wing loadings. Generally, a fighter with low wing loading will have a better instantaneous turning performance, especially at lower airspeed, than a fighter with high wing loading. However, fighters like the F-15 Eagle with a high thrust-to-weight ratio will have an advantage in their rate of climb, acceleration and high-speed performance. The fundamental aim of the Aggressors' dissimilar-air-combat training (DACT) programme is thus to demonstrate the strengths and weaknesses of both types of fighter, and to show the USAF and other NATO pilots how to force a fight that will capitalise on their own aircraft's performance. Initially, this is done during 'one-versus-one' missions, which serve as an introduction to DACT. The Aggressor pilot will begin by feeling out how good his opponent is, before starting to make things more difficult for him. Within two days there is usually a noticeable improvement in the performance of an inexperienced pilot. Indeed, it is the skill of the individual pilot that determines the outcome of a fight, irrespective of the basic qualities of the fighters engaged. As the Aggressors often put it, 'a hamburger is still a hamburger whatever the wrapping.'

The second stage of Aggressor training consists of defensive and offensive exercises, with the pilots fighting as members of a formation rather than as individuals. However, at this stage only small numbers of aircraft are involved (typically two-versus-one). The emphasis is on developing effective fluid tactics, with due regard for the need for teamwork, good radio procedures and flight discipline. As part of their instruction in offensive tactics, the Aggressors will teach disengagement techniques, so that their pupils will be able to complete their mission as a cohesive unit and not become separated during the combat. They will also learn how to fight from an initial position of disadvantage, maintaining the integrity of their formation while seeking to turn the tables on the attacker by achieving a good firing position. Once the skills of fighting dissimilar aircraft have been mastered in small-scale combats, the third stage of training will involve multi-aircraft

Far right: An external fuel tank waits to be fitted to a 'Bulldog' F-15 Eagle prior to Exercise Red Star 86-2. The nose of the F-15 contains a variety of combat avionics, including the APG-63 radar. Right: As a pilot runs over his flight briefing, one of the F-5E's 20mm M39 revolver-feed guns is clearly visible under the access hatch. The small size and sleek profile of the F-5E is an extremely useful asset in air combat – from head-on it is nearly invisible from a range of two miles. Below and below right: Pilots from the two opposing squadrons listen attentively as an officer outlines the nature of the exercise. Bottom right: After the 'combat', an Aggressor pilot writes up his flight report in preparation for the debriefing.

engagements, such as Exercise Red Star 86-2. This was planned to culminate in a 16 aircraft combat, with eight Aggressors attacking four F-15 Eagles and four F-111F Aardvarks. The intention was to give the Eagle pilots experience in dealing with a squadron-sized attacking force and Griffin thought that, realistically, these would be the largest enemy formations encountered in actual combat.

The job of providing dissimilar-air-combat training takes the Aggressors all over Europe on visits to USAF and NATO air bases. In addition, the squadron provides a six-aircraft detachment at Decimomannu in Sardinia for 48 weeks of the year. This is the location of the only air combat manoeuvring instrumentation (ACMI) range in Europe, over which all combats are electronically recorded and can be quickly reconstructed on computer displays for post-mission briefings. Usually, such a postmortem at Decimomannu takes only 45 minutes. However, since the ACMI range can handle only a maximum of eight aircraft at a time, it is not able to record the larger Aggressor missions. The excellent opportunities for travel around Europe make the 527th Aggressor Squadron a popular assignment for pilots. They also get rather more flying than the average, with each Aggressor pilot making around 200 sorties per year. It is the best job in the USAF, thought Captain Jeff 'Tico' Tice, a former F-111F pilot with the 48th Tactical Fighter Wing who has been at the Aggressor Squadron for over two years.

Like all the pilots serving with the squadron, Tice volunteered for the assignment. The squadron's

pilots are usually selected from the tactical fighter wings of the USAF in Europe, so that they are already familiar with conditions in the region. After a three-month training period with the Aggressor School at Nellis AFB, they join the squadron as fully qualified DACT instructors. They need to be skilled and experienced fighter pilots, but they also require a basic aptitude for the instructional side of their work.

Classroom instruction on the Soviet threat forms as valuable a part of the Aggressors' training work as their DACT sorties. Their time is divided about 50-50 between classroom and airborne work. The squadron is well provided with the raw materials of intelligence, and pilots spend many hours 'in the vault' studying various aspects of Soviet equipment, organisation and tactics.

Tice's area of special expertise is the Soviet fighter

Aggressors at 'war'

The Aggressor squadron simulates an attack on a flight of F-111s escorted by four F-15s. Over the week of Exercise Red Star 86-2 the F-15 pilots flew a series of 12 different types of mission against the Aggressor's simulated Soviet air tactics. The considerable experience gained by the F-15 pilots led to a

MiG Flight

significant improvement in their performance against the 'MIGs' of the Aggressors. On Day 3, shown here, the F-15s engaged the Aggressors in simulated air combat and four 'MIGs' were 'lost'. The F-111s got through unscathed.

Baron Flight

pilot and his views on the likely effectiveness of his Warsaw Pact counterpart in combat are of particular interest. Tice sees him as basically typical of the average fighter pilot, who is much the same the world over. If left to his own devices, he would probably develop in much the same way as Western pilots. However, the Soviet training system does not allow him to do so, as it places little value on individual initiative. Indeed, the Soviet commanders deride Western reliance on this quality, which they regard as no more than 'native wit' or muddling through. In their eyes, it is no substitute for strict adherence to 'The Plan' that has been carefully formulated by senior officers. The Soviet notion of strict subordination can be seen in the fighter pilots' relationship with their GCI controllers. In Tice's words: 'they are very dependent on the controllers and call them their third pilots' (the second pilot being the auto-pilot).

This factor is not the only constraint that tends to prevent the Soviet fighter pilot from realising his full potential. As a result of too great a concern with flight safety, he will not be allowed to fly his aircraft to the limits of its performance. Neither will he spend as much time in the air as his American counterpart,

who on average will accumulate 20 to 25 per cent more flying hours in a year. There are no Soviet equivalents to the Aggressor squadrons, but pilots do have the opportunity to train with the different fighter types in the Warsaw Pact inventory. They are also reasonably well informed about the NATO air forces and know what opposition to expect, although less knowledgeable in this respect than Western pilots. Tice is in no doubt that the Soviet pilots are very highly motivated, but he is nonetheless confident of the NATO pilots' ability to beat them.

It is a confidence born of the experience gained during numerous Aggressor engagements, and the outcome of the midday mission on the third day of Red Star 86-2 certainly confirmed this view. The Bulldogs' four F-15C Eagles lifted off from Alconbury's 9000ft runway and headed out for their rendezvous with the F-111Fs. They were followed by the Aggressors' F-5Es, led by Captain Burns. A last-minute problem caused by the unserviceability of one of the fighters scheduled for the mission had been quickly resolved by the allocation of a replacement aircraft. The Aggressors were therefore able to put up all eight of the F-5Es planned to provide the opposition to the Bulldogs. They had already decided on suitable Soviet-style tactics to meet the situation. The force was to be divided into three flights: Red Flight and MiG Flight, each with three aircraft, and Baron Flight with two aircraft. Red Flight was to mount a Barrier combat air patrol (CAP), with the primary objective of dealing with the Aardvarks. This is often flown as a counter-rotating CAP, with fighters circling in opposite directions over their patrol area in order to increase the chances of someone making contact with enemy aircraft. The other two flights were to carry out pincer attacks on the escorting F-15s in order to strip the fighter cover from the Aardvarks and so make Red Flight's job of intercepting them easier. An alternative stratagem,

Red Flight Three

Red Flight One

MiG and Baron flights manoeuvre to attack

F-15 escorts

Track of F-111 flight

Far left inset: Captain Jeff 'Tico' Tice of the 527th Aggressor Squadron. Far left above: Climbing into his aircraft, this Aggressor pilot will shortly undertake a systems check before taking to the skies with another F-5E (above left) and heading for the exercise area over the North Sea.

Back at RAF Alconbury, Aggressor pilot Cal Kemp strikes a proud pose for the camera. Every member of the squadron is an expert on one aspect of the Soviet threat, with specialisations varying from tactical doctrine to air-to-air missiles. This makes the Aggressors formidable opponents – and invaluable instructors.

also favoured by Soviet pilots, would have bee use MiG and Baron Flights as decoys to draw Eagles away from their charges.

At the opening stage of the fight the Eagles had significant advantage of good information about opponents' dispositions, thanks to their exce radars. This gave them the opportunity of asses the Aggressors' likely tactics before they enga them. The F-5Es, fitted with much less sophistic radars, were dependent at this stage on informa from their GCI controllers. However, once the ra closed, the Eagles' radar was of little help in pic up small F-5Es in a close-in fight. Moreover, since Aggressor pilots get a lot more practice in air-t combat than the average fighter pilot, their situa awareness is higher. In common with most mo air combats, the ensuing fight was a short one. North Sea training area used by the Aggresso well over a 100 miles from Alconbury and so mu the sortie was taken up with the flight out and re Typically, only three to five minutes of an hour-sortie will be spent in actual combat. Concern a fuel limitations also gives an added edge of realis the exercise.

The success of the opposition is, after all, only a reflection of the quality of their training

The Eagles entered the exercise area in a bro spaced line-abreast formation. Their intention to engage the Aggressors just before the Aardva ran through the area at high speed and at a m lower level (Mach 1.3 at 5000ft). Their reading o Aggressors' tactics was good, largely due to clues given them by their radars, and they were a to pick off four of the F-5Es before the latter co engage. Typically, this was a missile engagemen Griffin's experience guns are not so much use training, although radar-guided air-to-air miss have a kill probability of only some 25 per c Infra-red homing missiles, such as the AIM-9L, much better, however. It was only as the Eagles w breaking away, low on fuel, that the F-5Es were a to achieve a favourable attacking position on tw them. Apart from a fleeting glimpse by one p none of the Aggressors even saw the Aardva which would have been particularly difficult tar to pick up from above.

It was a somewhat subdued group of Aggres who landed back at Alconbury and assembled f flight debriefing, before the main debriefing with Eagle pilots. The details of the fight were worked on the blackboard, using a tape of the radio c versations as an aid to memory. Later, film from aircrafts' gunsight cameras would be available analysis to check the validity of kill claims. In ge al, though, the Aggressors' credibility is high, with their claims being subsequently upheld by evidence. In cases of disagreement between victor and his victim, the flight leaders have the jo arbitrating. The outcome of this mission was, pa doxically, a good result for the Aggressor squad As Tice reflected, 'our job is to die.' The succes the opposition is, after all, only a reflection of quality of their training. Tice's verdict was that 'if fly hard and they win, then we have done our jo

THE AUTHOR Anthony Robinson and the publish would like to thank the officers and men of the 52 Aggressor Squadron for their help in the prepa tion of this article.

MISSILE BOMBERS

OF THE
THIRD REICH

Equipped with the very latest in Luftwaffe missile technology, the pathfinders of KG 100 added a new dimension to aerial warfare

AT 2000 HOURS on 14 November 1940, two squadrons of Heinkel He 111H-3 bombers roared off into the darkness from their base at Vannes, in western France. They crossed the Channel and droned high over the darkened south of England, heading towards their target in the Midlands. Behind them, from a powerful transmitter on the French coast, a radio beam lanced out into the night, forming an invisible road in the sky for the aircraft. A steady signal in the pilot's headphones meant that he was on course; dots or dashes meant that he was straying to the left or right.

Each bomber was equipped with a special radio receiver known simply as 'X-Apparatus'. A signal, automatically triggered by a second beam cutting across the first at an angle from another station,

indicated that the bombers were now 10 miles from their target. As soon as this signal was received, each radio operator pressed a switch that set into motion a clock on his instrument panel. Five miles further on, in response to a signal from a third beam, the radio operator pressed the switch again, stopping the first pointer and starting a second.

It was now up to the pilot to hold the bomber steady on the final run-in to the target. Apart from opening the bomb-doors, that was his only task at this stage; everything else was automatic. When the second pointer on the radio operator's clock became superimposed on the first, it triggered the electrical bomb-release circuit and the Heinkel soared upwards as its load of 550-pounders fell away.

British Intelligence had been aware for some months that the Germans were using radio beams

On this fateful November night, the target was the picturesque cathedral city of Coventry, earmarked by Luftwaffe Intelligence as an important munitions centre and therefore a legitimate military target. During the hours that followed, 450 German bombers, guided by the fires started by the pathfinding Heinkels of Kampfgruppe (KGr) 100, dropped a total of 500 tons of high explosive and 30 tons of incendiary bombs into the expanding sea of flame below. When the last wave of bombers droned away in the early hours of 15 November, the heart of Coventry, together with its beautiful 14th-century cathedral, had ceased to exist. Night after night during that desperate winter of 1940-41, London, the Midlands, Lancashire, Wales, Tyneside, Plymouth, Exeter, Southampton and Bristol reeled under the avalanche of fire from the night sky. Many of the night raids on England during this period were led by Kampfgruppe 100.

British Intelligence had been aware for some months that the Germans were using radio beams as aids to navigation and bombing. As early as June 1940, Professor Lindemann, the scientific advisor to the British War Cabinet, had reported to Sir Winston Churchill that the Germans had developed a radio beam that enabled the Luftwaffe to conduct bombing operations by day or night, whatever the weather. On 21 June, the Prime Minister convened an emergency meeting that was attended by senior

Below left: Major Hans-Georg Bätcher, who commanded Kampfgruppe 100 during the bombing campaign against Britain. Below: Groundcrew attach SC 250 free-fall bombs to the external racks of an He 111. Designed for use against wooden bridges, the bombs contained an inflammable filling that was ignited by incendiary devices on the casing.

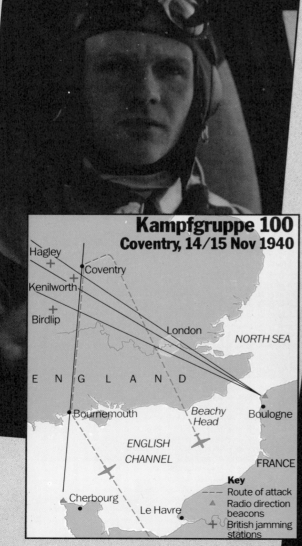

Kampfgruppe 100
Coventry, 14/15 Nov 1940

Hagley
Coventry
Kenilworth
Birdlip
London
NORTH SEA
E N G L A N D
Bournemouth
Beachy Head
Boulogne
ENGLISH CHANNEL
FRANCE
Cherbourg
Le Havre

Key
--- Route of attack
▲ Radio direction beacons
+ British jamming stations

Below left: A formation of Heinkel He 111s from KG 100 prepares to carry out a bombing mission over the Eastern Front. Right: A rare close-in shot of an He 111 in mid-flight. Previous page: Watching the skies for enemy fighters.

oyal Air Force (RAF) officers, scientists and the eputy Director of Scientific Research at the Air inistry, Dr. R.V. Jones. The latter informed the eeting that, for some months, reports had been oming in from sources on the continent indicating at the Germans possessed a novel night-bombing d on which they pinned great hopes. It seemed to e linked somehow to the codename 'Knickebein' Crooked Leg). British Intelligence had encoun- red the term several times without being able to xplain it.

Shortly after RAF reconnaissance aircraft photo- aphed three curiously-shaped towers on the Ger-

man-occupied coast of France, a German bomber was shot down near Liverpool. The subsequent examination of the wreck revealed that the aircraft carried radio equipment, the elaborate nature of which suggested that it was connected with some-thing other than the ordinary 'Lorenz' blind-landing system.

British scientists soon divined the significance of the Knickebein transmitters, and the first British countermeasures were operational by the middle of August 1940, their targets being the two 'Ruffian' stations – as the RAF codenamed the Knickebein transmitters – near Dieppe and Cherbourg. During

KAMPFGRUPPE 100

Kampfgruppe 100 (KGr 100 – whose insignia is shown above) was formed in the summer of 1939 as a special signals unit, and conducted operations during the Polish campaign under the direct command of Hermann Göring's headquarters in Potsdam. During the Norwegian campaign, the unit was based at Nordholz and operated Heinkel He 111Hs in the normal bombing role.

After seeing action in the Battles of France and Britain under the command of Hauptmann Friedrich Aschenbrenner, and becoming specialised in the art of precision bombing using the 'X' and 'Y' apparatus, KGr 100 was transferred to the Eastern Front.

In April 1943 the unit was withdrawn to Graz and re-equipped with the Dornier Do 217E-5. It was given full Kampfgeschwader status and expanded under the designation KG 100. In August 1943, the unit's number two squadron (2/KG 100) became operational with the Hs 293A air-to-surface missile, while 3/KG 100 was equipped with the 'Fritz-X'. Many successful missions were carried out with these weapons during 1943 and 1944. After D-day, the raids were directed against Allied invasion ports and beachheads. By 14 August 1944, 3/KG 100 was the unit's only surviving squadron. It was withdrawn from Orleans shortly after. By late September 1944, KG 100 had been disbanded, with its personnel re-assigned to other Luftwaffe units.

Above: The wreath on the 20mm cannon of this He 111 commemorates the 500th operational mission flown by Major Bätcher.

the last days of October, British Intelligence received indications that the enemy would shortly undertake a large raid with the help of the new equipment, and it concluded that the target would be either London or Liverpool. Intelligence, however, was tragically wrong; the objective of the German experiment was Coventry. Anti-aircraft defences there were pitifully light, and the Germans lost only one bomber during their raid on 14/15 November.

Early in 1941, the Germans went over to yet another radio-beam system – known as 'Y-Apparatus'. Again, it was pioneered by the Heinkels of KG 100. Whereas X-Apparatus had used three beams crossing on the approach to the target, Y-Apparatus used only one beam, in conjunction with a radio signal that indicated to the bomber pilot the distance he had travelled along the beam. The pilot was therefore able to keep a continuous check on his progress, dropping his bombs when the correct distance had been flown.

Although the weight of the German air offensive against Britain fell off markedly after the end of April 1941, KGr 100, now specialising in precision-bombing techniques, continued to operate against British targets for several more months. In the summer of 1941 it exchanged some of its Heinkels for Dornier Do 217s, and switched its main effort from land targets to the long series of anti-shipping operations that were to characterise its activities throughout the rest of the war.

In September 1942, several of the Kampfgruppe's most experienced crews were suddenly detached to Germany to take part in trials with two new secret weapons, both of which were air-launched radio-guided missiles for use against shipping. The first of these, known as the 'Fritz-X', consisted of a 3100lb armour-piercing bomb with four stubby fins set

midway along its body. The weapon was guided by radio signals and steered by a small control column installed in the bomb-aimer's compartment. Immediately after release, the pilot of the parent aircraft reduced speed to about 130 miles per hour, making it easier for the bomb-aimer to keep the missile in sight during the final stages of its trajectory. During the weapon's 42-second drop from 20,000ft, visual tracking was aided by a flare placed in its tail. However, the Fritz-X was not particularly accurate, and its use was complicated by the fact that the launch aircraft – usually a Dornier Do 217K-2 – had to fly straight and level while course corrections were being made.

When operational trials were completed in early 1943, a squadron of KG 100 (by this time, the unit had been given full Kampfgeschwader status) was assigned to Fritz-X operations and sent to Istres, near Marseilles. Under conditions of strict secrecy, stockpiles of Fritz-X missiles were positioned at German airfields in an arc from northern Norway to Italy. Detachments from KG 100 would shuttle from base to base as necessity demanded.

Meanwhile, parallel development had continued on the second type of anti-shipping missile, the Henschel Hs 293. Although its armour-piercing capability was not as great as that of the Fritz-X, this was a much more flexible weapon. Due to the addition of a rocket motor, the Hs 293 could be aimed over a greater range. The motor fired automatically after release and accelerated the missile to a speed

Below: Unteroffizier Horst Goetz of Kampfgruppe 100 in his He 111; the aircraft carries the unit's 'Viking ship' insignia.

Right: Major Bernhard Jope, the commander of 2/KG 100. Above: A Dornier Do 217. Top: Armed with an Hs 293 guided missile, a Dornier prepares for take-off.

GERMAN AIR-TO-SURFACE MISSILES

German air-to-surface missile (ASM) development began in 1915, when the Siemens-Schuckert firm began testing a series of glider bombs that were launched from aircraft or airships, and remotely controlled by wires. By the time of the Armistice in 1918, the testing of these weapons had reached an advanced stage.

In the late 1930s, the German Air Ministry sponsored the Blohm und Voss company to begin developing a series of aerial torpedoes. The series culminated in the SL 11 Schneewittchen (Snow White), designed for the Junkers Ju 88, and the BT high-velocity weapon, designed to be carried by fighter aircraft.

In 1942, following unsuccessful tests, the design of the BV 143 rocket-propelled sea-skimming anti-ship missile was modified to produce the BV 246 Hagelkorn (Hailstone). The latter was capable of homing in on Allied ground radar installations, but received only scant interest from the Luftwaffe. Anti-shipping operations remained the Luftwaffe's main preoccupation, and the Henschel firm developed the GT 1200 to this end. The latter was powered by two rocket motors, one of which came into operation underwater and directed the missile towards the target vessel. The Zitteroschen (Torpedo-fish) was also developed by Henschel, and it was believed to be the world's first supersonic, winged, guided missile. Data on this weapon is scarce, but the missile was rumoured to be ready for mass production when the project was suddenly terminated in October 1944.

Although many of the designs seemed highly promising, an enormous amount of research and development was needed before they could be classed as operationally reliable. It was left to the 'Fritz-X' and the Hs 293, with more orthodox configurations, to give the Luftwaffe the nucleus of an ASM capability.

of 370 miles per hour within 12 seconds. The Hs 293 also featured stubby wings and small tail surfaces, and was gyroscopically controlled to keep it stable in flight. Like the Fritz-X, it was steered by a small control column in the parent aircraft. Tracking was carried out by means of flare candles fitted to the tail for daylight operations, and a lamp with a red filter for night attacks. From a launch height of 19,500ft, the maximum range of the Hs 293 was 17,500yds.

In March 1943, KG 100's number two squadron – 2/KG 100 – re-equipped with Dornier Do 217E-5 bombers and later moved to Cognac, in southwest France, with its first batch of Hs 293 missiles. On 25 August, 12 of the squadron's aircraft were ordered to attack Royal Navy warships in the Bay of Biscay. On this occasion, each bomber carried two Hs 293s, one under each wing. Three British vessels were sighted and, in the attack that followed, one corvette was damaged. Two days later, during a second attack, the missile-armed bombers sank the corvette HMS *Egret* and inflicted damage on a British destroyer.

On 7 September 1943, 2/KG 100 joined its sister squadron, 3/KG 100, at Istres, in southern France. The two units were ordered into action against the Allied bridgehead at Salerno, in Italy. As a result of complete Allied air superiority in this area, the Dorniers were forced to operate at night and there was no confirmation of any hits by the missiles.

Those hectic days of September 1943 saw KG 100

take part in some of the most noteworthy attack missions carried out by Luftwaffe bombers during the entire war. On the 9th, the day the Allies went ashore at Salerno, 3/KG 100 was presented with a once-in-a-lifetime target. Earlier that morning, German reconnaissance had revealed that major units of the Italian fleet were at sea off the west coast of Italy. The Italian government had already capitulated, and the future of the fleet was uncertain. If it went over to the Allies, it could conceivably lend weight to their already overwhelming naval supremacy in the Mediterranean. On the other hand, if it sailed for harbours in southern France it would provide major reinforcements for the small German naval presence there. Accordingly, the order went out to 3/KG 100: if the Italian Fleet sailed north, it was to be protected; if it sailed south, it was to be sunk.

Two hours later, the Germans received the news that the Italian Fleet had in fact turned south. Three battleships, six cruisers and a whole armada of escort vessels were apparently heading towards Malta to surrender. In just a few hours, they would be in range of the Allied fighter umbrella which would ensure their safety. If action was to be taken against them, it had to be taken immediately.

At 1400 hours, two Do 217s – the only two on readiness – took off from Istres, each carrying one Fritz-X and a full fuel load. They flew low across the Mediterranean for over an hour to avoid the Allied radar, before climbing to 18,000ft. Minutes later, the two pilots sighted the Italian Fleet steaming in loose formation. The first bursts of flak started to come up towards them. In the leading aircraft, Oberleutnant Heinrich Schmetz selected the battleship *Roma* as his target, releasing the missile and then reducing speed to 130 miles per hour while the bomb-aimer tracked its flight. The battleship began evasive action with a wide turn, but Schmetz's bomb-aimer, Feldwebel Oscar Huhn, kept the white flare in the Fritz-X's tail directly superimposed on the ship's foredeck. At 1540 there was a red flash as the missile made a direct hit, ripping the ship's innards apart in a terrific explosion. In less than 20 minutes, *Roma* had vanished beneath the surface, killing 1254 Italian sailors, including the Italian Fleet Commander, Admiral Carlos Bergamini. Schmetz was awarded the Knight's Cross for his part in the operation, while his bomb-aimer received the Iron Cross. Schmetz was later appointed commander of III/KG 100.

The next few days saw the crews of 3/KG 100 operating intensively against the Salerno bridgehead, pressing home their missile attacks against Allied warships. Losses were high as the Germans had to fly through heavy flak and fighter cover, but 30 per cent of the missiles launched found their targets. On 16 September 1943, three Fritz-X missiles were launched against the British battleship HMS *Warspite*; one of them tore through several decks to blast a hole in the ship's bottom, while the other two cut a long tear in *Warspite's* side compartments, des-

troying one boiler room completely and flooding four out of the remaining five.

Only nine men were killed and 14 wounded, but the battleship was completely out of action, unable to steer and with her radar and armament rendered unserviceable. She shipped 3000 tons of water and had to be laboriously towed back to Malta for repairs. Other missile hits were scored on the cruisers HMS *Uganda* and USS *Savannah*. From now on, however, 3/KG 100's operations were severely curtailed – the Allies had established airstrips in the Salerno area, enabling fighters to maintain constant patrols.

Having suffered heavy losses over the Anzio beachhead during January 1944, KG 100 was destined to leave the Mediterranean theatre very soon. In the spring of 1944, with an Allied invasion of France a distinct possibility, KG 100 was once more transferred to bases on the Atlantic coast for operations against Allied shipping. On 30 April, 3/KG 100 used Fritz-X missiles for the first (and only) time against the United Kingdom. Fifteen Dornier Do 217s launched their weapons against shipping in Plymouth harbour, but no important target was hit.

The missile-equipped Luftwaffe units were assembled to counteract the Allied invasion when it finally came in June 1944, and the German High Command expected them to wreak havoc among the densely-packed shipping between the coasts of England and France. The Luftwaffe, however, had

Above: This photograph of a glider bomb was taken by a Royal Navy officer as it approached his vessel. The Hs 293 scored its first success on 27 August 1943 off the northwest tip of Spain. Above, far left: These two photographs show how a direct hit on HMS *Egret* caused the British corvette to sink with the loss of 222 lives. Above left: Despite taking evasive action, the Italian battleship *Roma* is unable to shake off one of KG 100's 'Fritz-X' guided missiles (right).

The Henschel Hs 293 glider bomb (left) was the first air-launched anti-shipping guided missile to be used in World War II. The missile contained a 1100lb warhead, and was guided onto its target by an observer located in the nose of the launch aircraft (top). The joystick passed guidance signals onto the Hs 293 via a radio link.

reckoned without total Allied air superiority, which made anti-shipping attacks completely impossible during daylight. Operations proved just as hazardous at night, with the bombers having to run the gauntlet of their own German coastal flak as well as the Allied nightfighters and anti-aircraft guns on the beachheads. Few of the crews managed to press home their attacks, and no major success was achieved. After D-day, the aircrews of KG 100 continued to carry out attacks on the Allied invasion ports and beachheads. Right from the beginning, Kampfgeschwader 100 had been the Luftwaffe's premier pathfinding force – in the face of fierce enemy fire, the men of KG 100 led the way.

THE AUTHOR Robert Jackson is a professional aviation historian and the author of over 60 books, including *The Royal Air Force in Action*.

On 18 April 1942, 16 B-25 bombers, under the command of Lieutenant-Colonel Jimmy Doolittle, took off from the carrier USS *Hornet* for the first American raid on Japan

WHEN THE UNITED States, staggering from the initial blows delivered by the Japanese in December 1941, determined to mount a retaliatory air raid on Tokyo, it was evident that a man of exceptional qualities should lead the raid. General Henry H. 'Hap' Arnold, chief of the US Army Air Force, chose Lieutenant-Colonel James H. Doolittle, a man who appeared to fit the specifications exactly. Doolittle was an experienced pilot, a gifted leader, an aeronautical engineer, and a man who got things done quickly. In the early months of 1942, as the elaborate preparations for the raid were carried out, Doolittle was to justify amply Arnold's faith in his ability.

The raiding force was to approach Japan aboard US Navy aircraft carriers before taking to the air. The first question facing the planners, therefore, was whether medium bombers, which normally required 1000-1500ft runways, could launch from the 500ft operational flight deck of an aircraft carrier. The aircraft would also need to carry a bomb load big enough to do appreciable damage, yet have enough range to reach their ultimate destinations, the American bases in China. Bearing these considerations in mind, Doolittle chose the B-25 Mitchell bomber for the raid. Calculations on paper suggested that the short take-off was within the Mitchell's capabilities, and immediately two of the aircraft were despatched to sea aboard the newly commissioned USS *Hornet*, the aircraft carrier designated to be the centrepiece of the strike force. They took off without difficulty from the pitching deck, finally confirming that the raid was feasible.

The unit selected to supply the B-25s for the mission was the 17th Bombardment Group, based at Pendleton, Oregon. The group immediately transferred to Columbia, South Carolina, and volunteers were sought for an 'extremely hazardous' mission. Virtually all the men came forward and the four squadron commanders of the group selected 24 crews. These would suffice, allowing for losses during training, to provide the 16 crews

DOOLITTLE'S RAIDERS

TARGET: JAPAN

Following the dramatic 'announcement', at Pearl Harbor on 7 December 1941, that Japan had become a combatant nation in World War II, her armed forces soon built up a reputation for invincibility. The raid on Pearl Harbor devastated the US Pacific Fleet, and Japanese aircraft quickly neutralised US airpower based in the Philippines. The British warships HMS *Prince of Wales* and *Repulse* were sunk in the Gulf of Siam, while Allied strongholds and territories in the Pacific, principally Hong Kong, Malaya, Singapore, the Dutch East Indies, Borneo and Burma, were swiftly falling to Japanese naval and air power. In January 1942, news of further losses shocked and baffled an American public still reeling from the Pearl Harbor disaster. Guam was lost, and then Wake Island fell after a gallant defence. It seemed as though nothing could slow the momentum of the Japanese juggernaut.

In Washington, the government became increasingly anxious to inflict upon Japan an injury great enough to demonstrate to the American people that the Japanese were not invulnerable. President Franklin D. Roosevelt demanded a bombing raid against Japan itself. A proposal was quickly put forward by Captain Francis S. Low, a senior operations officer on the staff of the Chief of Naval Operations. His idea was for medium bombers of the US Army Air Force to be loaded aboard a US Navy aircraft carrier and taken close enough to Japan to be launched for an air raid on Tokyo and other major cities. After the strike, the bombers were to fly another 1000 miles southwestward to join the American build-up at Chungking in free China.

Previous page, main picture: The strike weapon of the Doolittle Raid, the B-25 Mitchell, converted for long-range bombing. Inset: In a ceremony aboard USS *Hornet*, Jimmy Doolittle wires a Japanese medal to the fin of a 500lb bomb.

which would eventually sail with *Hornet*, and men would also be available as last-minute replacements. Major John Hilger, who commanded the 89th Reconnaissance Squadron of the group, was designated as Doolittle's deputy.

Time was short. The raiding force of 'Special

Below: Backed by the volunteer aircrews of the Doolittle Raid's 16 B-25 Mitchells, Jimmy Doolittle (left) stands on the flightdeck of the *Hornet* with her commander, Captain Marc A. Mitscher.

Aviation Project Number 1' had to be ready by 1 April 1942, leaving only slightly more than two months for all the necessary tasks to be completed. It was vital that the crews should be prepared for the conditions they were to face, and Doolittle ordered Hilger to move his men to Eglin Field in northern Florida to practise low-level approaches over water.

Each crew consisted of five men: pilot, co-pilot, navigator/bombardier, engineer and gunner. Some crews had separate navigators and bombardiers, in which case a single man would carry out the functions of the engineer and the gunner.

Doolittle's pilots were accustomed to landing strips of more than 1000ft, but now it was necessary to teach them techniques of getting their loaded aircraft off a rolling, pitching flightdeck less than 500ft long. Doolittle needed an experienced naval aviator to help with the job, and Lieutenant Henry L. Miller, USN, was called in. Hank Miller was a flight instructor at the nearby Pensacola Naval Air Station, and he went to Eglin to meet the B-25 crews. After two practice take-offs with Miller in charge, the group's lead pilots were convinced. They were able to lift the B-25B off the ground in 350ft – there was room to spare. White lines were painted on the Eglin runways to represent *Hornet's* flightdeck, and soon all

the pilots had mastered the take-off drill.

Doolittle shuttled between Washington and his crews at Eglin. He flew all the missions required of his men, and one of his pilots, Second-Lieutenant William M. Bower, later said of him; 'He demanded complete action. He'd give you the best, and then there wasn't any second best. Everything had to be completely done.' This was Doolittle's way of reducing the risks and motivating his men at the same time. His standards were high, and their standards rose accordingly.

While the crews were training, the US Navy was preparing its part of the operation. Submarine surveillance of the Japanese coast provided regular weather reports, which were essential information for the bombers. It was decided that two carrier task groups would merge into one for the raid, under the command of Admiral William F. 'Bull' Halsey. His flag would fly from USS *Enterprise*, which would sail with her escorts from Pearl Harbor. Captain Marc A. Mitscher, one of the Navy's most experienced aviators and carrier skippers, commanded the brand-new *Hornet.* He would sail from San Francisco. The combined force would rendezvous in the north Pacific, and be designated Task Force 16.

With training at Eglin Field completed, 22 aircraft left on 25 March for McClellan Field at Sacramento, California. (Two planes were damaged in training.) At McClellan, technicians performed final inspections of the aircraft, and replaced all propellers with new ones. The aircraft then flew the short distance from McClellan Field to the naval air station at Alameda on San Francisco Bay. *Hornet* was moored alongside, after a fast transit from Norfolk, Virginia, through the Panama Canal.

Doolittle's raid
18 April 1942

MONGOLIA

INNER MONGOLIA

SOVIET UNION

Vladivostok

JAPAN

SEA OF JAPAN

Tokyo
Yokohama

Peking

KOREA

Kobe

Nagoya
Osaka

Hiroshima

YELLOW SEA

C H I N A

Nagasaki

Nanking

PACIFIC

Hangkow

Shanghai

Chungking

Chuchow

EAST CHINA SEA

FORMOSA

Canton

HONG KONG

SOUTH CHINA SEA

Key
Route followed by
Doolittle's raiders

On 18 April 1942, as the
Japanese continued their
advance deeper into the central
and south Pacific, a small
American force of carrier-borne
B-25s under Lieutenant-Colonel
James Doolittle mounted an
historic raid against the
Japanese mainland.

Doolittle knew that, at most, 16 B-25s would fit aboard *Hornet*. He selected those that would make the voyage by meeting each aircraft as it landed from McClellan. If anything was wrong with the plane, he directed it into a hangar. If it was working smoothly, he sent it to the dockside. Although six aircraft were left behind, all of the crews sailed, ensuring that secrecy was preserved and spare crewmen were available if needed.

Lieutenant Hank Miller went ahead of the raiders to make arrangements with Captain Mitscher of *Hornet*, and on 31 March and 1 April, Navy yard cranes lifted 16 B-25Bs aboard the carrier. They were fitted together in tight rows and lashed down. Even so, the tails of the aircraft in the last row jutted out over the carrier's stern.

Hornet and her consorts sailed from San Francisco Bay on the morning of 2 April. When she was well at sea, the raiders and ship's crew were at last told their mission: to bomb Japanese cities. Cheers were heard throughout the ship and 'morale reached a new high'. The air crews then spent the time on board ship in training and familiarisation with the targets they would strike. Navigation classes were conducted, and Doolittle himself presented classes on gunnery and on targets to be bombed.

Doolittle let the pilots choose their targets. The target list was restricted to war industries, shipyards, power plants, and other installations of military use. The Imperial Palace in Tokyo was absolutely off-limits. Target folders were issued and the crews studied the enclosed target photos, using the maps to an their routes.

Admiral Halsey with *Enterprise* and her group left earl Harbor on 8 April. The two groups merged on londay, 13 April at the agreed point: 38 degrees orth, 180 degrees east. The seas were heavy as ask Force 16 ploughed westward towards the lanned launch point, 400 miles from Tokyo. Halsey unched scout aircraft daily to fly a 200-mile surveill- nce screen around the task force. Ahead of the hips and closer to Japan, two submarines kept atch for enemy ships and relayed weather informa- on. The Navy planned to close to within 400 miles of e coast before the launch, unless detected by the apanese. If that happened, the crews would take off, ut they would have further to fly and their chances of aving to crash-land would be increased.

Japanese early-warning capability was limited to string of patrol boats cruising about 600-700 miles ffshore, supplemented by reconnaissance aircraft n call. The Japanese military leadership thought at it would have enough warning to fly air strikes gainst any carrier task force before its planes could e launched against Japan, believing that US Navy arrier aircraft had an operational radius of only 300 iles. No serious Japanese intelligence officer ould have imagined that 16 B-25 medium bombers, epared for a one-way flight of more than 2000 iles, were at that moment approaching Japan.

On 17 April the fighting ships were refuelled. The ers then turned back towards Hawaii and Task

Force 16 began its dash towards the Japanese main- land. During the day, ammunition and bombs were brought up from magazines deep inside *Hornet* and wrestled aboard the B-25s. That evening, Doolittle gave the final briefing to the aircrews. Take-off was tentatively set for the evening of 19 April unless the force was intercepted earlier.

That night, long-range radar detected a Japanese ship ahead of the task force, and Halsey manoeuvred to avoid it. As the darkness gave way to dawn the sea was rough, with low clouds and rain squalls washing over the task force. In the early morning hours of 18 April, air patrols detected two more small ships closer to the force.

Admiral Halsey made the decision to prepare to launch the raiders immediately. At 0740 hours the loudspeaker blared, 'Army pilots, man your planes.' The escorts sighted a Japanese picket boat close by and the cruiser USS *Nashville* blasted it out of the water, but before sinking it sent off a short radio message to Tokyo.

Halsey had to assume that the Japanese were alerted. He ordered the bombers to be launched and his signalman flashed a message by light code to *Hornet*: 'Launch planes. To Col Doolittle and gallant command good luck and God bless you.' The dis- tance to the coast was 645 miles, not the planned 400, but there was no choice. The bombers had to launch before the Japanese could reach and attack the only two US aircraft carriers then operating in the north Pacific.

On board *Hornet*, disciplined haste was made. The bomber crews boarded the B-25s, stowing personal gear and flight equipment in pre-planned spots. Cockpit and crew checks were made. Captain Mitscher swung *Hornet* onto a course of 300 degrees to point her bow into the wind and increased speed to 27 knots. The carrier's bow slammed into rough seas cresting to 30ft, pitching up and down as she

Left: Observed by Captain Mitscher from *Hornet's* bridge, Doolittle's B-25, burdened by 6846lb of fuel and 2000lb of bombs, thunders down the flightdeck to begin the first American air attack on Japan.

rode through the waves, smashing spray high in the air to right and left. Halsey later said, 'The wind and sea were so strong that morning that green water was breaking over the carriers' ramps.'

The lashings were removed and the planes' wheels chocked. The nose wheel of Doolittle's air- craft, tail number 40-2344, was 467ft from the forward edge of *Hornet's* flightdeck, giving him the shortest take-off run. Lieutenant Hank Miller placed himself ahead of the aircraft with a blackboard, ready to relay instructions to the pilots if needed.

THE TOKYO BOMBERS

The North American B-25 Mitchell bombers selected by Lieutenant-Colonel Doolittle for what became known as the Doolittle Raid required extensive modifications for their long haul. Their normal range of 1300 miles had to be extended to over 2000 miles, and fuel capacity was increased to 1141 gallons, enough for a cruising range of 2400 miles after take-off with the planned bomb load. A 220-gallon tank was installed in the bomb bay, leaving room for four 500lb bombs or four 500lb incendiary clusters, and another rubber tank was installed in the crawl-way above the bomb bay – this tank collapsed on emptying to make the crawl-way available to the crew. In addition, a 60-gallon tank replaced the lower turret, and 10 five-gallon jerricans were carried to top up the turret tank during the flight. All expendable equipment was removed to save weight: the bottom turret was removed, and the 0.5in machine guns in the tail were replaced by dummy black-painted broomsticks. It was essential to the

Americans that the top- secret Norden bomb-sights normally carried by the Mitchells should not fall into Japanese hands. They were therefore replaced by a simple inclinometer-type sight suitable for bombing at a very low altitude.
Top: The insignia of the 34th Bomb Squadron, one of the units of 17th Bomb Group that went on the raid.

LT-COLONEL 'JIMMY' DOOLITTLE

Born in December 1896, James H. Doolittle enlisted in the US Army's Aviation Section in 1917. A natural pilot, he earned his wings in March 1918 and flew as an instructor for the rest of World War I.

Following the war, Doolittle remained in the Army. In 1921 he took part in bombing tests against naval vessels arranged by General Billy Mitchell. On 4 September 1922 he became the first person to fly across the United States in less than a day. He won the Schneider Trophy race in 1925 and set world seaplane records. He also earned one of the first doctorates in aeronautical engineering in 1925. In September 1929 he executed the world's first 'blind' take-off, extended circuit and landing in heavy fog, leading the way to the development of successful instrument flying. He won both the Bendix and Thompson trophies for speed.

In the 1930s he resigned his commission to head the aviation department of the Shell Oil Company. He remained in the reserves, however, and in July 1940 he returned to active duty. General Arnold set him to work converting the automobile industry to aircraft production in Indianapolis and Detroit. This work set in train, Arnold brought Doolittle to Washington for the raid on Japan.

Following the raid, he was promoted to brigadier-general and given command of the Twelfth Army Air Force in North Africa. He then took command of the Eighth Army Air Force for the D-day landings, leading it until the end of the war in Europe.

Right: Homing in on target, a bomber dives on the naval base at Yokosaku. Top right: Although the escort USS *Nashville* sank this fishing boat, it tried to warn Tokyo of the carrier's approach. Top far right: Doolittle sits on the wing of his B-25, ditched in China after the raid. Below far right: Surviving aircrews are photographed after regrouping in China.

Doolittle started his engines on signal, then ran them up. He was watching a launch control officer with a flag who was positioned on the port side, near the bow. On that officer's signal, Doolittle increased power to the B-25's engines. Plane handlers pulled the chocks blocking the wheels, and, as the deck began to rise, the launch officer signalled again with his flag. Doolittle released his brakes and his bomber began its run down the rainswept deck. Captain Mitscher watched from the bridge wing. Halsey on *Enterprise* also watched. He wrote later, 'Jimmy led his squadron off. When his plane buzzed down the *Hornet's* deck, there wasn't a man topside who didn't help sweat him into the air.'

Two white stripes were painted on the flightdeck, one for the nose wheel and one for the left wheel. If the pilot kept his aircraft on the stripes, his right wingtip would clear the carrier's 'island' superstructure. Doolittle's 40-2344 gained speed as the deck rose. He lifted it off, remained level for a time to gain airspeed, then climbed in a left-hand circle to come back over *Hornet*. It was 0820 hours.

In succession, the 15 remaining B-25s were launched the same way at about three-minute intervals. The take-offs were uneventful, except for No. 16. As it waited to take off, the ship pitched. A *Hornet* plane handler slipped on the deck and lost an arm to the aircraft's spinning left-hand propeller. He was pulled out of the way and the aircraft took off, piloted by Lieutenant William G. Farrow.

When each aircraft had made its take-off, it circled the carrier and flew right over the deck to read the course displayed on a large card. This gave them a last check of their compasses as they set their course for the heart of Japan.

The aircraft behind Doolittle flew in a loose stream of five groups of three, rather than in a tight formation. Consequently, although the bombers approached generally from the northeast, they were spread out across a 50-mile front. As they neared the target cities, the flights broke up. Individual bombers approached Tokyo, Yokohama, and Nagoya from different directions, giving the defenders the impression of a very large raiding force.

Jimmy Doolittle's B-25 was charging at low level from the north towards the centre of the city

In Tokyo that Saturday morning, an air-raid drill was planned. It began at about the time the last aircraft left *Hornet*. By noon, the activities were over and Tokyo returned to its normal Saturday routine. No-one suspected that Jimmy Doolittle's B-25 was charging at low level from the north towards the centre of the city. At 1230 hours local time, Doolittle pulled up to 1200ft and dropped his bombs.

Surprise was complete. Anti-aircraft batteries began firing, but Doolittle was away and headed south towards the sea. Right behind him came the other 15 raiders. Now that the defences were alerted, the flak grew more intense. It was inaccurate, however, and none of the raiders was lost to flak or fighter planes. Bombing reports filed later by the raiders vividly described the effects: 'Bombing from 900ft. Debris flew higher than the plane.' 'A chemical works burst into flame. Military barracks machine-gunned during withdrawal.' 'Smoke column from target billowing to several thousand feet . . .'

Now the raiders had to find the refuelling bases near Chuchow in China. They headed southwest, expecting to be able to detect radio homing devices

the bases. Unfortunately, through a series of
[err]ors, none was in place. In addition, Doolittle
[en]countered a lowering ceiling as he neared the
[Ch]inese coast. The ceiling dropped to 600ft, so he
[cli]mbed to 6000ft, then to 8000ft, to get above the
[ov]ercast. The raiders behind him followed suit. The
[on]ly favourable aspect of the post-strike flight was
[a 2]5mph tail wind, and with its help 15 of the aircraft
[m]ade it to the Chinese coast or inland.

One aircraft did not make it to China: it landed in
[th]e Soviet Union. The engines of Captain Edward J.
[Yo]rk's B-25 (plane No.8) were gulping fuel much
[fas]ter than anticipated. He decided to head north for
[Vl]adivostok in Russia. Barely enough fuel remained
[in] his tanks to get there. York and his crew were
[int]erned by the Soviets for 13 months before being
[re]patriated.

[L]ieutenant-Colonel Doolittle and his [c]rew baled out about 70 miles north of Chuchow

[Wi]thout the radio beacons, Doolittle and the other
[pil]ots relied on their own navigators to direct them
[to]wards Chuchow. But they were beaten by the bad
[we]ather and nightfall. Ultimately, they all had to bale
[out] or crash-land. Two crews (Nos.6 and 16) were
[cap]tured by the Japanese, and two men of Lieute-
[nan]t Dean Hallmark's No.6 drowned when the air-
[cra]ft ditched close to shore. The other three crew-
[me]n were captured and taken to Shanghai, where
[Ha]llmark was executed by the Japanese. The crew
[of] Lieutenant Farrow's No.16 baled out over
[Jap]anese-held territory and all five were captured.
[Far]row and Sergeant Harold Spatz were executed.
[Th]e other men from both crews were imprisoned by
[the] Japanese until the end of the war.

[L]ieutenant-Colonel Doolittle and his crew baled
[out] about 70 miles north of Chuchow. He found his
[ma]n the next day, and began the effort to find the
[oth]er crews. Chinese guerrillas helped some of the
[me]n; others contacted Chinese officials who moved
[the]m towards Chungking. Still others were treated
[as] heroes by Chinese villagers, who fêted them and
[tra]nsported them in sedan chairs westward to safety.
[T]he surviving raiders were assembled in Chung-
[kin]g and eventually made their way back to the US
[for] re-assignment. Doolittle was promoted to briga-
[die]r-general on 26 April, and President Roosevelt
[ord]ered him to leave Chungking on 5 May and return
[imm]ediately. He reached Washington in mid-May.
[At] the White House on 19 May, President Roosevelt
[de]corated General Doolittle with the Medal of Hon-
[or,] the nation's highest decoration.

[A]fter the news of the Doolittle Raid, America
[bel]ieved that the defeat of Japan was inevitable.
[Alt]hough the raid inflicted little real damage on the
[tar]gets, and all the bombers were lost, its effects
[we]re profound. The greatest effect was on the
[Jap]anese, who now knew that their homeland was
[vul]nerable from the air.

[I]n that gloomy mid-April of 1942, President
[Ro]osevelt had what he needed most, a strike at the
[he]art of Japan. The Doolittle Raiders had shattered
[th]e myth of Japanese invincibility.

[THE] AUTHOR F. Clifton Berry, Jr, is an aerospace
[wri]ter based in Washington, DC. He is a former
[par]atrooper and an active pilot, with land and
[sea]plane ratings.

FUERZA AÉREA
ARGENTINA

In May 1982, the FAA
(Argentinian Air Force),
under the command of
General Lami Dozo, was one
of the strongest air forces in
South America, fielding an
estimated 143 aircraft of
various types. These ranged
from medium-range
fighters, fighter-bombers
and bombers to short-range
attack aircraft,
reconnaissance planes,
transports, helicopters and
support aircraft. Of this
inventory, 46 were
Skyhawks.
During the Falklands
conflict, the FAA was
organised into four
commands: Air Operations,
Air Regions, Personnel and
Material. The FAA order of
battle for the conflict
consisted of seven Grupos:
Grupos 4 and 5 flew
Skyhawks, Grupos 6 and 8
flew Mirage IIIs and Israeli
Aircraft Industries Daggers
(a copy of the Mirage V),
Grupo 3 operated with
Pucará ground-attack
aircraft from bases on the
Falklands, while Grupos 1
and 2 were equipped with
Boeing 707 and Gates
Learjet 35A reconnaissance
planes, Hercules transports
and tankers, and Canberra
B 62 bombers.
The main bases from which
the FAA launched
operations against the
British were Rio Gallegos,
Rio Grande and Comodoro
Rivadavia. Situated in the
south of Argentina, these
bases were within 950km of
the Falkland Islands and all
had runways of at least
7000ft in length.
Above: The insignia of the
Vth Air Brigade.

In 1982 Argentinian Air Force jets attacked the Task Force in Falkland Sound – a stretch of water that soon became known as 'Bomb Alley'

DURING THE FALKLANDS conflict of 1982, the Argentinian Navy's Exocet missions garnered world attention as the first use of sea-skimmers in combat. However, of the six British ships sunk and 11 damaged during the war, only three were hit by Exocets. The other 14 were hit, some more than once, by pilots flying relatively unsophisticated and near-obsolete fast jets carrying iron bombs. Not only had the majority of the pilots in the Fuerza Aérea Argentina (FAA) – the Argentinian Air Force – not been trained to attack ships, but they also dropped surplus bombs, of which 75 per cent failed to detonate. In view of this,

and the dense anti-aircraft environment the FAA pilots were operating in, the Argentinian successes came as quite a shock to the British defenders.

Of all the Argentinian air units involved, by far the most successful was Grupo 5, flying A-4P Skyhawks (rebuilt versions of the A-4B) in the IVth and Vth Fighter Squadrons, attached to the Vth Air Brigade. Normally based at Villa Reynolds in the middle of Argentina, close to the Chilean border, the unit moved on the eve of the outbreak of hostilities to Rio Gallegos, on the coast, where Navy Skyhawk pilots gave their Air Force counterparts a concentrated course in how to attack ships at sea. Until then, the only tactical training given to FAA crews had been based on the possibility of a border war with Chile, the nation Argentinian military intelligence considered to be the greatest threat to national security.

On 1 May, the first day of the fighting, FAA Mirages and Royal Navy Sea Harriers tangled in the air, as

BOMB ALLEY

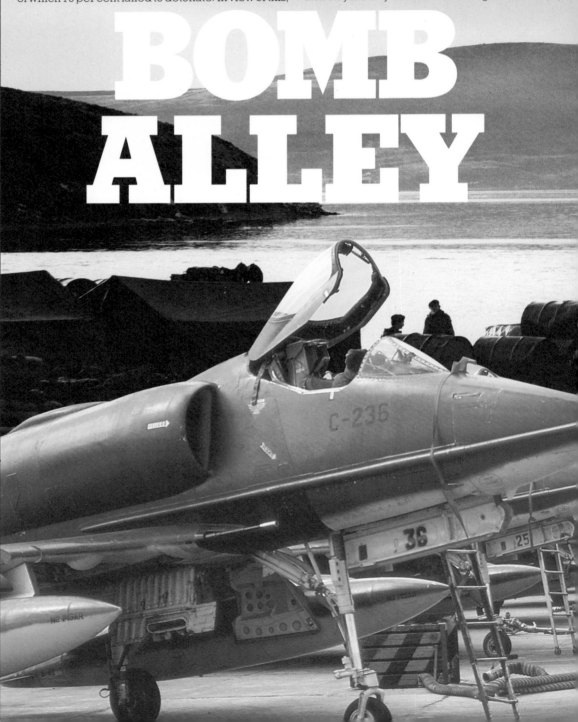

Below: While British troops unload supplies at the San Carlos beachhead, a Task Force vessel narrowly escapes the full force of an Argentinian bomb as it blows a sheet of spray high into the air. Below left: A line of Grupo 5 A-4 Skyhawks is prepared for battle. Bottom right: An A-4 taxies into Rio Gallegos air base after a sortie. Right: Thumbs up. An Argentinian Skyhawk pilot exudes confidence as he awaits the signal to take off.

Grupo 5's Skyhawks, along with Daggers, Canberras and other A-4s, attacked the British warships of the Task Force with total surprise. On that day, a total of 12 Dagger, six Canberra and 28 Skyhawk sorties were despatched, along with 10 Mirage sorties for air cover. At the end of 1 May, it was clear that the Argentinians were not going to be a threat to air superiority, but they were certainly likely to hit the British ships.

On 12 May, shortly after midday, Grupo 5 sent two flights of A-4s from Rio Gallegos to attack British warships engaged in bombarding Stanley airfield. The lead flight ran in to bomb, but found the destroyer *Glasgow* and the frigate *Brilliant* ready for them. HMS *Brilliant* engaged the attackers with Sea Wolf missiles and shot down Lieutenants Bustos and Nivoli. Lieutenant Ibarlucea crashed into the sea while trying to avoid a missile. As the fourth Skyhawk pulled clear, the second flight, led by Captain Zelaya, headed for *Glasgow*. The No.4 then broke off and made for *Brilliant*.

Again the Sea Wolf operators on *Brilliant* prepared to engage, but, at the critical moment, the

Main picture: A deceptively calm and peaceful view of the Task Force at rest. Superficially, the ships must have seemed sitting ducks to the attack pilots, but once they got in among them, intense anti-aircraft and missile fire and the pilots' lack of specific ship-attack training, often proved more than a match for their bravery and flying skills. Despite these shortcomings, the British ships still came in for some pretty nerve-racking moments (right). Below right: A Grupo 5 Skyhawk, bombed-up with three 500-pounders, takes on fuel from a tanker en route to 'Bomb Alley'.

system suffered a technical hiccup and went down – there was now no missile defence. The sailors watched helplessly as the Skyhawk closed in rapidly and released its bombs: they struck the water, bounced right over the frigate, and fell back into the sea on the far side.

Although Zelaya expected to see missiles, he could not see any in flight, but he could hear the explosions of anti-aircraft shells. The leader and his two wingmen pressed straight in on *Glasgow* and released their bombs. Lieutenant Fausto Gavazzi shouted over the radio, 'Viva la Patria! I hit it! I'm sure I hit it!' Gavazzi's 1000-pounder struck *Glasgow* amidships, smashed clean through her hull, emerged out the other side and exploded in the sea several seconds later when the ship was safely clear. On its way through, the bomb managed to miss all the ship's structural frames; it knocked over a high-pressure air bottle, without fracturing it, and smashed a fuel tank without starting a fire.

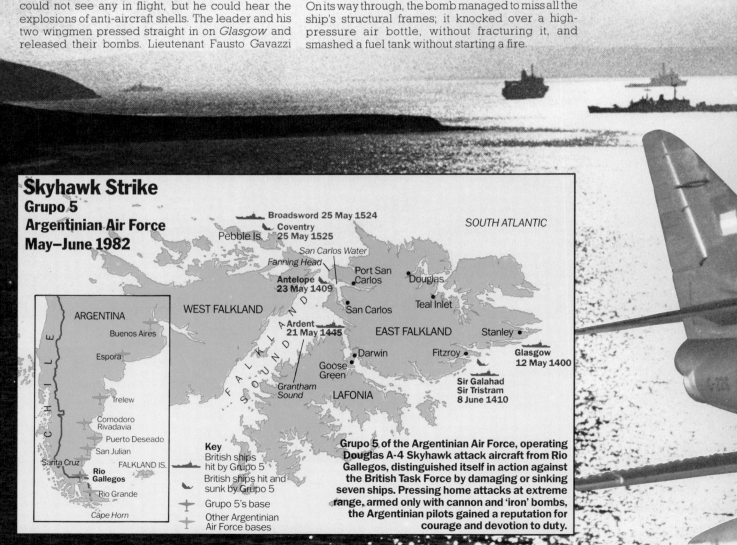

Skyhawk Strike
Grupo 5
Argentinian Air Force
May–June 1982

SOUTH ATLANTIC

Broadsword 25 May 1524
Coventry 25 May 1525
Pebble Is.
San Carlos Water
Fanning Head
Antelope 23 May 1409
Port San Carlos
Douglas
WEST FALKLAND
San Carlos
Teal Inlet
Ardent 21 May 1445
EAST FALKLAND
Stanley
Darwin
Fitzroy
Glasgow 12 May 1400
Goose Green
Grantham Sound
LAFONIA
Sir Galahad Sir Tristram 8 June 1410

ARGENTINA
Buenos Aires
Espora
C H I L E
Trelew
Comodoro Rivadavia
Puerto Deseado
San Julian
FALKLAND IS.
Rio Gallegos
Rio Grande
Cape Horn

Key
British ships hit by Grupo 5
British ships hit and sunk by Grupo 5
Grupo 5's base
Other Argentinian Air Force bases

Grupo 5 of the Argentinian Air Force, operating Douglas A-4 Skyhawk attack aircraft from Rio Gallegos, distinguished itself in action against the British Task Force by damaging or sinking seven ships. Pressing home attacks at extreme range, armed only with cannon and 'iron' bombs, the Argentinian pilots gained a reputation for courage and devotion to duty.

As the surviving A-4s flew past Goose Green on their way home, trigger-happy Argentinian anti-aircraft gunners opened up at the planes coming in from the east. Gavazzi's aircraft was hit and rolled over onto its back, smashing into the ground with the pilot still on board. The Skyhawks then pressed down to just a few metres above the water. The pilots were learning that, regardless of who was firing, if they were to survive they would have to fly very low indeed and at maximum speed. Salt collected on their windscreens to the point that it was impossible to see straight ahead. Although everyone got back, Lieutenant Vazquez, the sole survivor of the lead attack flight on *Brilliant*, had almost the entire forward portion of his canopy covered in salt and as he landed, his aircraft ran off the runway. It had been a hard day for Grupo 5; four aircraft and pilots lost, one aircraft damaged on landing, and another crippled with battle damage.

On 21 May the British amphibious landing on East Falkland was finally launched

The encounter on 12 May demonstrated that Sea Dart, the sole anti-aircraft missile system fitted to *Glasgow* and her sister Type 42 destroyers, although effective against high-flying targets, was far less so against aircraft approaching at ultra-low altitude; and it was clear that the Argentinian pilots, who had practised attacks against their own Navy's Type 42 destroyers, knew of this weakness. Also, when used to engage low-flying aircraft, the Type 42's gun-control radar suffered considerably from 'surface clutter' and the accuracy of fire from the 4.5in gun was reduced accordingly. HMS *Brilliant's* Sea Wolf had shown that, when it functioned properly, it was extremely effective against low-flying aircraft; but, like many computer-controlled systems, it was liable to 'sulk' at the worst possible time. In view of the narrow escapes experienced by *Glasgow* and *Brilliant,* the British commander, Admiral Sandy Woodward, decided that there would be no further naval bombardments of Port Stanley airfield during daylight hours.

On 21 May the British amphibious landing on East Falkland was finally launched from a host of ships, towards San Carlos Water. Just over one mile in width and four miles in length, the inlet formed a slit trench, surrounded by hills on all sides, except for the southeast and the entrance at the northwest; it served as a natural protection from air attack. The first attack force to be launched from the Argentinian mainland was led by Major Carlos Martinez, who took in six Grupo 6 Daggers on an armed reconnaissance. Grupo 5 sent out four A-4s as the next force led by Captain Pablo Carballo. From the outset, the Skyhawks ran into trouble. Rendezvousing with a KC-130 tanker off the Argentinian coast, one of the planes was unable to take on fuel and had to turn

back. Later, another of the fighter-bombers was unable to transfer fuel from one of its drop tanks and it, too, aborted.

The two remaining Skyhawks flew on, crossed over the centre of West Falkland, and entered Falkland Sound. In the channel, the pair sighted a large ship in front of them; in fact, it was the Argentinian freighter *Rio Carcaraña*, lying abandoned after an attack by Sea Harriers five days earlier. Carballo turned to attack, but then saw that it was not a warship, and was probably one of their own. Carballo broke off, but his wingman, Ensign Carmona, was so busy concentrating on the attack that he swept in and dropped his bombs. Ordering Carmona to return to base, Carballo pressed on alone up the eastern side of Falkland Sound. Carballo recalled the run in:

Above: The A-4P Skyhawk. Top left: In time-honoured tradition, an Argentinian crew 'dedicates' a bomb. This particular weapon would seem earmarked for HRH The Prince Andrew. Left: A Skyhawk is bombed-up prior to a mission. Below: Two pilots from Grupo 5; Lieutenant Fausto Gavazzi (right), who was shot down by his own side's AA fire on 12 May, and Ensign Alfredo Vasquez, who fell victim to a Sea Harrier from No.800 Squadron on 8 June. Right: HMS *Exeter* looses off a Sea Dart.

'I was passing rapidly by the small bays and entrances to the sea when all of a sudden, on entering Bahía Ruiz Puente [Grantham Sound], in front of me there appeared a frigate. My first thought was, "It's not as big as I had imagined!" Then I ran in to attack. As I closed in, almost touching the water to avoid being picked up on their radar, the frigate grew larger and larger.'

On board the frigate *Ardent*, the first anyone knew of something happening was when a cry came from the bridge, 'Aircraft closing!' Four thousand yards away, coming straight for the ship from the southwest, over land and closing fast, was Carballo. He was right on the bow. *Ardent's* captain, Alan West, was on the bridge – he put on full wheel and called for full speed.

The A-4 flashed over the ship just as she was beginning to turn. Her 4.5in gun had no time to get on the Skyhawk and the only thing that could fire was the

between the boiler room and the engine room, demolishing several steam pipes, causing a boiler to explode, and then wrecking a part of her steering gear. The other bomb impacted below the waterline, further forward, and passed through a couple of fuel tanks, across a sonar compartment, and ended up in the forward Sea Cat magazine, where it caused two missiles to detonate and killed two of the ship's crew. Although both bombs caused secondary explosions, neither detonated, but the attack left *Argonaut* in serious trouble, with both engines and the steering gear out of action.

By 1445, yet more aircraft were streaking in to attack the warships and transports.

SKYHAWK

The Douglas A-4 single-seat Skyhawk attack aircraft was in continuous production for some 26 years (1954-79) and has seen combat in various

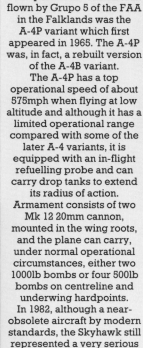

20mm Oerlikon. Carballo's two bombs fell away – one fell short and the other passed over the ship. The Argentinian pilot dropped to just above the water, turned and flew off down the sound. Alan West and his crew had experienced at first hand how rapidly things could change if fortune ever deserted them.

Later that day, at 1430 hours, the FAA pressed in another attack. A force of A-4s came around the north of the island and reached Falkland Sound without interference. Six of them went for HMS *Argonaut* and she was hit with two 1000-pounders. One bomb smashed into her hull just above the waterline,

Brilliant was strafed by A-4s and 20 hits from cannon shells penetrated to the fighter-control radar room. One controller was hit in the stomach, and the controller talking to Sea Harrier pilots Lieutenant Commander Sharkey Ward and Lieutenant Steve Thomas was hit in the arm. The British fighter pilots moved into position over Pebble Island to catch the attackers on the way out, or new ones inbound.

Five A-4s of Grupo 5 attempted to hit the ships unloading in San Carlos Water. The Argentinian pilots found the high ground surrounding the anchorage difficult to see over during their approach, forcing them to attack the ships, regardless of position, as they topped the last hill. As Ensign Marcelo Moroni remembered, 'There were eight or nine ships in the bay. The moment they saw us, they opened up with everything they had. Two of the Skyhawks went for one frigate, another two headed for another ship, and I was last of the five.' Each A-4 dropped its bombs and got back to Rio Gallegos with only one suffering damage from smallarms fire.

conflicts including Vietnam, with the US Navy and Marine Corps, the Middle East, with the Israeli Air Force, and the Falklands with the FAA.

One of the outstanding features of the Skyhawk was its capacity to incorporate design changes to keep it in step with the changing face of aerial warfare. In its long history, 23 operational variants on the original production model have been produced. The aircraft flown by Grupo 5 of the FAA in the Falklands was the A-4P variant which first appeared in 1965. The A-4P was, in fact, a rebuilt version of the A-4B variant.

The A-4P has a top operational speed of about 575mph when flying at low altitude and although it has a limited operational range compared with some of the later A-4 variants, it is equipped with an in-flight refuelling probe and can carry drop tanks to extend its radius of action. Armament consists of two Mk 12 20mm cannon, mounted in the wing roots, and the plane can carry, under normal operational circumstances, either two 1000lb bombs or four 500lb bombs on centreline and underwing hardpoints.

In 1982, although a near-obsolete aircraft by modern standards, the Skyhawk still represented a very serious threat to the ships of the British Task Force.

THE BOMBERS' DILEMMA

Although it was apparent that most of the Argentinian bombs were failing to detonate, the FAA pilots were on the horns of a dilemma. They could either release their bombs from altitudes above 200-300ft and court almost certain death from the ships' missile defences, or they could avoid the missiles by flying in at under 50ft and pop up to 100ft at the last minute to release their payload. However, using the latter strategy, the bombs' two-second arming systems would not have had time to operate before the weapons struck their targets. Technically, it was simple to make a bomb live immediately after it left the aircraft, but doing so would have meant that when making low-level attacks, the plane would have been blown up by its own bombs.

There was also another problem. Even if the bomb did arm itself properly before it struck the target warship, there remained the question of how long a delay should be set on the fuze between impact and detonation. If a short delay was used, about a quarter of a second, then, to avoid falling debris from bombs dropped by preceding aircraft, the succeeding planes had to attack with at least a 25-second gap between each attack run. To attack at shorter intervals in order to swamp the defences, the detonation of the bombs had to be delayed after impact by between 12 and 30 seconds so that the last aircraft was clear before the first bomb exploded.

Far left: An Argentinian armament technician prepares a bomb. Left: Grupo 5 pilots celebrate what they believe was a kill on HMS *Glasgow* after a sortie on 12 May. In reality, when the bomb hit the ship it passed clean through and exploded harmlessly in the water. Far left below: Lieutenant-Colonel Ruben Zini stands beside the Skyhawk in which he led the attacks on the Task Force on 25 May. Left below: HMS *Antelope* slips beneath the waves, a victim of an FAA bombing attack. Left inset: Lieutenant Luciano Guadagnini who, seconds after attacking *Antelope*, was blown out of the sky by a British missile.

Other Grupo 5 A-4s ran in to attack *Ardent*, already the victim of a bomb from a Grupo 6 Dagger, as she was pulling out of Grantham Sound. In two flights, the Argentinian fighter-bombers fired cannon as they pressed in. The ship was deluged with bombs, most of which failed to detonate, but two which struck her went off, causing further damage to the stern. *Ardent* was now in a very bad way.

The final attack made on *Ardent* was by A-4Qs of the 3rd Naval Fighter and Attack Escuadrilla, which succeeded in putting two 500lb Snakeye bombs onto her stern. *Ardent* was flooding badly and listing. Captain Alan West called for *Yarmouth* to come and put her stern against *Ardent's* bow. In Navy tradition, West was the last man off. Twenty-two of the ship's crew had been killed and 30 injured. Six hours later, after taking seven 1000lb and 500lb bombs which exploded, and two which did not go off, *Ardent* sank.

The bombs punched deep into the destroyer and exploded, blowing a great hole in her port side

Despite this success, the Argentinians' lack of combat training was painfully obvious: they had no tactics for mutual support with cannon or missiles if enemy fighters attacked. Lieutenant-Colonel Ruben Zini of Grupo 5 noted, 'We were briefed to avoid dogfights and escape at low level and alone. Every man for himself.' While this puzzled British pilots, who expected to be hard pressed, the Harrier pilots gave their Argentinian adversaries nine-and-a-half out of 10 for sheer guts and courage.

On 23 May HMS *Antelope* was attacked by Grupo 5's Skyhawks. Lieutenant Filipini actually hit a mast with his droptank, losing one fin. Lieutenant Luciano Guadagnini, just after releasing his bombs, was engaged by a Sea Wolf from HMS *Broadsword* and possibly a ground-launched Rapier. The aircraft broke up into a ball of flaming wreckage and crashed into the sea, killing Guadagnini. With two bombs lodged in her hull and a smashed rear mast, *Antelope* limped to the far end of San Carlos Water for the bombs to be made safe. That night, one exploded and the frigate sank.

After a few attacks on the morning of 25 May against the San Carlos landing area, the FAA came back in the afternoon with great determination. Ruben Zini led six Skyhawks of Grupo 5 from Rio Gallegos to attack the warships at Pebble Island. Zini and his wingman went for *Broadsword*, which got a radar lock-on and waited for the targets to come within range of her Sea Wolf missiles. At the time, Lieutenant Commander Neil Thomas was leading a pair of Sea Harriers from No. 800 Squadron which had just arrived on patrol. Thomas accelerated to maximum speed and was diving in to intercept when, before he could get into a firing position, he received orders to break off the chase so as not to follow the enemy aircraft into the missile engagement zone.

The two Sea Harriers pulled away, but at this critical moment *Broadsword's* missile-control radar tripped out and broke lock, making it impossible to launch. Unopposed, the two A-4s went in and dropped their bombs. Three missed, but the fourth skipped off the water, struck the ship's stern, came out of the top of the flight deck, carried away part of the nose of the Lynx helicopter and continued on, to fall back into the sea on the other side without exploding.

A second pair of Skyhawks, flown by Jorge Neuvo and his leader, was about 10 miles from HMS *Coventry* and closing at maximum speed. Again the Sea Harriers moved to intercept, again *Broadsword* achieved a lock-on with Sea Wolf and again the British fighters were ordered to break away. *Coventry* fired a Sea Dart at the approaching aircraft, but it missed, as did the shots from her 4.5in gun. *Broadsword* was just about to open fire with Sea Wolf when, suddenly, *Coventry* manoeuvred to make the attackers' task more difficult and cut across her bow, shielding the Skyhawks; again the missile control radar broke lock. Neuvo saw three of the bombs hit the ship and the planes swept away from the target.

The three bombs punched deep into the destroyer and exploded, blowing a great hole in her port side. There was immediate flooding, fire, and loss of all power and communications. *Coventry* rolled right over until she was upside down with only her propellers showing.

Not until 8 June was another major attack launched against British ships. Five Skyhawks of Grupo 5, unable to spot targets at Fitzroy, turned around and started to head for home. Suddenly, the formation leader heard a call from one of the pilots at the rear, 'There are the ships!' In the distance, back towards shore, were the faint silhouettes of the landing ships. By sheer chance, the formation attacked *Sir Galahad* and *Sir Tristram*. They released from high enough to arm the bombs and *Sir Galahad* went up in flames as the bombs exploded; *Sir Tristram* also caught fire. Altogether 51 men were killed and 46 injured, the worst single loss inflicted on British forces during the conflict. The Argentinian Air Force had forcibly demonstrated that it was still very much in business, but follow-up attacks on the Fitzroy area, later in the day, met far stronger defences and were able to achieve little.

The Argentinian fighter-bomber pilots gave a salutary demonstration that brave pilots, flying near-obsolete or unsuitable aircraft, armed with iron bombs, can penetrate sophisticated missile defences and inflict major, even fatal, damage on modern warships. However, although the men showed that they were competent flyers, this was their first war and their tactics were often poor.

During the conflict, the most successful Argentinian unit against shipping was Grupo 5, whose A-4 Skyhawks inflicted death blows on *Coventry* and *Sir Galahad*, probably dropped the bomb which caused the loss of *Antelope*, scored hits on *Ardent* and *Broadsword*, and inflicted damage on *Glasgow* and *Sir Tristram*. In action Grupo 5 lost 10 aircraft and nine pilots.

THE AUTHOR Jeffrey Ethell has written numerous articles and more than 20 books on aviation subjects. Having learnt to fly before learning to drive a car, he regularly flies current high-performance aircraft with the US Air Force, Navy and Marine Corps. His recent books include *Air War South Atlantic, Fox Two* and *Pilot Maker*.

617 Squadron, one of the most successful RAF units during World War II, now plays a key role in the front line of NATO's defences

After a remarkable career in World War II (above), No. 617 Squadron is now flying the RAF's most sophisticated aircraft, the Tornado (left). Above right: Two modern-day Dambusters in g-suits pose in front of the squadron's famous insignia.

TORNADO SQUADRON

No.617 SQUADRON is unique among the flying units of the Royal Air Force in having been formed to carry out a specific operation – the famous attack on the Ruhr dams in May 1943. The brilliant execution of this raid and the 'Dambusters' outstanding record of precision attacks on targets of special importance during the following two years of the war, earned the squadron a special place in RAF history. Consequently, it was decided to retain No.617 Squadron on the RAF's much-reduced peacetime establishment after the end of World War II. Normally, the RAF's squadrons are reformed or disbanded strictly according to seniority and so most of today's squadrons can trace their origins back to World War I, or earlier in some cases.

No.617 Squadron, now based at RAF Marham in Norfolk and flying Tornados, is a notable exception to the rule and, as the USAF's Strategic Air Command bombing competition of 1984 demonstrated, the present-day Dambusters are worthy heirs to a great tradition.

No.617 Squadron began operations on the Panavia Tornado GR Mk 1 in January 1983, as 'the second, but premier' RAF Tornado squadron. The Dambusters' primary roles are tactical strike and conventional attack in the European theatre. The squadron is subordinated to No.1 Group, RAF Strike Command and is part of SACEUR's (Supreme Allied Command, Europe) force within NATO.

The squadron is equipped with 12 Tornado GR Mk 1s and, to operate and maintain them, has a strength of 30 pilots and navigators, 150 technicians, various administrative personnel and a British Army ground liaison officer. Initially, its aircrews were drawn from pilots and navigators with previous experience of operating fast jets, but to an increasing extent new crews are now 'first tourists', straight from training.

All Tornado aircrews pass through the Tornado Weapons Conversion Unit at Honington before being posted to a squadron. Nonetheless, crews with no previous operational experience require additional training on the squadron before they are fully proficient in their very demanding role. The Tornado GR Mk 1 is a comparatively new aircraft in RAF service and the full operational capabilities of this complex 'weapons system' are still being explored.

No.617 Squadron is commanded by Wing Commander Pete Day, who relieved Wing Commander Tony Harrison on 21 June 1985. The squadron's aircrews are organised into two sub-units: A Flight and B Flight – the OC A Flight being a pilot and the OC B Flight a navigator. The present 'OC A' is Squadron Leader Pete Dunlop. In addition to running his flight of seven Tornado crews, Dunlop is responsible for all flying operations, including alerts, exercises and war plans, and acts as the deputy squadron commander.

The system, however, does not operate rigidly. Crews and aircraft are allocated to various squadron tasks according to availability, rather than being permanently segregated into two flights. Similarly, although pilots and navigators team up as a crew during training, they do not always fly together. Squadron Leader Tim Boon, a highly-experienced navigator who has previously operated on Phantoms in both the strike/attack and air-defence roles, thought that this was beneficial. He has found that when operating with a new flying partner he felt obliged to make an extra effort to put on a good performance.

A recently-joined pilot, who had better remain anonymous, saw things rather differently. He discovered that when flying with an experienced navigator, his partner was inclined to do rather too much 'back-seat driving'. However, he did concede that there is a tremendous amount to be learned from the more experienced crews.

In general, it seems that there is little distinction made between the squadron's aircrew on the

POST-WAR HISTORY

After the fall of Germany in May 1945, 617 Squadron transferred to the Far East for proposed operations against the Japanese. However, the squadron arrived as Japan surrendered and, after a spell in India in the first four months of 1946, returned to the UK.
Early in 1952, the squadron took delivery of its first Canberra jet bombers and, in July 1955, a detachment flew bombing sorties against communist guerrilla forces in Malaya. This section returned to Britain in November and the squadron was temporarily disbanded in the following month.
The squadron was reformed at RAF Scampton in May 1958 to fly the Vulcan bomber as part of Britain's strategic nuclear deterrent. In the following year, the squadron received its standard, a distinction usually only awarded after 25 years' service.
Other noteworthy events of 1959 were the winning of all three trophies in Bomber Command's annual Bombing and Navigation competition and a round-the-world flight by four of its Vulcans.
In mid-1969 the Vulcan's strategic deterrence role was passed over to the Royal Navy's Polaris submarines, and the squadron then retrained for tactical nuclear operations, flying at low level in all weather.
The squadron's long association with the Vulcan ended in December 1981 and, after being disbanded at Scampton, the Dambusters prepared for conversion to the Tornado.
Above: An unofficial badge worn by 617 Squadron's ground staff.

grounds of rank or seniority and that there is only a barely perceptible rivalry between pilots and navigators, or 'navs' as they are known. Another newly-joined pilot, Flight Lieutenant Steve Forward, found the atmosphere on an operational squadron a tremendous improvement over the more formal student-instructor relationships of the training units.

The servicing of No.617 Squadron's Tornados is carried out by the unit's own technicians under the command of Squadron Leader Sean Murphy, the squadron's Engineer Officer. He works directly under Day and is responsible to the officer in charge of RAF Marham's Engineering Wing for the overall technical efficiency of his team.

The senior NCO in charge of the squadron's 25 electrical specialists, Chief Technician Wally Rogers, whose experience goes back to 1959 when he worked on Shackletons, sees the Tornado as the first RAF aircraft designed from the outset with the engineer in mind. All the aircraft's systems are readily accessible, a situation that helps to speed up the process of servicing and fault rectification. This characteristic was recently demonstrated when a Dambuster Tornado suffered a birdstrike and was forced to land away from base with a damaged engine. A small team of specialists from the squadron, led by Sergeant Bob Longmore, succeeded in replacing the damaged powerplant in only five hours, a performance which Longmore entirely attributed to the Tornado's ease of maintenance.

In general, the groundcrews appreciate the protection from the elements provided by RAF Marham's hardened aircraft shelters (HASs) in contrast to a flightline in the open. However, Chief Technician Rogers has found that, whereas under the old system it was easy to see where everyone was working, he was now liable to lose track of members of his team inside the shelters.

In terms of performance, the Tornado's greatest single advantage over earlier strike/attack aircraft is undoubtedly its ability to operate at high speed and low-level in darkness or bad weather. The RAF has found it essential to fly at low level when penetrating heavily-defended airspace in order to minimise the effectiveness of enemy radar. With the Tornado, fitted with terrain-following (TF) radar and highly accurate navigation and attack systems, the RAF would positively welcome darkness and bad weather, as this would render the Soviet Union's visually directed surface-to-air missiles (SAMs) and anti-aircraft weapons impotent, without degrading the accuracy of the aircraft's weapons delivery.

In flight, the terrain-following radar senses the profile of the ground ahead of the aircraft and this data is then used to maintain a pre-selected height clearance over all obstacles. The system usually operates automatically, but a manual terrain-following system can be selected. Should the system fail, the aircraft will automatically climb to a safe height.

In addition to operating in the automatic terrain-following mode, the Tornado's autopilot can be set to follow a pre-selected track or to carry out an ILS (instrument landing system) airfield approach, so that in theory the aircraft could be

Below: Wings swept back for speed, a lone Tornado makes a low-level pass over Niagara Falls en route for the Prairie Vortex bombing competition in the western United States. In a sustained bout of precision flying, the squadron's teams almost swept the board – winning three trophies. The announcement of the results (right) was met with unrestrained jubilation. Never before had the USAF surrendered the trophies to a foreign team. Far right: Squadron Leader Pete Dunlop and Flight Lieutenant Dick Middleton pose with the fruits of this famous victory.

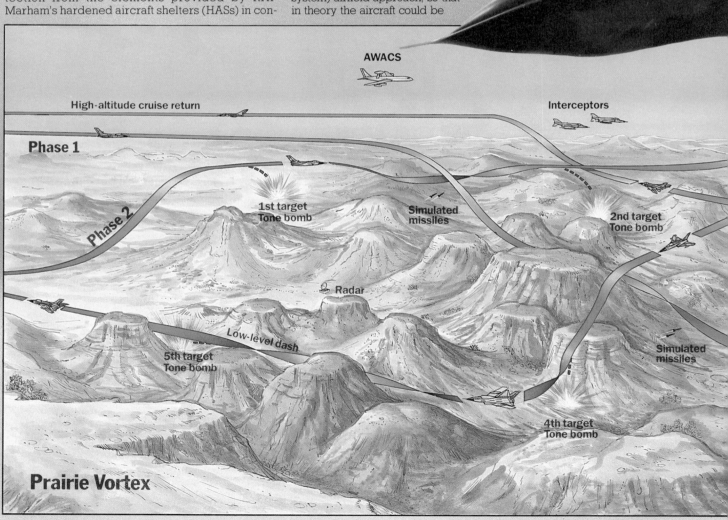

AWACS

High-altitude cruise return

Interceptors

Phase 1

Phase 2

1st target
Tone bomb

Simulated
missiles

2nd target
Tone bomb

Radar

Low-level dash

5th target
Tone bomb

Simulated
missiles

4th target
Tone bomb

Prairie Vortex

OPERATION PRAIRIE VORTEX

In 1984 No. 617 Squadron's Tornados were selected to take part in the USAF's Strategic Air Command (SAC) bombing competition. Held at Ellsworth Airbase, in South Dakota, over three weeks, the trials were conducted across several mid-western states and involved sorties over both flat and mountainous terrain.

Two teams, each of two aircrews, were selected to represent the squadron: Team A consisted of Squadron Leader Dunlop and Flight Lieutenants Middleton, Hunter and Dolan; Team B comprised Squadron Leaders Bussereau and Dyer-Perry with Flight Lieutenants Legg and MacDonald.

Phase One of Prairie Vortex was designed to test the crews' abilities on a long-range bombing mission. After a two-hour flight to the exercise area, the Tornados descended to low level to carry out attacks on 'no-show' (hidden) targets, using radar off-set techniques. During the terrain-following part of the raid, lasting nearly two hours, the Tornado crews had to deal with simulated surface-to-air missile attacks and fighter interceptions. The results of each team's sorties were judged on bombing accuracy, timing and evasion tactics.

Phase Two of the competition was a two-part exercise of two six-hour sorties flown during the day and night. The trials began with a high-level bomb release against a radar target and followed by a mid-air refuelling test. It was then down to terrain-following height for a four-hour stint of high-speed flight and attacks on a further four radar targets. All of these manoeuvres were scored for accuracy and some for timing. As in Phase One, missile and interceptor threats had to be countered.

The outcome of Prairie Vortex was an unprecedented success for the RAF. The teams from 617 Squadron won two out of three competitions and took second place in the third. The LeMay Trophy, awarded to the crew with the highest points for the three sorties, went to Dunlop and Middleton with their team-mates Hunter and Dolan taking second place. The Meyer Trophy, given to the team with the best damage-expectancy rating, went to the squadron's Team A. Team B took third place.

Team A came second in the Mathis Trophy, given for the best high and low-level bombing score. The BAe Trophy for the best Tornado crew went to Dunlop and Middleton.

The squadron's performance was remarkable: never before had a non-American unit won the LeMay and Meyer Trophies.

3rd target
Tone bomb

lated
les

No-show targets

THE TORNADO

Originally designated the MRCA (multi-role combat aircraft), the Tornado was the brainchild of Panavia Aircraft, a joint British, West German and Italian enterprise formed in 1969. In 1976, the MCRA received its present title and the three NATO governments involved in the project placed an order for 809 aircraft. The first British Tornado made its maiden flight on 11 July 1979 and, following successful trials, the RAF ordered a total of 385 aircraft. Of these, some 220 will be the Mark 1 strike/interdiction version,

some 165 Mark 2 Tornados for air defence, and the remainder will be IDS (interdiction/strike) models. Of all-metal construction, the Tornado makes use of variable-geometry wings which, in conjunction with turbofan engines and sophisticated computer-assisted avionics, allows the two-man crew to fly low-level penetration raids in all but the very worst weather conditions. Powered by two RB 199-34R engines, the Tornado is capable of reaching Mach 2.2 at high altitudes, and has a tactical radius of around 870 miles with a full load of weapons.

The Tornado has been tailor-made to fit the combat requirements of three air forces and is deployed in six main roles: battlefield interdiction, counter air strike, naval attack, air superiority, air defence and reconnaissance. Armament includes two 27mm cannon and up to 18,000lb of ordnance carried on three fuselage and two wing weapons stations. The air defence variant (ADV) is fitted with Foxhunter radar which can detect enemy aircraft at ranges up to 115 miles, and carries two Sidewinder and four Sky Flash air-to-air missiles.

flown 'hands off' for an entire sortie with the pilot only taking over for the take-off and landing. However, in practice, by no means all tactical flying can be performed satisfactorily by the autopilot and such exercises as in-flight refuelling and combat manoeuvring require considerable piloting ability.

By itself, the ability to fly safely at low level in any weather is of no practical use unless the attack aircraft is also able to find its targets and bomb accurately. Navigation and weapons' management are the primary responsibilities of the Tornado's navigator. He also contributes to the aircraft's considerable self-defence capabilities by monitoring the electronic-warfare systems and providing an

additional lookout during air combat.

The nav's cockpit is dominated by two TV displays and associated keyboards, which give him access to the aircraft's main computer, and a combined moving-map and radar display. Pre-flight planning is carried out using a system known as the Cassette Preparation Ground Station, which transfers onto a magnetic tape all the essential navigational data associated with the sortie. The tape is then loaded into the aircraft's computer and the nav is able to call up a plan of the entire mission on one of his TV displays. Using this system, it is comparatively easy to re-plan a sortie after take-off.

The Tornado's primary navigation aids are the

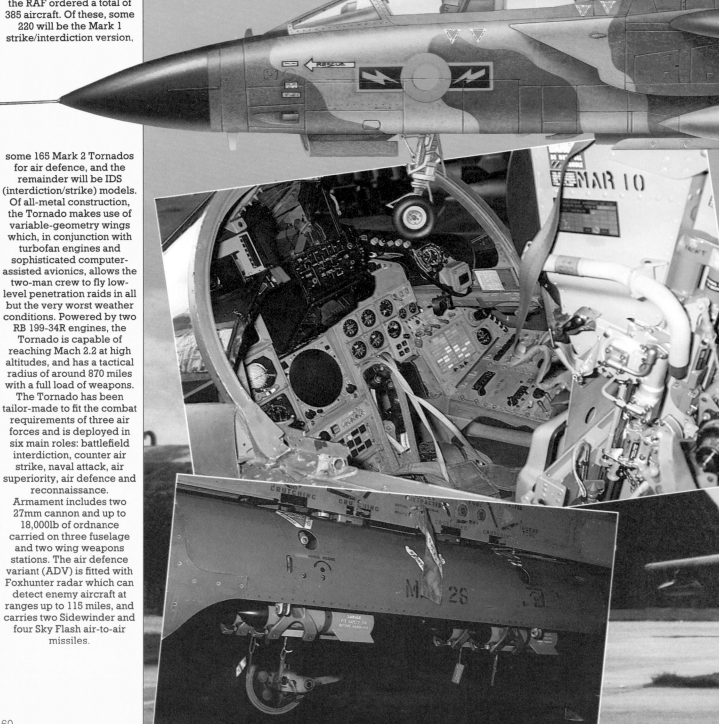

Below: A Panavia Tornado GR Mk I as flown by No. 617 Squadron. This sideview shows the aircraft fitted with a long-range fuel tank (with red lines) and the Ajax electronic counter-measures pod. Below left: A daunting prospect for any novice pilot – the dazzling array of flight controls in the Tornado's cockpit. Bottom left: During the frequent training sorties, crews used small practice bombs to simulate the characteristics of larger ordnance. Bottom: A Tornado taxis along the runway of RAF Marham in preparation for a training mission to the Pennines.

inertial navigation system (INS) and the Doppler radar. Both systems are capable of sensing the aircraft's velocities continually throughout its flight and, since the Tornado's starting point is known with absolute accuracy, this data can be used to calculate the aircraft's present position.

In addition to psychological pressures, the crew is subjected to intense physical stress during high-g manoeuvring

The most important of the pilot's displays is the HUD (head-up display): a glass screen, like a larger version of the traditional gunsight, mounted at the top of his instrument panel. Not only does it provide the pilot with all the essential data he needs to fly the aircraft, without the need to look down at his main instrument panel, but it is also used to aim bombs, guns and air-to-air missiles (AAMs).

During a bombing run, both the pilot and the navigator work together to get the bombs onto the target. The nav will select which bombs are to be released and the method of aiming them, using a computerised Stores Management System which reduces much of the work of arming weapons, and selecting the sequence and intervals at which they

are to be released. The run-in begins at a pre-selected IP (initial point), typically only one minute's flying time from the target.

It is easy to form the superficial impression that the Tornado's advanced, automatic systems make the aircraft so simple to operate that the crew really only goes along for the ride. Nothing could be further from the truth. In the first place, the pace of high-speed jet flying can be fast and furious, with everything happening in a short space of time. For example, should a Tornado be slightly off the planned track during the final approach to a target, the pilot has only seconds to recognise the situation and correct it. Moreover, in a hostile environment many things will be happening at once, with the crew having to identify and deal with threats from enemy ground-based air-defence systems and interceptors, at the same time as flying and navigating the aircraft accurately.

Such flying often requires intense concentration and the pilots are always acutely aware of the ever-present dangers. In addition to these psychological pressures, the crew is subjected to intense physical stress during high-g manoeuvring (for instance, under a load of 4g the heart will weigh four times as much as normal).

Standard flying kit includes an anti-g suit that applies pressure to the legs and abdomen in order to counteract the tendency of the blood to drain away from the head during positive-g manoeuvres. A protective flying helmet is invariably worn, but, when this becomes several times heavier than its normal weight under g-loading, then even the nav's job of turning his head to keep a lookout to the rear represents a considerable physical feat.

During the months of autumn, winter and spring, the sea temperatures off Europe are so low that the crews must wear a rubberised immersion suit. This will prolong their lives for an appreciable period if they are forced to eject into the sea. However, it is a

Below: A Tornado climbs into the night sky. With wings swept forward, it is able to fly from air strips less than 3000ft in length.

hot and uncomfortable garment, which is particularly prone to chafe the neck. The aircrews' NBC protective suits, worn if there is a risk of contamination from nuclear or chemical weapons, are even more uncomfortable and restrictive.

Before the day's flying begins for No.617 Squadron, the crews attend a weather briefing. Then, a total of 15 sorties is planned, including some night flying, and this represents a fairly typical daily effort. Pre-flight preparation not only involves the route and target planning already described, but also a check on the likely hazards to low flying. Around Marham, the extensive aerial crop-spraying activity over the eastern counties during the summer is a particular threat.

The Tornados will avoid densely-populated areas and controlled airspace during their training flights, which are usually carried out over such areas as north Wales and the Scottish Highlands. Recently, the Dambusters visited Canada, for low-level training and the crews found the limitless expanses of sparsely-populated forests, mountains and lakes a refreshing change from the UK with its numerous restrictions on low flying. In Britain, a training sortie

Below centre: Watched over by a member of the squadron's ground staff, a pilot jumps into his cockpit. Bottom left and right: After pre-flight maintenance, a Tornado emerges from its hardened shelter at RAF Marham.

usually lasts about two hours and might take a single Tornado to Scotland, flying at high altitude and then letting down to low level.

Such is the accuracy of the Tornado's navigation systems that the aircraft can even let down through cloud without the crew needing to worry about the danger of the aircraft being off course and crashing into high ground. Once the Tornado is flying in the 'auto TF' mode, it could then carry out a simulated strike on Leuchars airfield followed by an attack over the electronic-warfare training range at Spadeadam.

Perhaps, the crew would then finish with a practice-timed first-run attack, using the loft-bombing technique on one of the coastal ranges, before landing back at Marham. A first-run attack requires the Tornado to fly straight into the range area, locate its target and then release its practice bomb, all in a single pass.

As the RAF aims to train in the same way as it would fight, many aspects of the Dambusters' war missions have already been covered in describing the squadron's day-to-day activities. However, the main elements of the unit's operational capabilities are worth emphasising. In the event of a war in Europe, the priority targets for the RAF's Tornado squadrons would be the Warsaw Pact's armoured and air forces. Tornados could be used to blunt the enemy's initial armoured thrusts, seal off the battle area and prevent the build-up of reinforcements and support in the enemy's rear areas. At the same time, the Warsaw Pact's airfields could be targets of primary importance.

Such offensive air operations will be fiercely contested by Soviet SAMs, anti-aircraft gun defences and fighter aircraft. To a large degree, Soviet SAMs and anti-aircraft guns can be evaded by the Tornados by flying fast and low, preferably in conditions of poor visibility.

The Tornado can also counter any radar-directed weapons with its electronic-warfare equipment and, when the Alarm radar-homing missile becomes available, will be able to attack them directly. And, since Soviet interdiction aircraft are likely to attempt to knock out the RAF's squadrons on their airfields, the practice of operating from hardened facilities, where men could live as well as work during an offensive, is an equally important defensive measure.

In the Tornado, with its unique combination of offensive and defensive capabilities, the aircrews of No.617 Squadron have a potent weapons system with which to carry on the proud record and tradition of the original Dambusters.

THE AUTHOR, Anthony Robinson, and publishers would like to thank the Commanding Officer of No.617 Squadron, Wing Commander P.J.J. Day, Squadron Leader Tim Boon and the other members of the squadron for their kind help in the preparation of this article.

WING COMMANDER DAY

Invariably known as 'The Boss', Wing Commander Pete Day took charge of No. 617 Squadron in June 1985. Born at Maidstone, Kent in 1945, he was educated at a local grammar school before joining the RAF in 1963. After basic flight training, Day's first operational tour was in the Far East, flying all-weather Javelin fighters.
He then returned to the UK and became an instructor on Jet Provosts at the RAF College, Cranwell. In 1971. he was selected as a member of the RAF's aerobatic display team, the Red Arrows, and flew with them for three seasons.
After leaving the Red Arrows, Day underwent an operational conversion course onto the Jaguar GR Mk1 strike/attack aircraft.
There then followed postings to No. 6 Squadron at RAF Coltishall and to No. 14 Squadron at RAF Bruggen in West Germany. In 1980 he took up a staff appointment with Headquarters, RAF Germany at Rheindahlen and then attended the RAF Staff College at Bracknell in 1983. Promotion to wing commander, and another desk job at Headquarters, RAF Strike Command, preceded a refresher flying course and operational conversion onto the Tornado.

NYE'S
ANNIHILATORS

322ND BOMBARDMENT GROUP

The 322nd (Medium) Bombardment Group was activated at McDill Field, Florida, on 19 June 1942 and comprised the 449th, 450th, 451st and 452nd Squadrons. Training began immediately on the B-26 Marauder. The group was then ordered to Britain, but a shortage of aircraft delayed the arrival of the first air squadron at Bury St Edmunds until March 1943.

The 3rd Bomb Wing, to which the 322nd had been assigned, had adopted a strategy of 'zero' altitude bombing, in order to avoid German flak and maximise the number of missions possible under low cloud cover. Targets within a radius of 400 miles were to be attacked by forces of no more than 12 aircraft, flying below radar range to achieve surprise.

The 322nd's first mission, on 14 May 1943, also marked the first bombing sortie of a UK-based Marauder. Three days later, the group lost an entire strike force on a low-level attack, forcing a fundamental change in USAAF thinking. Then on 31 July the 322nd flew its first medium altitude operation, attacking Triqueville airfield. An Fw190 was shot down by a waist gunner, and the raid signalled a change of fortune for the group.

In October, by which time the 322nd had completed 34 missions, the proposed invasion of Europe necessitated the formation of a new tactical air force to support ground operations, and on 16 October 1943 the group was assigned to the Ninth Air Force (whose shoulder sleeve insignia is shown above).

Following the cessation of hostilities, the group returned to the USA and was deactivated. In 1954 it re-emerged flying F-86s and F-100s, but it survived only a few years.

The 322nd Bombardment Group's early operations were dogged by disaster but the group soon became the scourge of German airfields

THE DUTY FLYING control officer in the Bury St Edmunds watch-tower glanced at the wall clock as the minute hand moved to 1330 hours. It was two and a half hours since the bombers had set out from the airfield and his worst fears were now realised; all 10 aircraft were missing in action. Their estimated time of arrival (ETA) at Bury was 1250, and when they failed to appear the hope had been that the force had landed at another English airfield on the east coast to refuel. But no USAAF or RAF base had any such news, increasing the apprehension felt by the senior officers waiting in the Bury tower. The next hint of disaster was an RAF intercept of Luftwaffe radio messages which mentioned the shooting down of enemy aircraft. Now, 40 minutes past the ETA, there was no hope of the aircraft still being airborne as fuel would be exhausted.

The officers left the tower. Little was said, but each one knew that the Eighth Air Force's attempts at conducting low-level bombing operations with medium bombers had proved disastrous. Moreover, this débâcle threw serious doubt on the combat future of the aircraft involved, the Martin B-26 Marauder. Indeed, 17 May 1943 was the blackest episode in the extraordinary story of the Marauder. It was also the darkest day in the history of the 322nd Bombardment Group, the unit involved in this, the only total loss of a strike force, albeit small, suffered by American air forces in Europe during World War II.

When the prototype Martin B-26 Marauder first flew in November 1940 it was hailed as the most advanced medium bomber in the world. So far, however, its record had left a great deal to be desired. Since its introduction into service in the summer of 1941 there had been a spate of accidents. Pilots had experienced great difficulty adjusting to

Page 165: **Never an aircraft to suffer from a lack of armament, the B-26 Marauder eventually carried almost as many guns as the heavy American bombers. Later variants of the B-26 had a pair of 0.5in Colt-Browning machine guns mounted in individual blisters on each side of the forward fuselage. Left: Colonel Stillman briefs crews of the 322nd before their first low-level operation. Below left: B-26 'Mister Period Twice', so named because it missed the group's first two raids due to mechanical problems. Below: One B-26 was severely damaged by flak on the first raid and crash-landed at Bury St Edmunds, killing the pilot. Bottom: A formation of Marauders warms up on the runway.**

the aircraft, especially to the unfamiliar necessity of landing at high speed, and mechanics could not quickly grasp the complex electrical and hydraulic systems. As the rate of accidents rose, the plane had become notorious as the 'Widowmaker' and the 'Martin Murderer'.

Although the Marauder had performed badly in service in the Pacific and then in North Africa, high hopes were held for operations from England, where airfield facilities were good and many enemy targets in occupied Europe were within range. The first Marauder group sent to Europe flew its aircraft across the North Atlantic via Greenland and Iceland during the autumn of 1942, and in December the ground echelon of the 322nd Bomb Group arrived, the first squadrons of the air echelon being delayed until the early spring of 1943 by a shortage of new aircraft. The 322nd immediately began training for low-level attack, hedge-hopping over the East Anglian countryside, for their operational plan was to come in low to escape the enemy's radar detection screen and, with the advantage of surprise, strike the targets and escape before defences could be brought into action.

The 322nd Bomb Group set out on its inaugural mission on 14 May 1943, when a dozen Marauders attempted to bomb an electrical power station at Ijmuiden in western Holland. The force was met with heavy ground fire and several aircraft were dam-

aged, one so badly that the pilot lost control when the aircraft was in the landing circuit at Bury St Edmunds, resulting in a fatal crash. The cost of this accident, and of the hot reception at the target, was accepted in the belief that the target had been badly damaged, but two days later Colonel Stillman, the Group CO, was summoned to 3rd Wing, the controlling headquarters. He was informed that reconnaissance photographs showed that the target was untouched and, in consequence, the group was to be sent back to try again. Stillman objected, opining that the enemy would be expecting a return, and without the advantage of surprise the B-26s would suffer heavily. His objections overruled, Stillman decided to lead the next raid himself. Only 11 B-26s were available

Ijmuiden raid
322nd Bomb Group, 17 May 1943

Ten B-26 Marauders of the 322nd Bomb Group set out to bomb Ijmuiden in Holland on 17 May 1943. Not one returned. But with the adoption of new tactics after the raid, the 322nd became one of the most successful units in the Allied bombing campaign against Germany, earning the nickname 'Nye's Annihilators.'

Key
→ Route flown 17 May 1943
--→ Intended route
✱ Raid on Amsterdam
→ Enemy fighters

for the mission and they took off at 1100 hours on the next morning, 17 May. One aircraft turned back over the North Sea when a generator failed; the others continued on course for the enemy coast, never to return.

Two days later, a British destroyer picked up two crewmen from a life raft, survivors from a Marauder which had been shot down by an enemy fighter. These men were able to provide some information on what had happened, but the full picture did not emerge until after the cessation of hostilities. It appears that after leaving Orfordness on the Suffolk coast, the 322nd formation had gradually veered south in a brisk cross wind, eventually making landfall on the Dutch coast some 30 miles from the briefed entry point. Moreover, landfall was made near the Maas estuary, one of the most heavily defended points in the Low Countries. The Marauders were met with a hail of ground fire and the lead aircraft, commanded by Stillman, was hit and crashed inverted on a sand dune. Stillman and two airmen were extracted from the wreck alive but badly injured. Another bomber also fell to the coastal barrage while the rest found themselves hopelessly lost. Two collided and went down, and another had to crash-land after being struck by wreckage. After unsuccessfully trying to locate their briefed target the remaining five aircraft had bombed a gasometer near Amsterdam and then turned west. Crossing the coast, misfortune again took a turn for they flew over another defensive stronghold and four were brought down by ground fire. The remaining aircraft escaped out to sea only to fall to the guns of a Messerschmitt Bf 109 that had been despatched to intercept.

Further B-26 operations were suspended while the USAAF reviewed the situation. Three more B-26 groups were in the process of moving to the United Kingdom, but the Eighth Air Force had come to regard the aircraft as a liability. As a result, pending a decision on their future use, all the B-26s in Britain were moved from Bomber Command to Air Support Command, which was non-operational, and all further movement of B-26 groups from the US was called to a halt.

A staff officer from 3rd Wing Headquarters, Lieutenant-Colonel Glenn Nye, was given command of the demoralised 322nd Group. Nye was one of a small band of US officers in England who had been

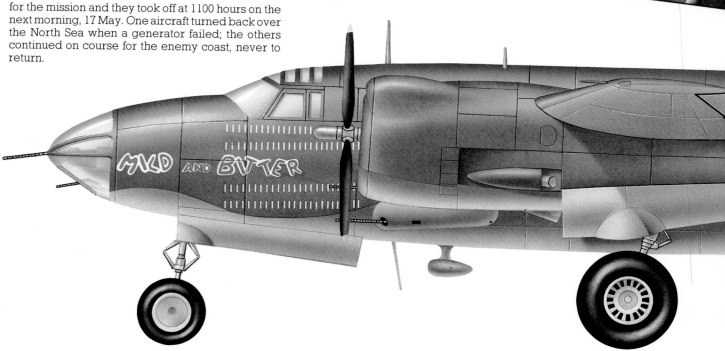

THE MARAUDER

The Martin B-26 Marauder was designed to provide the USAAF with a fast, heavily armed medium bomber, and so impressed was the Air Corps with its characteristics that 200 aircraft were ordered 'straight off the drawing board'.

The B-26 introduced many innovations in aircraft construction, including high strength clear plastic mouldings, large alloy castings and advanced electrical and hydraulics systems. It featured a streamlined, cigar-shaped fuselage, circular in cross-section, and its top speed of 315mph equalled that of many single-engined fighters of its day. The bomb bay was larger than that of the B-17 Flying Fortress and it could carry an equivalent weight of bombs, 4000lb, for half the distance of the heavy bomber. It was powered by twin 1850hp Pratt & Whitney R-2800-5 Double Wasp radial engines, and in addition to nose, ventral and tail-cone guns there were two 0.5in Browning machine guns housed in an electrically-operated Martin 250CE dorsal turret, the first powered turret to be installed in an American bomber.

However, one design feature of the B-26 was to help create the plane's early reputation as a killer. To gain maximum speed, the wing span and area had been cut to a minimum, and low-speed handling proved hazardous. The aircraft also required a long take-off run, and its fast landing speed of 100mph was well beyond most USAAF pilots' experience at the time. With the introduction of design improvements and better training, however, the Marauder went on to record the lowest losses in action of any US bomber type over Europe.

Above: Marauders arriving straight from the production line were named by their first commanders. 'Pappy's Pram', for instance, was Captain 'Pappy' Pursel's aircraft. 'Mild and Bitter', the first B-26 to complete 100 missions, went on tour in the US covered with the autographs of 322nd Bomb Group personnel. 'Flak Bait' completed 200 missions, the only US bomber to do so.

involved with the B-26 since its introduction into service and he had analysed the problems. Nye knew that the Marauder's bad name was primarily due to weaknesses in the original crew-training programme. In the hands of good pilots and competent mechanics, he believed it to be as reliable as any other combat aircraft in the USAAF inventory. He further believed that the operational failures of the B-26 were due to its method of employment. As CO of the 322nd, his first priority was to build confidence in the aircraft, but this was to prove a difficult task, particularly after the tail broke off a B-26 flying low in the vicinity of the airfield. The aircrews inevitably saw this event as yet further proof that the Marauder was not fit to fly, let alone fight. However, investigation of the wreckage revealed that securing bolts had failed, and to prove that the mishap was peculiar to that particular aircraft, Nye took up an identical B-26 and performed a series of manoeuvres to prove that the tail unit was robust. Through such incidents, the men of the 322nd gradually warmed to their new boss.

Going back to war again in the B-26 was another matter. A series of top-level meetings had brought a decision to operate the B-26s at medium altitude, as they had been forced to do while operating from North Africa. The bombers were to adopt the large, tight formations that the B-17 heavy bombers were using so successfully over Europe, and arrangements were made with the RAF to furnish strong Spitfire escorts. The first operation of this type was flown by a new bombardment group in late July 1943, and was conducted without loss. Following three more successful raids, the 322nd forsook its low-level training and joined the operations being flown at between 9000 and 14,000 feet, altitudes beyond the range of German light flak. From a new base at Great Saling in Essex the 322nd led three other groups in a sustained campaign of bombing enemy airfields during the following three months; sometimes two

missions were flown in one day. The bomb group became the scourge of German air bases within its range, at the same time sustaining very low losses.

Having found a role for the Marauder where it could contribute to the Allied aerial onslaught on Europe with telling effect, the USAAF ordered four B-26 groups still retained in the USA to Europe. A tactical air force, the Ninth, was formed in Britain during the autumn of 1943 with the object of supporting the cross-Channel invasion planned for the following spring, and to this the Marauder units were transferred to form the basis of IX Bomber Command. Under the new command, target priorities were initially unchanged, with enemy airfields at the top of the list. Late in 1943, however, the Marauders were given a new objective, the destruction of the V-1 flying-bomb sites that were being rapidly constructed in the Pas de Calais region. The 322nd Group opened the campaign on 5 November, and found that the flak defences in the target area were vicious. Many Marauders were to fall to the guns of the Pas de Calais during the next few months.

Like the heavy bombers of the Eighth Air Force, the Ninth's B-26s were frequently prevented from

Right: The 322nd's 'Lil' Pork Chop' banks away as trains of bombs pound the dispersal area of a Luftwaffe airfield at St Andre de l'Eure in France. Below right: Groundcrew use a trolley jack to arm a Marauder with 500lb M43 bombs. Background: A Marauder strike force led by 'Mild and Bitter' heads for Schipol in Holland on a diversionary raid.

Bombardier, Medium Bombardment Group, USAAF, 1944

First Lieutenant Benjamin McCartney is wearing light uniform of the US Army Air Force. Under the life vest, a light khaki shirt (with one silver bar on the collar to denote rank) is worn with khaki dress trousers, russet shoes, and the standard officer's peaked cap.

bombing their targets by cloud cover. Following the lead of the strategic air force, the Ninth turned to the British for help in the form of radar blind-bombing devices. Such special equipment was in short supply, but a few sets of 'Oboe II', an American-made version of a British system, were at last obtained. Major Robert Porter, a survivor of the 322nd's first Ijmuiden raid, was selected to head an experimental unit at Great Saling. The airborne Oboe set allowed the operator to receive signals from two transmitting stations in England and enabled him to pin-point his aircraft's exact position to within 200yds. Apart from its accuracy, Oboe had the advantage that its signals were almost impossible for the enemy to jam. Porter's little unit was formed into a provisional squadron at the 322nd's base in February 1944, providing Oboe pathfinders for all the other B-26 groups in IX Bomber Command.

On 26 March 1944, the 322nd Bomb Group, now known as 'Nye's Annihilators', was given its long-awaited opportunity to avenge the 10 Marauders destroyed on the disastrous second raid on Ijmuiden in 1943. An enormous force of 380 aircraft from several bomb groups was despatched, with veterans from the 322nd's inaugural mission of 14 May 1943 aboard the leading Marauders. This time their objective was Ijmuiden harbour and installations used by E-boat strike forces in the North Sea. The formation of bombers flew into a maelstrom of flak over the port, but this time their loads of high explosive found their mark. All but one of the bombers returned to England, many of them bearing scars from the hail of steel fragments they had endured.

Following the Allied cross-Channel invasion in June 1944, the Marauders flew most of their missions against tactical targets whose destruction would aid the advancing ground forces. Particular success was obtained against bridges and other communications targets, and the Annihilators were usually in the forefront of these attacks. In September the Ninth Air Force began moving its bombers into Europe to extend their range, the 322nd moving to Beauvais/Tille in France, and from there to Le Culot in Belgium in the following March. After more than a year in command of the group, Glenn Nye was assigned to higher headquarters and replaced by Colonel John Samuel, who continued in command until after the end of hostilities. For the intensely active period of Nye's command, the 322nd received the coveted Distinguished Unit Citation.

When the war in Europe came to a close in May 1945, Nye's Annihilators and their brother bombardment groups had fully vindicated the much-maligned Marauder, proving it more durable than any other American bomber in Europe. The first Marauder to complete 100 sorties from Britain had been the 322nd Group's 'Mild and Bitter', which had achieved this feat as early as 8 May 1944. Many Marauders from numerous bombardment groups survived 150 sorties over Europe, but the supreme champion was the Annihilators' 'Flak Bait', which on 18 April 1945 completed its 200th mission, the only Allied medium or heavy bomber of the war in Europe to amass such a record. Holed some 900 times by enemy flak in 21 months of combat flying, that battered aircraft has come to symbolise the 322nd's determination to contribute towards Allied victory.

THE AUTHOR Simon Clay is a leading authority on the history of the US Army Air Force in World War II and has written numerous books on the subject.

NIGHT FIGHTING

It takes a cool head and a great deal of self-confidence to make an effective night fighter. Under the blanket of darkness the agitated mind teems with imagined dangers and irrational fears can trigger off a full-scale panic. Most people have a natural fear of darkness, and so the first step towards becoming a successful night fighter is to overcome this fear.

A good starting point is to remember that the enemy is just as afraid of the dark as you are. He will be sitting there in the darkness wondering when you are going to spring from the shadows, or creep up behind him, knife at the ready. A very common mistake made by inexperienced soldiers is to overestimate grossly the enemy's ability to cope with fighting in the dark.

Darkness breeds confusion and the key to overcoming a great many of your fears is to be extremely well organised. To be able to lay your hands on any piece of your equipment without having to search around for it will greatly increase your confidence. Always pack your kit in exactly the same way, so that you know its layout like the back of your hand. Strong leadership has the same effect. If you are commanding a squad on a night operation, make doubly sure that every man knows exactly what he has to do, and get the men to work together closely. Always act decisively and keep the men well informed.

To instil the confidence that is crucial to night fighting you must practise all the various relevant skills until they are second nature. The first of these is learning to use your eyes in the dark. In broad daylight, you look straight at an object in order to observe it as clearly as possible. Not so at night. Due to certain characteristics of human vision, in darkness it is better to direct your gaze slightly away from the object you wish to inspect and look at it out of the corner of your eye. It takes about 30 minutes of darkness for your eyes to adjust fully to night vision,

Left: The night sky of Korea is illuminated by tracer.
Above: In night operations it is advisable to move in tightly-knit groups, keeping all individuals

COMBAT SKILLS OF THE ELITE

COMBAT SKILLS Of The Elite

equipped with a night scope, you should aim your rifle by 'pointing' it, a technique similar to that used by wildfowlers hunting with a shotgun. To fire, you should raise the rifle to your shoulder, into a position in which your normal sighting eye is about two inches above the top of the receiver. Concentrate on the base of the target – if you aim at the centre of it your shot will go high – and then fire off a round with a sharp pull on the trigger. This firing technique requires a great deal of practice, but once you have mastered it you should be able to hit targets up to a range of 50yds fairly consistently.

It should be remembered, however, that the muzzle flash from a rifle fired at night will be clearly visible to the enemy, who will respond by saturating your position with fire. Grenades are very useful weapons in close-quarters night firefights since it is impossible for the enemy to identify their source.

In modern warfare there are a great many technological aids available to help the soldier cope with the disadvantages of fighting blind. Infra-red equipment, image intensifiers and night sights are fitted to modern weapon systems and a night action can be lit up by a variety of flares and illuminating rounds. These range from simple trip flares to parachute flares dropped by an aircraft circling over the battlefield. If you are digging in for the night, trip flares should be placed around your night perimeter on the most likely avenues of enemy approach. Any incoming troops attempting to probe the perimeter will be floodlit in the harsh glare of the flare when they set off the trip mechanism, but they will not be able to see you. Illuminating rounds can be called in

so make sure that they are acclimatised to the dark before going into action. If you are preparing for a night action it is a good idea to wear sunglasses during the preceding day, since bright sunlight degrades night vision for as long as 36 hours.

Because your vision is very restricted at night, movement becomes extremely difficult. An enemy sentry will be relying a great deal on his hearing to detect any approach to his position, so stealth and the ability to move over unfamiliar terrain in complete silence are absolutely essential. When walking forward you should take very short steps. Lift one foot high off the ground and then place it forward with the toe downwards, feeling for loose rocks or dry twigs as you slowly lean your weight onto it. Pause for a second, and then repeat the movement with your other foot. If you are stalking an enemy you should crouch down as you move in.

Stealth requires immense self-control and discipline and the basic rules should be observed at all times. Move forward in bounds. Stop for a few seconds while you listen and look around you, and then move on a few more paces. On occasion, outside sources of sound – overflying aircraft, trains, thunder – can be used to cover the sounds of your movement. Try to stay in fairly open ground as much as possible, since moving through woods or scrub can be very noisy, but avoid wide, open spaces where you can be caught by an enemy flare. Never run, except in cases of extreme emergency or during a combat assault.

Your lack of clear vision at night will also affect the way in which you use your rifle. Unless you are

Movement by night

Above: A trooper training with the 'Nova' night vision goggles. The goggles incorporate a single image intensifier and are compatible with helmets, respirators, NBC and Arctic headgear. They are used for surveillance, foot patrol, night maintenance and vehicle driving. The Nova goggles can be either hand-held or head-mounted.

from mortar teams, artillery batteries, and even warships stationed offshore.

If you spot a flare going up, try to conceal yourself as best you can before it bursts, and above all do not move. Flares have a short life span and if an enemy is scanning your area for a target he will immediately shoot at anything that is moving.

Night fighting is frightening, but once you have acquired the necessary skills and feel confident in your abilities you will have overcome many of its problems. Team work is essential, and if you and the men in your squad can keep a steady nerve at all times you will be able to operate very effectively.